"Body image dissatisfaction is particularly well-suited to an acceptance-based approach, yet there has been little to guide therapists in confronting this sensitive topic with their clients. I commend the authors for taking on this challenging issue and providing a clear-eyed yet empathic approach that is equally useful whether a client's concerns reflect primarily distorted perceptions, or, at least to some extent, more reality-based apprehensions regarding others' potentially negative responses to their physical presentation."

—Linda Craighead, Ph.D., professor of psychology and director of clinical training at Emory University in Atlanta, GA

"After observing her for over a year in complex psychological settings, I have been impressed by how Adria Pearson 'walks the talk' of acceptance and commitment therapy. She seems always to be ACT-consistent by embodying genuineness, honesty, and courage in all her actions. This book is just like that... she knows the concepts well enough to express them in ways that are equally meaningful for both therapists and clients who struggle with body image dissatisfaction."

—Kenneth D. Cole, Ph.D., director of training at the VA Long Beach Healthcare System

Acceptance & Commitment Therapy

for Body Image Dissatisfaction

A Practitioner's Guide to Using Mindfulness,
Acceptance & Values-Based Behavior Change Strategies

ADRIA N. PEARSON, PH.D.
MICHELLE HEFFNER, PH.D.
VICTORIA M. FOLLETTE, PH.D.

New Harbinger Publications, Inc.

Publisher's Note

Distributed in Canada by Raincoast Books

Copyright © 2010 by Adria N. Pearson, Michelle Heffner, & Victoria M. Follette
New Harbinger Publications, Inc.
5674 Shattuck Avenue
Oakland, CA 94609
www.newharbinger.com

Acquired by Tesilya Hanauer; Cover design by Amy Shoup;
Edited by Jean Blomquist; Text design by Tracy Marie Carlson

Library of Congress Cataloging-in-Publication Data

Pearson, Adria N.
 Acceptance and commitment therapy for body image dissatisfaction : a practitioner's guide to using mindfulness, acceptance, and values-based behavior change strategies / Adria N. Pearson, Michelle Heffner, and Victoria M. Follette.
     p. cm.
 Includes bibliographical references.
 ISBN 978-1-57224-775-8
 1. Body image--Social aspects. 2. Acceptance and commitment therapy. 3. Self-acceptance. I. Heffner, Michelle. II. Follette, Victoria M. III. Title.
 BF697.5.B63P43 2010
 616.89'1425--dc22

                    2009052767

12 11 10

10 9 8 7 6 5 4 3 2 1   First printing

To Dr. Linda Craighead, my undergraduate mentor at the University of Colorado at Boulder. Thank you for encouraging me to pursue this wonderfully rewarding career, including the joys of research, writing, and clinical practice.

—ANP

This book is dedicated to all of my clients. My experiences with you inspired me as I worked on this book.

—MH

For Laura and my friends, who teach me about love every day.

—VMF

Contents

A Letter from the Series Editors   vii

Foreword   ix

Acknowledgments   xi

PART 1
Introducing ACT for Body Image Dissatisfaction

CHAPTER 1
Body Image Dissatisfaction: An Introduction   3

CHAPTER 2
Acceptance and Commitment Therapy: An Introduction   17

CHAPTER 3
Using ACT to Treat Body Image Dissatisfaction   37

PART 2
Applying ACT to Body Image Dissatisfaction

CHAPTER 4
Introducing ACT to Your Client   55

CHAPTER 5

Creative Hopelessness: Openness to Trying
Something Different   73

CHAPTER 6

Control as the Problem, Acceptance as the Solution   89

CHAPTER 7

Mindful Acceptance of Thoughts, Emotions,
and Physical Sensations   105

CHAPTER 8

Clarifying Values and Defining Goals   129

CHAPTER 9

Barriers to Values and Commitment to Valued Living   147

CHAPTER 10

Adapting ACT to Group Therapy   167

AFTERWORD

Endings and New Beginnings   179

References   181

Index   195

Dear Reader:

Welcome to New Harbinger Publications. New Harbinger is dedicated to publishing books based on Acceptance and Commitment Therapy and its application to specific areas of mental health. New Harbinger has a long-standing reputation in the mental health community as a publisher of quality, well-researched books. We offer an effectual forum for you to get this pertinent information to a wider audience.

As part of our commitment to publishing sound, scientific, clinically-based research, Steven C. Hayes, Ph.D., Georg Eifert, Ph.D., and John Forsyth, Ph.D., oversee all prospective ACT books for the *Acceptance and Commitment Therapy Series*. New Harbinger is at the forefront of publishing books that make ACT skills available to a trade and professional audience.

As ACT Series Editors, we review all ACT books published by New Harbinger, comment on proposals and offer guidance as needed, and use a gentle hand in making suggestions regarding content, depth, and scope of each book. We strive to ensure that any unsubstantiated claim or claims that are clearly ACT inconsistent are flagged for the authors so they can revise these sections to ensure that the work meets our criteria (see below) and is true to its roots (e.g., not passing off other models and methods as ACT).

Books in the *Acceptance and Commitment Therapy Series*:

- Have an adequate database. Those meant for the public will have at least one reasonably well-done and successful randomized trial showing that the methods are helpful.

- Be theoretically coherent—they will fit with the ACT model and underlying behavioral principles as they have evolved at the time of writing.

- Refrain from making excessive claims, and orient the reader toward unresolved empirical issues

- Not overlap needlessly with existing volumes

- Avoid jargon and the needless creation of new terms, or unnecessary entanglement with proprietary methods

- Keep the focus always on what is good for the reader

- Support the further development of the field

- Provide information in a way that is of practical use to readers

Sincerely,

—Steven C. Hayes, Ph.D.
 Georg H. Eifert, Ph.D
 John Forsyth, Ph.D.

Foreword

How did it come to be? How is it possible that nearly 90 percent of adult women in our culture want to be thinner, and year after year the female physical ideal becomes thinner yet? Why are so many men more worried about their apparent muscle mass than about the quality of their character? How did it come to be that we find it harder and harder to live inside our own skin?

The acceptance and commitment therapy (ACT) model applies to a wide variety of human problems because it targets common core processes in psychopathology and psychological health. The negative processes ACT targets have never been so dominant; the positive targets never so needed. Through media and technology, we have created a culture that disproportionately favors a problem-solving, discrepancy-based mode of mind. Nowhere is this more obvious and more needlessly destructive than in the area of body image dissatisfaction. Our culture is smothering us with beautiful ideals and negative self-judgments. The verbal tools that evolved to analyze situations and to predict and compare possible outcomes of actions are being used instead to compare our body shape to an ideal, to detect our own anxiety and insecurity about our physical form, and to predict illusory forms of self-esteem to be found in yet another restrictive attempt to lose weight.

It is not possible to turn off the flow of words and images that create idealization and shame. They bombard us from every corner. They leer out at us from our TVs, from our computer screens, from our cell phones, and from the checkout stands at the grocery store. With all the subtlety of a Times Square LED display, poured over fifteen floors of vertical real estate, commercial images splash into our consciousness, using those beautiful ideals and negative self-judgments to sell, sell, sell. It is not possible to turn off the flow and remain part of the modern world.

We need to do something more creative and more broadly useful. We need to strengthen an alternative mode of mind that can stand up to the modern world we have created—one based on appreciation, mindfulness, and engagement. Standing firmly in consciousness itself, we need to learn to notice the flight of thoughts, as they jump like nervous birds from branch to branch. Cupping our hand so we can better hear the echoes of our own history, we need to see how our past projects into the present with feelings, and memories, and sensations; yet we need to see them as they are, not as our fearful, self-critical minds declare them to be. Our thoughts and feelings are not our enemy. We can learn from them. But we dare not turn our lives over to them. We dare not. Not when commercial culture has programmed them so deeply. And as we become more open and centered, we need to learn to move our attention flexibly toward what we really value, and to step boldly in the directions we choose—directions that sustain us and give meaning to this very moment.

This book is about empowering you, as a therapist, to heal these cultural wounds and to create modern minds for the modern world. This book is about how to move from a problem-solving mode of mind to an engagement mode of mind in the area of body image dissatisfaction. In example after example, the authors make the ACT model accessible and relevant for those treating body image concerns. Practically, sensitively, and wisely, the authors address the nuts and bolts of clinical work with this population, from assessment to therapy transitions. This book builds on other ACT books but does not assume knowledge that not everyone will have. The practitioner who knows ACT will see how to link that knowledge to this problem area, and will find case examples and techniques to get over rough spots. The practitioner who does not know ACT will learn enough to get going and will have an excellent structure into which new knowledge can be placed. Thus the book works as a starting place or as an addition to a library of ACT methods. Experienced ACT therapists will find new exercises, examples, and ideas; newcomers will find a new path into a healthier response to the pain of body image dissatisfaction.

And if the process data and early controlled treatment data continue to hold, our clients will find something else: an empowering and self-compassionate space in which to stand amid the cacophony of words and images that invite us all to look down at our own bodies and find ourselves wanting. Our clients will find a place to live inside their own skin.

—Steven C. Hayes, Ph.D.
Reno, Nevada
December 2009

Acknowledgments

We would like to thank Tesilya Hanauer and Jesse Beebe at New Harbinger for their helpful feedback throughout the development of this book. Their knowledge of acceptance and commitment therapy (ACT) was evident in their suggestions, which were consistently helpful. Additional thanks to Jean Blomquist for the copyediting on this manuscript, to Jesse Burson for his assistance in the prepublication phase of the manuscript, to Amy Shoup for our cover design, and to all others at New Harbinger who helped in the development, editing, and publication of this book. It was a pleasure to work collaboratively with New Harbinger during the entire process of writing and editing this book. Without a doubt, this was a wonderful collective effort!

—ANP, MH, and VMF

First and foremost, I would like to thank my coauthors, Dr. Michelle Heffner and Dr. Victoria Follette, who contributed their clinical, research, and writing experience to this book. I would like to acknowledge and thank my research and clinical mentors at the University of Nevada, Reno's clinical psychology doctoral program for providing me with a strong foundation of training. It is with gratitude that I acknowledge Dr. Steven Hayes and Dr. Victoria Follette, from whom I received my clinical training and research experience in acceptance and commitment therapy. Thank you to my clinical supervisors at the VA Long Beach Healthcare System for continued clinical training and instrumental support while I worked on this book during my internship year. Special thanks to Dr. Kenneth Cole and Dr. Richard Tingey for our helpful discussions about the use of ACT by clinicians with diverse theoretical orientations and training backgrounds. Your feedback helped make this book user-friendly for a broad range of clinicians within different clinical settings. Enormous thanks to my fellow intern class of 2008–09: Dr. Colleen Clemency, Dr. Emily Fine-Foster, Dr. Heather Eisele, Dr. Marya Schulte, and Dr. Maggie

Syme. Your friendship, company, encouragement, and feedback while I was working on this book were wonderful! Thank you also to my family and friends for encouraging me, without fail, to live in a manner consistent with my values.

—Adria N. Pearson, Ph.D.

I would like to thank Dr. Michelle Rodoletz of HealthForumOnline.com (an online source for continuing education credits) for granting permission to reprint portions of my eating disorder courses featured on HealthForumOnline. I also would like to thank Center for Hope of the Sierras (CHS), a residential eating disorder treatment center. I worked at CHS for two years, and my experience with the clients and professionals there was invaluable as I wrote portions of this book.

—Michelle Heffner, Ph.D.

I am grateful to Adria for asking me to go on this journey with her. Her dedication to helping those with body image concerns has been an inspiration to me. As always, I am particularly thankful to Steve Hayes for opening the door to ACT for me. His mentorship and support have been invaluable. I appreciate the support and guidance in learning about body image that Linda Craighead has provided. As always, I am thankful for the support of the New Harbinger staff who have been so generous with their time. Finally, I am so appreciative of the support of my friends Heather, Don, and Stacy. They nourish my heart, body and soul.

—Victoria Follette, Ph.D.

PART 1

Introducing ACT for Body Image Dissatisfaction

CHAPTER 1

Body Image Dissatisfaction: An Introduction

Release me from this pain.
Everything my spirit longs to have fulfilled, fulfill.

—Sappho

The Complexity of Body Image Dissatisfaction

Body image dissatisfaction, a complex construct, is the negative evaluation of one's weight and shape. In their developmental contextual theory, Lerner, Skinner, and Sorell (1980) proposed that experience with one's body is influenced by a variety of factors, including cultural, developmental, biological, and historical. Specifying the relative impact of these contexts on body image satisfaction versus dissatisfaction is complex, and it likely varies by individual (McKinley, 2006). However, body image dissatisfaction impacts a wide range of individuals, both women and men, including those with subclinical levels of disordered eating and those without eating disorders.

Consider these questions: When was the last time you heard an individual remark negatively about his or her body? Was it last year? Last week? Was it today? Was the individual a man or a woman? Have you experienced a judgmental thought about your body today? If you cannot recall the last time you listened to someone negatively judge her body, take a trip to the local mall, grocery store, or gym and conduct your own research study. See how long it takes before you hear a comment related to weight loss, body fat, or changing body shape in some way. Our guess is that it won't take long. The Western society in which we live offers plenty in terms of food available. However, we also live in a society with a daunting ideal of beauty. That ideal dictates that bodies should not only be increasingly thinner but also have less body fat and more muscle, a reality that, for most people, is impossible to achieve. We face a difficult dichotomy between food that is hard to resist and an ideal body image that is hard, if not impossible, to achieve.

When did we humans begin to evaluate the body, and how did that evaluation acquire so much importance? Why are we so frequently obsessed with appearance? Several sociological and evolutionary theories offer possible answers to these questions, yet a definitive answer eludes us. The topic, however, provides good material for a lively philosophical discussion. In each time period and culture, people adhere to a narrative "truth" about what is beautiful (for example, "You can't be too rich or too thin" or "Thin is in"). Likewise, within each individual, a certain narrative "truth" reverberates in the mind (for example, "I've always been the fat girl," "I'll never look good enough," or "I've always been the scrawny guy"). In our minds, we tell ourselves various stories: what we think might happen in the future, why we think something happened in the past, what is beautiful, what is desirable, and so on. Like the thoughts we have on a daily basis, the stories we tell ourselves and others vary in accuracy with respect to our actual experience. When we become attached to thoughts or to a particular story as "truth," our behaviors may change accordingly. For example, if you're attached to the thought "Fat is ugly" as truth, your eating behavior may change in order for you to avoid becoming fat. Alternately, if you're overweight or perceive yourself to be, you may experience negative feelings when you tell yourself the "truth" that "Fat is ugly."

Just as individuals have personal stories, societies also have stories or myths that are passed down through generations. These are reflected in art, music, and literature, and they become social symbols of what is considered important, timely, and desirable. Today the media, including advertising, television, and movies, powerfully convey the "ideal" body image. The societal idea that thin is beautiful and that physical attractiveness is a valuable asset has roots in antiquity and is reflected in the Greek myth of the judgment of Paris (sixth century BC). In this myth, which appears in classical texts and artwork, three goddesses—Hera, Athena, and Aphrodite—are judged on their beauty by Paris of Troy, a male mortal. The prize for the fairest goddess is a golden apple, which Aphrodite wins with her beauty. She then causes Helen, wife of Menelaus and the most beautiful woman in the world, to fall in love with Paris, who takes Helen home with him to Troy. To avenge the insult to his brother Menelaus, Agamemnon follows with troops. The Trojan War ensues in a quest to bring Helen home.

For centuries, women have waged personal wars with their bodies as they have sought a "winning" appearance and all that is associated with it. The casualties of these wars are the women who lose vitality, time, and energy fighting for the weight, shape, or appearance that is attached to the perception of a prize. Each decade of the twentieth century had its own representation of female attractiveness. Each promoted a new look—the flat-chested, slender figure of the flapper style popularized during the 1920s; the more curvy figure that emerged in the 1930s and 1940s, highlighted with Marilyn's hourglass figure in the 1950s; Twiggy's stick figure in the 1960s; and, closer to the end of the century, the emergence of the athletic shape of the 1980s and the waif-thin appearance popularized in the 1990s. The twentieth century evidenced a continued emphasis on physical attractiveness as being associated with success. In the first ten years of the twenty-first century, we've observed an increase in advertisements to the public regarding both surgical interventions for weight loss and medical interventions for reducing signs of aging. New dietary strategies for weight loss and over-the-counter products marketed toward weight loss and reduction of the signs of aging are also prominent in television infomercials and magazines. As part of our popular culture, the marketing of these interventions continues to cultivate the message that it is important to remain youthful and thin. Since Greece in the sixth century BC, we've seen thousands of variations on Helen of Troy, the woman whose beauty was fought over, sought after, and idealized.

And what about men and body image dissatisfaction? It may seem that marketing for weight loss and beauty products is aimed primarily at women. Given the high rates of eating disorders among women, much of the research on body image concerns and eating disorders has historically focused on women and used women as research subjects. Because this is the case, we will present information pertaining to women first in this chapter. However, body image dissatisfaction is not just a female problem. With rates of obesity increasing across genders and in a culture with plentiful food yet with a high value on thinness, youth, and physical fitness, body image dissatisfaction is a human problem, not only a women's problem. In this chapter, we address gender differences with respect to the different manifestations of body image dissatisfaction in men and women. Yet, while body image dissatisfaction may manifest differently in men and women, the relative impact is the same. Therefore the treatment presented in part 2 of this book is for anyone, man or woman, struggling with body image dissatisfaction. Our clinical case examples include both men and women to illustrate issues relevant to both genders.

Women and Body Image Dissatisfaction

Since 1959, the image of the ideal female figure has decreased in size, becoming thinner (McKinley, 2006). Over the past thirty years, research on body dissatisfaction and disordered eating has frequently assessed symptoms in college-aged women, an age cohort showing a particularly high level of disordered eating behaviors and attitudes. As many as 88 percent of normal-weight college women report a desire to be thinner (Raudenbush & Zellner, 1997). Disordered eating behaviors such as calorie restriction, bingeing and purging, and use of other compensatory behaviors occur at a high frequency among college samples (Schwitzer, Rodriguez, Thomas, & Salimi, 2001; Protinsky & Marek, 1997; Harris, 1995; Hesse-Biber, 1992; Mintz & Betz, 1988). However, body image dissatisfaction is not only a problem among young women. Levels of body image dissatisfaction remain stable across the life span in women (Tiggemann & Lynch, 2001), with cohorts of women in their fifties showing relatively similar levels of body dissatisfaction to women in their twenties (Bennett & Stevens, 1996).

Contemporary research conceptualizes *body image* as one's cognitive, emotional, and behavioral reactions to body weight and shape (Tiggemann & Lynch, 2001). If, theoretically, body dissatisfaction is related to a constellation of thoughts and stories people tell themselves based on history, biology, culture, and development, the stability of dissatisfaction makes sense. Consider the enduring nature of stories across generations and, with our Greek myth, centuries! Using this pattern as a model, individuals' personal stories about what is attractive would easily be maintained over the course of a lifetime.

Biological, social, familial, and individual factors all impact the level of body dissatisfaction. The most predictive factor shown to increase rates of body dissatisfaction is body mass index (BMI), a mathematical ratio between height and weight (McLaren, Hardy, & Kuh, 2003; Tiggemann & Lynch, 2001). Higher BMIs are associated with higher levels of body dissatisfaction. Given our cultural ideal of thinness, this is not surprising. Social contextual factors, such as the popular media, play a large role in triggering body dissatisfaction across Western culture (McKinley, 2006).

Biological factors in women—including age of menarche (earlier onset), number of pregnancies, onset of menopause (earlier onset), and use of hormone replacement therapy— also impact the level of body image dissatisfaction (Hardy & Kuh, 2002). Additionally, a study by Clark, Skouteris, Wertheim, Milgrom, and Paxton (2009) showed body image problems increased in the months following pregnancy. Clark and colleagues also showed that, during pregnancy and in the first year postpartum, body image dissatisfaction was positively correlated with rates of depression. To the extent that these biological factors increase weight or change body shape, they also increase body dissatisfaction. Signs of aging also appear to increase body dissatisfaction, given that age moves one farther away from the Western cultural ideal of beauty (McKinley, 2006). For example, a man or a woman may be dissatisfied with sagging skin, wrinkles, or loss of muscle tone, which are not changeable through exercise and diet. We have a youth-obsessed culture. Take a look at the market in the United States for beauty products aimed at eliminating signs of aging as well as more extreme measures of cosmetic surgical procedures to see the anecdotal evidence of this.

Gender Considerations and Body Image Dissatisfaction

Historically, as we mentioned above, literature on body image has focused on female samples. Thompson, Heiburg, Altabe, and Tantleff-Duff (2002) suggest that much of the literature on body dissatisfaction is focused on women because it is related to eating disorders, which statistically are more common among females. In addition, the generalized sociocultural norm does not tend toward men having a small or thin ideal shape. While the ideal female form has consistently become smaller and thinner since the 1960s, the ideal male image has stayed relatively constant (Thompson et al., 2002). However, men experience body image dissatisfaction also. Instead of aiming for weight loss or a smaller or thinner shape, men's desire tends to focus on increased muscle mass (Filiault, 2007; Grossbard, Lee, Neighbors, & Larimer, 2009). The desire for more muscle in men has been termed the Adonis complex (Pope, Phillips, & Olivardia, 2000). Within samples of men, sexual orientation impacts rates of body image dissatisfaction. Specifically, gay men evidence greater levels of body dissatisfaction and related distress when compared to samples of heterosexual men (Siever, 1994; Lakkis, Ricciardelli, & Williams, 1999); heterosexual men evidence lower levels of body dissatisfaction than samples of gay men, lesbians, and heterosexual women (Beren, Hayden, Wilfley, & Grilo, 1996). Kimmel and Mahalik (2005) examined minority stress as a factor impacting degree of body image dissatisfaction in gay men. Their findings showed that factors including internalized homophobia, stigma, and experiencing an antigay physical attack all were associated with increased levels of body image dissatisfaction and distress in gay men who endorsed conforming to masculine norms. The authors relate the increase in body image and related distress to be a reaction to minority stress factors in order to conform to the traditional masculine image.

Body dissatisfaction in men and women predicts poor psychological well-being in both genders (Ganem & Morera, 2009). Filiault (2007) points out that men who are dissatisfied with their muscle mass have been shown to exhibit increased psychological distress, including higher levels of depression and lower self-esteem, in addition to lower perceived sexual efficacy. A study by McFarland and Kaminski (2009) showed lower self-esteem and higher rates of depression and anxiety to be predictive of body image problems in a sample of men. A study by Grossbard and colleagues (2009) also showed self-esteem to be related to a drive for body image changes, specifically in men who showed a high drive for increased muscularity. Research has consistently shown that samples of women with subclinical disordered eating also show increased rates of psychological distress such as depression and anxiety, poorer quality of life (Niemeier, 2004), and overall poor mental health (Ganem & Morera, 2009). For women, Grossbard and colleagues (2009) also showed a relationship between weight concerns and lower self-esteem. Additionally, high levels of weight-related anxiety have been associated with high rates of unemployment and an increase in anxiety and depressive symptoms (Bennett & Stevens, 1996). This draws attention to the gender differences that exist in the manifestation of body image dissatisfaction, but it also shows that the relative psychological impact of body image dissatisfaction is similar across genders. Whether a man is distressed about his muscle mass or a woman is concerned about her shape, size, or weight, the psychological impact appears to be similar.

This book and the treatment we offer here are intended to address the range of body image problems men or women may experience. Body image dissatisfaction can manifest itself in a myriad of ways. We have only touched on some general trends that have been shown to vary by gender with respect to body shape and size. This does not account for manifestations of body image dissatisfaction that relate to facial appearance, height, or other issues related to shape and size that distress individuals. For our purposes in this book, "body image dissatisfaction" includes any negative evaluation of the body. From an acceptance and commitment therapy (ACT) theoretical perspective, the most important aspect of body image dissatisfaction is determining how it functions for a person, as opposed to the specific aspects of the body that evoke the dissatisfaction. Just as body image dissatisfaction has similar psychological impact in both men and women, the same may be true with different manifestations of body image dissatisfaction. Whether people are unhappy with their weight or other aspects of appearance, research shows that persistent body dissatisfaction results in decreases in psychological well-being. As we move ahead in this chapter, we will review some risk factors for body image dissatisfaction, its various manifestations, and the resulting impact on quality of life.

Experiential Factors in Body Image Dissatisfaction

Within society, there are additional contextual factors at group level and individual level associated with higher rates of body dissatisfaction and disordered eating. Individuals with trauma histories, those in performance groups (including sports), and those with chronic or severe medical conditions have each exhibited high rates of body dissatisfaction. It is important to state, however, that body image dissatisfaction is not limited to these groups, nor should a causal relationship be drawn between the group membership (for example, those with a trauma history) and the occurrence of body dissatisfaction. The old research adage "Correlation does not equal causation" is important to remember in that respect. We have included a brief review of body image dissatisfaction as it occurs in these subgroups in this first chapter. Later you'll find case examples related to some of these subgroups as well as other populations. We hope these examples will make this book salient to your clinical work while also providing a flexible approach to treat anyone struggling with body image dissatisfaction.

Research has consistently shown higher rates of trauma histories in individuals with eating disorders than those without eating disorders (Briere & Scott, 2007), making for a complex clinical presentation. Much has been hypothesized about sexual trauma being a predictive factor for the development of eating disorders and associated symptoms. The research is mixed on this. However, there have not been consistent empirical findings that childhood sexual abuse is a specific risk factor for eating disorders or the severity of disordered eating symptoms (Levitt, 2007). In addition, Billingham and Patterson (1998) showed no correlation between rates of sexual victimization and levels of body image dissatisfaction in a college sample. Yet, within this sample, higher rates of body image dissatisfaction were shown in subgroups within dating relationships. With regard to body weight, Weiderman, Sansone, and Sansone (1999) examined rates of body image dissatisfaction in obese women with and without a sexual trauma history. They found that obese women with a history of sexual trauma had less body dissatisfaction than women who had not been sexually abused. The authors hypothesize that obesity may serve as a protective factor—that is, if women aren't fitting the "ideal image" of the thin body portrayed in Western society, they may feel more protected from male attention.

Given the high rates of comorbid disordered eating symptoms (including body dissatisfaction) and historical sexual trauma, it is important to recognize this correlation. However, given the mixed research outcomes, it doesn't appear to be a stable, consistent, or a causative relationship. Therefore, as you encounter women with body image dissatisfaction, disordered eating, or a trauma history, the literature to date suggests caution in assuming that one would coexist with or predict the other. Briere and Scott (2007) suggest that trauma be treated separately, and that the treatment of trauma would not necessarily result in a reduction of disordered eating symptoms.

Other subgroups also experience higher rates of body dissatisfaction than the general population. Individuals involved in activities or subcultures that place a value on thinness and appearance experience higher rates of body dissatisfaction (Allison & Park, 2004; Connor-Greene, Striegel-Moore, & Cronan, 1994). Certain athletic groups are a good example of this. Gymnastics, figure skating, wrestling, and long-distance running, for example, promote a low weight. In these contexts, individuals have added pressure to maintain a certain body weight and shape. Holm-Denoma, Scaringi, Gordon, Van

Orden, and Joiner (2009) compared eating disorder symptoms, including body dissatisfaction, among nonexercisers, varsity athletes, club athletes, and independent exercisers. They found that, overall, women who participated in sports had higher levels of eating disorders than nonexercisers, and that those who had high levels of sports anxiety and who participated in athletics had higher levels of body dissatisfaction.

Contextual factors have an additive effect on the rates of body image dissatisfaction. Specifically, Clemency (2009) conducted a study examining the role of self-objectification (that is, self-evaluative thoughts about the body) on rates of body dissatisfaction in individuals in multiple performance groups (acting and dancing). The findings showed that individuals in multiple performance groups experienced higher rates of body dissatisfaction than those individuals in only one performance group, and those rates were higher than that of the general population. This research supports contextual factors as having an additive effect on body image dissatisfaction.

Presumably any number of factors, alone or in combination, may explain preoccupation with the body and dislike of appearance. It is likely not possible to determine the specific etiology of preoccupation with the body, dissatisfaction, and associated features. We do know that certain risk factors exist—such as sexual trauma or involvement in athletics or multiple performance groups—and that their effect is additive. In addition to risk factors for developing body image dissatisfaction, life events may change or threaten the body. Individuals whose weight or body image is somehow compromised by physical illness also show higher rates of body dissatisfaction than that of the general population. Let's take a closer look at that population now.

Medical Populations and Body Image Dissatisfaction

Individuals with chronic health conditions are susceptible to high levels of body image dissatisfaction. Health problems that result in weight increases or changes in physical features can impact self-perception and increase body image dissatisfaction and disordered eating attitudes (such as believing foods are either "all bad" or "all good," having rigid rules around eating, or exhibiting subclinical eating disorder symptoms). We hope that this book and the treatment approach we offer will be useful to medical professionals as well as to mental health professionals practicing in an integrated care setting. We will briefly review below the manifestation of body image dissatisfaction in three medical conditions: diabetes, multiple sclerosis, and cancer. Obviously body image dissatisfaction may occur in a myriad of disease processes. We chose to highlight these three diseases because, in these disease processes, several issues—including medication, diet, and potential disability—may impact body image. The impact of cancer on body image is related to treatment options, such as chemotherapy and surgery, that often alter the appearance of the body. Studies have shown body image dissatisfaction within samples with these disease processes, and that the rates are higher than in healthy control groups.

Diabetes

Erkolahti, Ilonen, and Saarijarvi (2003) examined self-image in adolescents with diabetes mellitus (type 1) and rheumatoid arthritis and compared these groups to healthy controls. Their findings showed no differences between the groups overall. However, the chronically ill adolescents showed lower scores on the body image scale of the self-image measure. The authors conclude that chronic illness does not predict poor self-image. By adolescence, individuals who have been living with chronic illness have incorporated the illness into their self-image instead of letting the illness define them.

In both type 1 and type 2 diabetes, diet is a key component of disease management. Carroll, Tiggemann, and Wade (1999) examined the relationship between body dissatisfaction, bingeing, and self-esteem in women with type 2 diabetes compared to a nondiabetic control group. Overall, findings indicated that women in the diabetic group were more dissatisfied with their bodies than the control group, and that they were heavier on average. This result supports BMI as being the strongest predictor of body image dissatisfaction. Given that the sample represented a wide age range (twenty-five to eighty-three old), with a mean age of fifty-eight, this also provides further support that body image dissatisfaction is present across age cohorts. Specific to the diabetic population was a stronger relationship between binge eating and self-esteem than in the nondiabetic control group (Carroll et al., 1999). The authors conclude that binge eating for women with type 2 diabetes may evidence the lack of control they already feel about their body due to the diabetes, thus impacting self-esteem. They suggest that "general self-esteem enhancement strategies" (1999, 72) be used to increase blood glucose control in women with type 2 diabetes. Presumably decreases in binge eating would moderate this change.

Multiple Sclerosis

Multiple sclerosis (MS) is another chronic health condition that impacts self-perception of the body; it is also a disease with high rates of comorbid depression (Siegert & Abernethy, 2005; Goretti et al., 2009). While MS may sometimes result in a physical disability, the disease often presents with symptoms for which the effect is invisible to society. An individual may appear healthy, yet suffer from symptoms of fatigue, sensory problems, and weakness. In addition, a common treatment for acute exacerbations of the disease is intravenous and oral corticosteroids (Beck et al., 1993; Myers et al., 2004; Frohman, 2007), which often result in weight gain (Langer-Gould, Moses, & Murray, 2004; Stanbury & Graham 1998). A study by Halligan and Reznioff (1985) compared MS patients in early stages of the disease to those in middle and later stages of MS. The study showed that patients with a newer diagnosis (first five years), when the disease is less severe, had comparatively higher body anxiety than those in the middle to later stages of the disease. In support of this research, Barak, Lampl, Sarova-Oinchas, and Achiron (1999) showed lower body esteem in patients with relapsing-remitting MS than in healthy controls. This research points to the changes in self-perception that occur early, before patients experience noticeable changes in body function.

Cancer

Cancer may not be the first disease we think of with respect to weight gain and associated body dissatisfaction. We more commonly associate weight loss with cancer because *cachexia*, weight loss despite maintaining a normative caloric intake, is associated with several types of cancers (Denmark-Wahnefried, Rimer, & Winer, 1997). Breast cancer, commonly associated with weight gain, is an exception to this. In fact, weight gain occurs in up to 80 percent of women with breast cancer (Helms, O'Hea, & Corso,

2008). Weight gain as a side effect of a specific type of chemotherapy, increases in caloric intake (due to stress), and decreases in physical activity may all contribute to weight gain in breast cancer patients. Helms and colleagues also describe hair loss and the degree of invasiveness of the surgical intervention to the breast as being other factors impacting body image concerns. Distress related to self-image has been shown to impact treatment decisions and coping ability with treatment in general (Quintard & Lakdja, 2008). Sheehan, Sherman, Lam, and Boyages (2008) examined what factors lead to decision regret with respect to choosing immediate versus delayed breast reconstruction following a mastectomy. Their findings show that decision regret was associated with negative body image. They suggest that physicians work with surgical candidates during the decision process to dispel any unrealistic expectations with respect to surgical outcomes. With respect to degree of distress, body image distress was higher in cohorts of younger breast cancer patients (Helms et al., 2008).

Of course breast cancer is only one of many disease processes that include potential physical changes. Consider the potential of disease or accidents to result in permanent damage to the body. One such disease process impacting the face and neck is head and neck cancer. Body image changes in patients with head and neck cancer have been investigated. Medical interventions for head and neck cancer, such as radiation and tumor resection, often leave patients with noticeable physical changes without the possibility of entirely recapturing the predisease physical appearance (Liu, 2007). Facial disfigurement impacts various areas of life, including personal identity, self-image, and social functioning (List et al., 1996; Lockhart, 2000). Liu (2007) conducted a research study examining changes in body satisfaction in patients with head and neck cancer. In the study, ninety-seven Chinese patients with head and neck cancer were surveyed following reconstructive microsurgery. Liu found that self-image significantly decreased following surgery. Factors impacting self-image were gender (women experienced higher levels of dissatisfaction), employment status (unemployment was associated with higher dissatisfaction with appearance), type of treatment (more aggressive treatment was associated with higher levels of image dissatisfaction), and age. This study was conducted in an Eastern culture. However, the result of women showing higher levels of image dissatisfaction is consistent with research from Western cultures.

In another study with head and neck cancer patients, Terrell, Manavati, Esclamado, Bradford, and Wolf (1999) showed that the subjective report of disability in a Western culture was associated with the number of treatments that were implemented. An increased number of treatments in these head and neck cancer patients was associated with the perception of a more advanced disease process, additional complications, and greater physical changes caused by the treatments and their side effects. This research draws upon the relative impact of treatment side effects on body image dissatisfaction.

Medication

Compliance with medical treatments is impacted by weight gain and also by associated body dissatisfaction. One example is compliance to HAART (highly active antiretroviral therapy) to treat HIV disease where compliance is impacted by perceived body image changes. Plankey and colleagues (2009) showed that self-perception of fat gain around the central part of the body (stomach area) was the strongest predictor of noncompliance with the HAART regimen. The authors suggest that more attention should be given to the impact of perceived body changes on adherence to HAART. In addition to this example, weight gain is associated with several different pharmacotherapies for psychological disorders, including antidepressants, antipsychotics, and mood-stabilizing agents (Vanina et al., 2002). The side effect of weight gain is one among many factors that have been implicated in reducing compliance in psychotropic medication (Allison et al., 1999; Masand, 2000). Theoretically any medication that impacts weight may impact compliance, and this may be especially salient in those with body image dissatisfaction with fear of weight gain.

We have highlighted three disease processes (diabetes, multiple sclerosis, and cancer) that impact body image. The impact on body image and weight from treatments such as surgery and medications affects treatment decision making and treatment compliance across various medical and psychiatric populations. Given that this book may be used in medical settings by health care practitioners, these may be salient clinical issues to assess and target. In part 2 of this book, we provide case examples of individuals with medical conditions and associated body image dissatisfaction to illustrate treatment application.

Therapeutic Issues and Body Image Dissatisfaction

Now that we have considered various aspects of body image dissatisfaction, let's briefly look some therapeutic issues. First, we will present some basic research on acceptance and commitment therapy as an intervention for body image dissatisfaction. Second, we will look at using the treatment approach presented in this book with clinical and nonclinical populations. Third, we will revisit some gender and cultural considerations. And finally, we'll discuss the necessity of intervention.

ACT and Body Image Dissatisfaction

Preliminary investigations of ACT as an intervention for eating- and weight-related issues are promising. Lillis, Hayes, Bunting, and Masuda (2009) applied a one-day ACT workshop to a sample of obese men and women. The study showed significant decreases in experiential avoidance, greater maintenance of weight loss, less psychological distress, and improved quality of life. Pearson (2009) applied ACT in a one-day workshop format to treat body image dissatisfaction in adult women (ages eighteen to sixty-five). The study showed significant decreases in disordered eating attitudes and body image–related anxiety and experiential avoidance, and significant increases in acceptance. The treatment presented in this book is modeled after the Pearson (2009) study. We hope that the promising treatment results shown in that study will someday be replicated with men, adolescents, and individuals with other types of image-related distress.

Use with Clinical and Nonclinical Populations

The treatment we present in this book is primarily targeted to those individuals with body dissatisfaction who do not have an eating disorder. However, disordered eating behaviors such as binge eating, purging, and excessive dieting and associated attitudes about food and eating often co-occur with body image dissatisfaction (Mintz & Betz, 1988; Tylka, 2004; Tylka, & Subich, 2002; Lewis & Cachelin, 2001). Disordered eating attitudes encompass a variety of beliefs and feelings that occur in individuals across diagnostic spectrums of eating disorders. Anxiety with respect to one's body, dichotomous thinking (that is, black-and-white or all-or-nothing thinking), rigidity with respect to thinking and rule making, perfectionism, and avoidance of experiencing emotions may all be considered disordered eating attitudes or characteristics. Negative evaluation of weight and shape, or body dissatisfaction, may also be considered part of the larger constellation of disordered eating attitudes and is a diagnostic criterion for both anorexia and bulimia. *Anorexia* is characterized by a refusal to maintain normal weight due to fear of fat, whereas *bulimia* is characterized by repeated episodes of binge eating followed by compensatory behavior (for example, self-induced vomiting, laxative abuse, excessive exercise, and so on).

Body dysmorphic disorder (BDD) is another clinical diagnosis related to body image dissatisfaction. In BDD, an individual experiences a negative perception and psychological distress related to a specific body part or feature without any apparent physical deformity. Like body image dissatisfaction, associated problems in social functioning, depression, and anxiety are evident in BDD (Didie et al., 2006). As in anorexia and bulimia, symptoms similar in scope to BDD may be evident in nonclinical populations. Manifestations of body image dissatisfaction may appear similar to BDD, given the preoccupation with body shape, weight, or appearance. Therefore, accurate assessment and diagnosis are always important to differentiate between BDD and body image dissatisfaction.

Given the comorbidity of body image dissatisfaction with eating disorder symptoms and the similarity in clinical features of BDD, it is not necessary to exclude clinical populations in application of ACT for body image dissatisfaction. We discuss some applications to disordered eating patterns and provide measures for assessment of eating disorders. However, ACT for body image dissatisfaction is not, by itself, a treatment for a clinically severe eating disorder or body dysmorphic disorder. We encourage you to utilize an empirically supported treatment for these psychological diagnoses when available. We hope that the treatment described in part 2 of this book will be useful for nonclinical populations, as an adjunct to an empirically supported treatment in a clinical population, or in addressing body image dissatisfaction that may persevere after an eating disorder or body dysmorphic disorder has remitted. Body image dissatisfaction is also the strongest predictor of relapse for eating disorders (Keel, Dorer, Franko, Jackson, & Herzog, 2005). Therefore this book and the treatment in it may be useful as a relapse-prevention intervention for patients recovering from an eating disorder.

Gender and Cultural Considerations

The treatment in this book is applicable to both women and men, as well as to individuals from diverse cultural backgrounds. As we indicated earlier, body dissatisfaction and disordered eating attitudes are not problems exclusive to women, and they certainly aren't exclusive to Western cultures either.

Given that research has consistently shown a higher prevalence of body image dissatisfaction and disordered eating attitudes in women and in Western cultures, however, much of the research we cite in this book was conducted with related samples. Therefore, as with any clinical issue, sensitivity to cultural and gender differences should be used when considering the problems discussed in this book and when applying the treatment to individuals from diverse backgrounds. Because it is impossible to adequately capture each individual and cultural difference in one book, the responsibility of cultural competence is, as always, that of the clinician applying the treatment.

The universality of human suffering, experience of painful emotions, and having a body we must live in (for better or worse) crosses boundaries of time, age, and culture. While differences in presentation of clinical problems and response to treatment may exist at the level of individual, gender, and culture, our common thread is our humanity. Our goal as clinicians and researchers is to be helpful in dealing with individual suffering across culture, gender, and individual differences.

The Necessity of Intervention

To date, there is no empirically supported, efficacious treatment for body image dissatisfaction and associated attitudes. An *empirically supported treatment* is a manualized treatment that has been shown to be superior to pill, placebo, or other treatment in a randomized clinical trial (Chambless & Ollendick, 2001).

Most treatments that address body image dissatisfaction are more broadly designed for eating disorders or have been included in eating disorders prevention programs. A review of eating disorder prevention programs by Mussell, Binford, and Fulkerson (2000) showed an overall poor outcome of these interventions in terms of their ability to prevent eating disorders at long-term follow-up. Currently, cognitive behavioral therapy (CBT) for bulimia is an efficacious treatment. While there are some promising studies, to date there are no treatments for anorexia that meet the strict criteria for an empirically supported treatment. While efforts at preventing eating disorders and treating eating disorders are important, treatment aimed at addressing the more common constellation of disordered eating and body image dissatisfaction is needed also. Even though body image dissatisfaction may not present the extreme clinical picture evident in anorexia and bulimia, it is an insidiously chronic problem.

Body image dissatisfaction has varying levels of psychosocial, mental health, and medical impact on individuals. The term "normative discontent" has been used describe the prevalence of body dissatisfaction in women. Given the long history of focus on body image concerns and the high prevalence of disordered eating behaviors among women, it may be that body image dissatisfaction has become a socially acceptable problem among women. The term "normative discontent" itself would certainly support this. For men, the issue of body image dissatisfaction is just beginning to emerge in the literature as a problem with a similar psychological impact as for women. As we discussed above, research shows that the impact of continuous dissatisfaction with one's body in men and women is associated with a variety of mental health variables, including depression, anxiety, and lower self-esteem. In addition to associated mental health issues, body dissatisfaction alone has been associated with poor quality of life and other adverse health-related behaviors, such as avoidance of physical activity (Reboussin et al., 2000; McLaren & Kuh, 2004).

Given that BMI is the strongest predictor of body dissatisfaction, the associated psychological and physical problems with having either a high or a low BMI are also relevant. Body dissatisfaction and other areas of psychological distress appear to be more prevalent among those with high and low BMIs (as opposed to a normative BMI). McLaren, Beck, Patten, Fick, and Adair (2008) investigated mental health variables (that is, anxiety and depression symptoms) among cohorts of men and women with a range of BMIs. Within samples of men and women with either low or high BMIs, a higher incidence of anxiety and mood disorders was shown compared to cohorts with normative BMIs.

In addition to impacting quality of life, body image dissatisfaction impacts medical populations in various ways, including compliance and treatment decision making. Because contextual factors are additive with respect to increasing body image dissatisfaction, patients with health problems may be at especially high risk for body image problems. Decreased medication compliance is a wide-reaching problem with medications that impact weight and shape. In terms of treatment success and decision making regarding treatments, it appears that body image is a relatively important factor. The literature addressing the impact of medical interventions on body image repeatedly suggests that clinicians attend to this. When a physician diagnoses a patient with a serious illness such as cancer, the physician's goal is to save the patient's life; the impact of the treatment on body image is likely to be, at best, a secondary consideration. Therefore health psychologists, nurses, and psychologists in private or community practice who treat patients with medical problems have an important role. Attending to the perceived importance of body image changes resulting from treatment may, in fact, help individuals adhere to the treatment or make a balanced treatment decision. By helping patients clarify their values with respect to all areas of life, including health, the perceived impact of body image changes may be considered with the patients in the larger context of their life functioning.

Given the psychological, social, and health consequences of body image dissatisfaction and associated disordered eating attitudes and behaviors, we hope that acceptance and commitment therapy may offer a solution. Some benefits of this treatment are that it is brief, it has successfully been applied in group and individual formats across a wide age range of populations, and it can be applied flexibly to various types of body image problems.

Who Will Benefit from This Book?

This book is for any clinician whose clients include people who have become attached to the myth that personal value is determined by appearance. It is for you to help your clients see that the stories their minds tell them do not need to shape their personal truth. We hope that those who read this book, those who apply the treatment, and those who benefit from the treatment gain some insight into the various factors that have shaped (1) the story of what is attractive, (2) the energy spent in the quest to attain that, and (3) what the cost has been. We offer, in this treatment, a way to begin living a more broad and flexible life based on personal values instead of living in accordance with stories that are held in the mind.

Our hope is that the treatment in this book will help a diverse range of individuals with varying presentations of body image dissatisfaction. The examples we use provide some common clinical presentations of body image dissatisfaction, but we understand that we have not come close to capturing every clinical picture. We hope that use of this book by a broad range of clinicians will diversify the utility of the treatment.

Conclusion

To review, body image dissatisfaction affects both men and women. Although it may manifest differently across genders, it appears to have similar psychological impact. Certain populations have been shown to exhibit high levels of body image dissatisfaction, especially those in performance groups and sports and those with chronic medical conditions. The effect of being a member of multiple high-risk groups has been shown to be additive. Other individual factors may also play a role in the development of body image dissatisfaction. Therefore, it is important to consider all contextual and historical factors that may have contributed to your client's body image dissatisfaction and may be serving to maintain it. This book is intended to guide clinicians in treating body image dissatisfaction with acceptance and commitment therapy. We hope this treatment helps your clients let go of an overemphasis on body image and clarify what else really matters in life, and thereby live a more vital, meaningful life.

And so, what comes next? In the following chapter, we describe the theory and application of acceptance and commitment therapy, including specific application to body image problems. We also recommend various assessment tools. In chapter 3, we discuss using ACT in various settings and modalities, as well as considerations for various populations. In part 2, Applying ACT to Body Image Dissatisfaction, we guide you through the application of each component of acceptance and commitment therapy in an individual therapy format, provide recommendations for specific application of each component, and offer relevant case examples. We also provide specific guidance on implementing this treatment in group or workshop format. And, in closing, we offer a few thoughts on ending treatment and on life for clients following therapy.

CHAPTER 2

Acceptance and Commitment Therapy: An Introduction

One's suffering disappears when one lets oneself go, when one yields—even to sadness.

—Antoine de Saint-Exupéry

The Pervasiveness of Human Pain

Emotional pain is an inescapable part of the human experience. Humans are subject to a full range of emotions that we have labeled as either "unpleasant" (for example, sadness, anxiety, anger, disgust, grief, disappointment, and so on) or "pleasant" (amusement, happiness, joy, and so on). When we are distressed, we often look for ways to cope with or relieve that distress. Some of these strategies can be adaptive and healthy, such as having a cup of tea, taking a warm bath, or going for a walk to cope with negative experiences. These responses, which are part of a generally accepted convention of dealing with difficulties, can be useful when employed in ways that do not interfere with general psychological functioning.

However, humans sometimes go to great lengths to avoid the emotions we label "unpleasant." Behaviors such as substance abuse, working unreasonably long hours, self-injury, binge eating, purging, extreme dieting, or social isolation may be employed in order to avoid uncomfortable emotions. We conceptualize these behaviors as serving the function of avoiding emotional pain. While some of these behaviors may work in the short run, it's easy to see how many of these behavior patterns create additional suffering (painful emotions on top of the source of the original painful emotions) in the long run. The original pain doesn't really go away, but instead is embedded in a layer of suffering produced by the very means used to avoid the pain. One example of this may be eating to cope with uncomfortable emotions, such as sadness or anger. Indulging in our favorite treat after a stressful day is not a bad thing or even unhealthy when done in moderation. However, if we overuse this coping strategy and overeating is a primary strategy of avoiding uncomfortable emotions, additional suffering may be created. Additional suffering may result in the form of unhealthy weight gain and other health-risk factors such as high cholesterol, high blood pressure, and other problems associated with obesity. Therefore, the original painful emotions still exist, and on top of that is the suffering brought on by the avoidance strategy.

Acceptance and commitment therapy encourages individuals to accept the experience of emotional pain as something that is part of any human life. Of course, this challenges our societal notion that we should always be happy and avoid pain at all costs. We would argue that this is a culturally created myth that joins other thoughts and ideas about what is normal and how people should strive to live their lives. With the help of ACT, our task as clinicians and humans is to develop a different relationship with those myths, thoughts, and ideas for ourselves and our clients. To accomplish that task, instead of always attempting to change emotional experience, ACT promotes (1) acceptance of what exists and (2) behavior change based on what is meaningful in terms of having a rich life. This doesn't mean that we expect people to just sit with any pain that shows up. After all, pain can serve a useful function: it can convey the need to make change, such as pulling your hand from a hot stove or leaving an abusive relationship. However, when the avoidance of pain becomes a way of life, the suffering and problems associated with that avoidance can drain life of its vitality and meaning. In short, in the face of the pervasive pain of life, ACT helps people to accept and be present for all of their life experiences and to change their behavior based on what is meaningful to them.

Some Basic ACT Resources

Before we move into a discussion of the historical context and theoretical bases of ACT, we want to acknowledge that you—the mental health professionals reading this book—may have a range of clinical experiences from a variety of theoretical orientations. Some of you may already have experience using ACT as an intervention. Others may be learning about ACT for the first time. While we provide a fundamental foundation in this book for using ACT with clients who have issues associated with body image, we encourage you to explore the wealth of additional theoretical and applied books that can enrich your understanding of acceptance and commitment therapy. If you are new to ACT, we recommend these books:

- *ACT in Practice: Case Conceptualization in Acceptance and Commitment Therapy,* by Patricia A. Bach and Daniel J. Moran (2008)

- *Learning ACT: An Acceptance and Commitment Therapy Skills-Training Manual for Therapists,* by Jason B. Luoma, Steven C. Hayes, and Robyn D. Walser (2007)

- *A Practical Guide to Acceptance and Commitment Therapy,* edited by Steven C. Hayes and Kirk D. Strosahl (2004)

These books provide a thorough review of the theoretical principles of ACT and methods of application of the therapy. Several other books apply ACT to specific populations, including those with post-traumatic stress disorder (PTSD), anxiety disorders, and others. Over the past five years, ACT has been applied in a growing number of research studies to a range of eating disorder populations, including anorexia, overeating, weight loss, and body image dissatisfaction (Lillis, Hayes, Bunting & Masuda, 2009; Pearson, 2009; Heffner, Sperry, Eifert & Detweiler, 2002). An ACT self-help manual for the treatment of anorexia—*The Anorexia Workbook: How Accept Yourself, Heal Your Suffering, and Reclaim Your Life*—is available (Heffner & Eifert, 2004). However, our book is the first to provide clinicians with a step-by-step guide on applying ACT to treat body image dissatisfaction, which occurs across various populations. In this chapter, we review historical and theoretical underpinnings of this therapy approach and then provide a discussion of its clinical application to treat body image dissatisfaction. Following this, we offer recommendations for assessment.

The Historical Context of Acceptance and Commitment Therapy

Acceptance and commitment therapy is a behavioral therapy that is part of a tradition referred to as the third wave of behavioral interventions. Initial behavioral interventions were based on operant and classical conditioning theories. These initial interventions were innovative in that they were aimed at direct and observable behavioral changes, such as treating a fear response by exposing the client to feared objects and situations until the fear response was extinguished. Behavior therapy was at the forefront of the movement for evidence-based treatments. Because the targeted behaviors were observable and could be directly assessed, behaviorists were able to empirically measure change as a result of their interventions. This interest in theory and measurement has been described as the first wave of behavior therapy. The second wave of behavior therapy included addressing internal experiences such as thoughts and feelings, which had been largely unaddressed in earlier models. These therapies include cognitive behavioral therapy interventions, where the aim is to change observable behaviors by first restructuring maladaptive thoughts. The idea behind this approach is that if the thoughts are changed, behavior change will follow and feelings will change as a result.

Cognitive behavioral interventions have been successfully applied to treat several psychological disorders using step-by-step manualized treatments. These treatments are tailored to treat the symptoms present in diagnostic categories of the psychological disorders in the *Diagnostic and Statistical Manual of Mental Disorders* (American Psychiatric Association, 2000). Over the past thirty years, empirical studies have shown a great deal of success, with many CBT interventions now being considered efficacious treatments for depression (Segal, Williams, & Teasdale, 2001), anxiety disorders (Barlow, 2002), and bulimia (Fairburn, Marcus, & Wilson, 1993) among others. There are many benefits to manualized CBT treatments, including ease of dissemination to a wide range of clinical practitioners and settings, time efficiency, and cost efficiency. However, even as these therapies have continued to gain acceptance, a number of concerns about their utility have emerged. Some of the issues have included questions about the mechanism of change and concerns about "nonresponders" or dropouts. Over the past twenty years, a new behavioral tradition began to emerge, sometimes referred to as the third wave (Hayes & Smith, 2005), that addresses the broader context of the human experience. One focus of the third-wave behavioral interventions is on identifying and changing the function of behaviors versus changing their form or content. In short, the goal is no longer to get rid of dysfunctional thoughts, but rather to move toward the acceptance of thoughts and feelings, and to move toward behaviors that are more consistent with the client's valued life goals.

In addition to expanding the context of what is included in behavioral therapies, some third-wave therapies have added a focus on mindfulness, adopted from a traditionally Eastern meditation practice. Given its success, mindfulness has now been integrated into several different psychotherapies. Mindfulness-based cognitive behavioral therapy (Segal et al., 2001), for example, expanded upon traditional CBT for depression. Acceptance and commitment therapy was developed in the tradition of the third wave of behavior therapies, with a focus on addressing the function of behaviors and utilizing mindfulness and acceptance as tools for change (Hayes, Strosahl, & Wilson, 1999). In ACT, gaining awareness of context and the cues in the given context are emphasized by teaching skills such as mindfulness and meditation. In this way, individuals are taught to broaden their behavioral repertoire to respond to present-moment stimuli. In many ways, a focus on mindfulness and acceptance fits a broader zeitgeist that is changing our approach to a wide range of cultural problems.

The Theoretical Bases of ACT:
Relational Frame Theory, Cognitive Fusion,
and Experiential Avoidance

We believe that in preparation for practicing acceptance and commitment therapy, it is important to understand the theoretical foundations of ACT. If you already practice ACT, you may already understand the importance of the theoretical underpinnings. In that case, this may be a review with specific attention to how relational frame theory, cognitive fusion, and experiential avoidance apply to an ACT conceptualization of body image dissatisfaction.

Like other psychotherapies, ACT has treatment components, which we will review in part 2 of this book. The tools within the treatment components (that is, therapy exercises, handouts, and so on) serve a particular function. To use the tools without having at least a basic understanding of the theory on which they are based is like using a hammer without knowing why you are using it. You may still be quite successful at operating the hammer (you might know that it changes the shape of things when you hit it upon an object). However, knowing its intended function is quite important to both the process of using it and the outcome. Understanding the theoretical underpinnings of ACT will allow you to apply the tools of ACT in a meaningful way, which hopefully will provide a workable and effective experience for you as a clinician.

Relational Frame Theory

ACT is a psychotherapy based on the conceptual foundation of relational frame theory (RFT). Hayes, Barnes-Holmes, and Roche (2001) provide a detailed description of RFT and the supporting research. In keeping with the scope of this book, only the basic tenets of the theory will be covered.

All humans, assuming normative cognitive development, acquire language and begin to make associations between objects and words. Once children acquire language, they begin to name objects in their environment. A learned relationship is made between the object and the word that is bidirectional in nature (that is, hearing or thinking the word will bring to mind the object, and seeing the object will bring to mind the word). In RFT terms, this is called a *verbal referent*, and it is based on form (that is, the appearance of the object; Hayes et al., 2001). For example, when children learn the word "apple" for that fruit, they will be able to imagine an apple (versus a banana or a pear) when hearing the word, and will also be able to identify the fruit by its name when they see it.

As children develop cognitively and have more life experience, verbal referents become more complex. For example, a child will learn that the person known as "Mommy" also has a first and a last name. Mommy might be called "Susan" by the child's father and "Mrs. Smith" by someone calling on the telephone. Through these experiences, the child learns that Mommy, Susan, and Mrs. Smith are all the same person; she now has three verbal references for her mother.

RFT proposes that verbal references can also be comparative, hierarchical, and evaluative (Hayes et al., 2001). For example, a comparative verbal referent might be this: "I'm smarter than you" (based on a child learning he has scored higher on a test than his friend). The function of scoring higher on a test becomes paired with level of intelligence. An example of a hierarchical verbal referent would be the association of thinness to the word "beautiful" in Western culture. The thinner a woman is, the more beautiful she is considered to be. An example of an evaluative verbal referent would be a child feeling shame or sadness upon hearing "You're a bad boy." The word "bad" becomes evaluative, functioning as punishment and evoking unpleasant feelings. In these ways, associations with words become a matter of function instead of being associated merely through the form of an object.

An example often used in RFT literature (Hayes, Strosahl, Bunting, Twohig, & Wilson, 2004; Luoma et al., 2007) to illustrate the shifting from form to function in a relational frame is that of a dime and a nickel. If a child who does not know the value of money is shown a dime and a nickel and is asked, "Which is bigger?" he will choose the nickel based on form: the nickel is larger in size. However, an older child, knowing that a dime has more value, chooses the dime as bigger based on function (that is, "bigger" has extended its association from a larger size to greater worth).

It's not too much of a leap to apply this example to body image. Consider the statement "You're a big girl." This statement may be used as a compliment to a two-year-old during toilet training as an association to being more independent (and also perhaps "dry"). As such, in childhood, being a "big girl" or a "big boy" may be a statement of praise, associated with independence, responsibility, and perhaps greater worth as a person. This same phrase may also be used by a parent as a reprimand to stop unwanted behaviors—for example, "Stop that. You're a big girl now." In this way, "You're a big girl now" might be associated with feelings of shame or less worth for the child. Arbitrary associations are already being made at this early age. That a two-year-old has a larger body than an infant, in part, promotes successful toilet training. Size may help a child with the skills necessary for toilet training. However, the relationships between "big girl" and responsibility, or "big girl" and praise, or "big girl" and punishment are arbitrary associations. These associations are subsequently learned by the child.

Consider now if this same statement is made to the same girl at age thirteen by her mother's adult, female friend: "You're a big girl." Depending on her experiences in childhood and her current experiences in puberty, the words "big" and "girl" probably won't have positive associations. By the time she is thirteen, hearing these two words together may have multiple functions that are context dependent. This includes the association between the words and the person saying them, the words as they relate to prior experiences, and also the words "big" and "girl" as associated in social contexts.

Now consider the same statement said by a seventeen-year-old boy to the same girl, now age fifteen, when he sees her in her bathing suit at the pool: "You're a big girl." The scenarios are becoming painful, and their associations are much different. "Big girl" may now have hierarchical associations (such as less liked than a small or thin girl) and evaluative associations (such as lonely or worthless). The words in these scenarios have not changed, yet their function has shifted. We can almost promise the reader that, unlike the two-year-old did when successfully using the potty, the fifteen-year-old girl does not associate pride, responsibility, or independence when hearing the statement at the swimming pool. The function of these words has changed, based on the contextual factors of her history, prior learned associations of the words "big girl," and the contextual factors of the current situation (the boy, the tone of voice, and hierarchical and evaluative associations that may exist with these words). In short, she will experience these words differently based on their relational frame.

Cognitive Fusion

Language has a great deal of utility in many aspects of our life. However, when *cognitive fusion*—that is, fusion with verbal stimuli—begins to control our life choices, problems frequently arise. Words do not in and of themselves carry pathological functions. As we illustrated above, the functions of words are learned. As humans, using language and learning verbal relations is unavoidable if we are to interact in the world.

The problem occurs when cognitive fusion, brought about by derived verbal relations, becomes more powerful in determining behavior than other important factors, such as emotional experience. Fletcher and Hayes (2005) identify three problems that occur with cognitive fusion: (1) thoughts are associated with internal experiences, such as fear; (2) attachments are made to thoughts that describe the self, which people spend energy attempting to either prove right or change (consider the woman with anorexia who is fused with the thought "I am fat" and dies trying to change this); and (3) present-moment experience is blunted and overtaken by thinking about the future or the past. Thinking, reasoning, and explaining (that is, verbal processes) become entangled in a never-ending web. Results of attachment to thoughts and loss of contact with the present moment include the narrowing of behavioral choices, which become based only on thoughts instead of on experiences.

Consider the story of the girl who was told, "You're a big girl," at different points in her life, beginning at an early age. The phrase "You're a big girl" may become a story she hears, like a tape replaying itself, in her mind. In the process of cognitive fusion, the girl will make an attachment to the phrase and all other variants of it, despite any evidence to the contrary. Other verbal networks related to the statement will have been formed, likely shifting in form and function depending on the context. For example, the verbal network may include "You're ugly, unattractive, fat, and you have no self-control" and other variants that are evaluative of "You're a big girl" or explain to her why she is "a big girl." Noticing that her body becomes bigger as she grows up and physically matures will be one context that triggers these thoughts. However, the actual form of her body (whether or not she is overweight or tall, or literally bigger on average than other girls her age) won't shift the function of this story in her life. If she is cognitively fused to that story, her behavior will be controlled by that verbal network instead of other factors. For example, she may not respond to hunger by eating but instead respond to the thought "I'm a big girl." This could perpetuate food restriction, even when she is hungry. Theoretically, she may behaviorally respond to any number of thoughts in this verbal network (such as "I'm fat," "I need to diet," or "Big girls aren't attractive") versus responding to her actual experiences in life. In this way, behavior in other domains of life may also be impacted. After the incident at the swimming pool, she may decide that "big girls shouldn't go to swimming pools." The cognitive fusion or inability to shift behavior in response to present-moment demands (versus verbal ones) has been termed psychological inflexibility (Dahl, Plumb, Stewart, & Lundgren, 2009). This is theoretically on the far end of a continuum of psychological flexibility, a concept first introduced by Hayes, Strosahl, Bunting, and colleagues (2004). The inflexible or narrow behavioral response set that is generated from cognitive fusion is, theoretically, one factor that leads to psychopathology. If taken to the extreme, the story "I'm a big girl" and its variants could continue to drive her eating behavior until the individual becomes anorexic. In her quest to avoid the fear, shame, and other emotions that all the variants of her story evoke, she will change her behavior accordingly. She would literally behave in response to the story her mind has created instead of responding to her experience in life. This brings us to the next component of the theoretical framework of ACT, which is experiential avoidance.

Experiential Avoidance

Hayes, Wilson, Gifford, Follette, and Strosahl (1996) define *experiential avoidance* as occurring "when a person is unwilling to remain in contact with particular private experiences (e.g., bodily sensations, emotions, thoughts, memories, behavioral predispositions)" (1996, p. 1154). The term describes the function of any behavior engaged in for the purpose of attempting to avoid or reduce unwanted experiences. Several behavior classes have been conceptualized as serving the function of experiential avoidance. Substance abuse is a clear example of behaviors that belong to the class of experiential avoidance, generally serving to immediately reduce or numb unpleasant emotions. Moreover, this is not just relevant to the issue of abuse. Using alcohol to address distress or anxiety is a socially sanctioned way of dealing with discomfort. Experiential avoidance is not only associated with "disorders," but rather is a general approach to dealing with negative experiences. Thus it is not surprising that avoiding or getting rid of uncomfortable feelings is something that people view as an appropriate manner of responding. Familiar advice such as "Put a smile on," "Stop thinking about negative stuff," or "Don't worry so much about food" is a part of the typical human experience. However, when avoidance becomes a way of life that pervades all aspects of existence, people run into all types of trouble.

Experiential avoidance has been described as a functional diagnostic dimension that is relevant to a range of psychological phenomena (Hayes et al., 1996). Recently, the relationship of experiential avoidance to eating disorders has become a focus of investigation (Heffner, Sperry, Eifert, & Detweiler, 2002; Hayes & Pankey, 2002). Heffner and colleagues (2002) describe bingeing, compensatory behaviors, and excessive dieting as behaviors whose function is avoidance of thoughts and feelings evaluated by the individual as negative and uncomfortable (such as anxiety and guilt experienced after eating). Thus disordered eating behaviors and attitudes, including body image dissatisfaction, may serve a common function of experiential avoidance. We provide a conceptualization of this set of behaviors as a functional class below.

Functional Relationships of Disordered Eating Behaviors

Dieting, binge eating, and purging (and other compensatory behaviors) are three overt behaviors that comprise the primary diagnostic criteria for anorexia, bulimia, and binge eating. In considering experiential avoidance as a possible functional dimension across all three eating disorders, it is important to assess how disordered eating behaviors may function in relation to each other, and in relation to negative thoughts, feelings, and physical states. Research on the functional links among these three behaviors, as well as research on the etiology and risk factors for these behaviors, theoretically supports the concept that they may each function as experiential avoidance.

In relation to experiential avoidance, compensatory behaviors may serve as avoidance of the thoughts, feelings, and body sensations that result from either an objective binge (in bulimia or binge-eating disorder) or a subjective binge (in anorexia). Theoretically, eating large amounts of food (in bulimia) or what one perceives as large amounts of food (in anorexia) may trigger thoughts and feelings regarding weight, shape, and associated family or sociocultural values of thinness. These standards may then be compared to the individual's own perceived failure with dieting after a binge, and escape behavior (such as purging, laxative abuse, or excessive exercise) may ensue. The consequence of these behaviors may be the immediate lessening of negative affect regarding the inconsistency between one's high standards (or values) of control of food, thinness, and associated attributes, and the perceived failure at achieving those when bingeing (either subjectively or objectively). If the compensatory behavior results in weight loss or physiological sensations of hunger, these may serve as reinforcers for the behavior, which is theoretically mediated by experiential avoidance.

Body Image Dissatisfaction

In addition to disordered eating behaviors serving as a form of experiential avoidance, focus on body image dissatisfaction to the extent that it causes distress or becomes time-consuming may be conceptualized similarly. In a sample of women over the age of twenty-two with bulimic attitudes (as measured by a widely used eating disorders attitudes inventory), there was greater cognitive avoidance of emotional material than nonemotional material using a measure from a basic laboratory task (Seddon & Waller, 2000). In a comparison group of younger women (under twenty-one years), Seddon and Waller also showed cognitive avoidance of both positively and negatively emotionally valenced items. This suggests a trend in adolescent women toward avoidance of emotion, both positive and negative, and is one of the pieces of the scientific foundation that supports intervention targeting experiential avoidance in order to address body image dissatisfaction issues.

As is found in clients with clinical levels of eating disorders, where high rates of desire for self-control are evidenced (Mizes & Klegses, 1989), women in nonclinical or subclinical populations may also exercise internal attempts to control thoughts and feelings. By focusing on thoughts related to the body, food, calories, and eating, other, more difficult topics (or less "controllable" events) may be avoided. In this way, cyclical efforts at dieting and chronic body dissatisfaction may serve as avoidance strategies for approaching more emotionally difficult or less personally controllable situations (such as relationships). The chronic nature of body image dissatisfaction and disordered eating attitudes suggests they are being maintained by avoidance of a more unpleasant stimulus.

ACT Core Processes and Treatment Components: Treating Body Image Dissatisfaction

ACT is a flexible treatment with six core processes that are implemented within a framework of six treatment components. Describing the relationship between the core processes and the treatment components is not linear. Rather, the processes that theoretically facilitate change in ACT are interwoven into each component of treatment in a flexible and fluid manner. The benefit to this is that the treatment components create a framework within which therapeutic work can be individualized to the varying needs of each client. Below we describe how the core processes of treatment may be implemented within each treatment component.

Overarching Themes of Acceptance and Commitment Therapy

Acceptance and commitment therapy targets experiential avoidance and cognitive fusion in the service of broadening behavioral repertoires to provide a more vital, meaningful life. In this section, we provide a guide to applying the treatment's six core processes within the framework of the components of treatment. Application of each treatment component to body image dissatisfaction is thoroughly described in part 2 of this book.

ACT involves six core processes, which are implemented in the therapy:

- Self-as-context

- Defusion

- Acceptance

- Contact with the present moment

- Values

- Committed action

The therapy itself is structured into the following treatment components:

- Creative hopelessness

- Control as the problem

- Mindfulness and acceptance

- Values clarification

- Barriers to values and committed action

Of course it would be easiest to describe how to conduct ACT if each of the core processes aligned neatly with each of the therapy components. This is not the case. Each core process may be integrated into any of the therapy components. The therapy components serve as a framework and a guide. The core processes are the theoretical points of intervention within that framework. As mentioned above, in part 2 of this book, we will provide a detailed description of the methodology used in each treatment component, which serves to target core processes. When you utilize exercises or therapy tools in each component of treatment, pay attention to which therapy process you are targeting. In other words, what is the desired effect in that moment?

While the overall model can seem quite complex, breaking the treatment down into its basic components can help to clarify the bigger picture. It is often useful to remember the two overarching themes present in ACT: (1) mindfulness and acceptance and (2) behavior change and committed action. Within any treatment component, reorient to whether mindfulness and acceptance or behavior change and committed action are needed in that moment. Knowing which of these is targeted with a particular therapy exercise is useful in determining which core process you target (Orsillo & Roemer, 2005).

The table below provides a conceptualization of each of the six core processes as they are subsumed under the themes of mindfulness and acceptance, and behavior change and committed action.

Mindfulness and Acceptance	Behavior Change and Committed Action
Self-as-context	Self-as-context
Contact with the present moment	Contact with the present moment
Defusion	Values
Acceptance	Committed action

Hayes, Strosahl, Bunting, and colleagues (2004) indicate self-as-context and contact with the present moment occur in behavior change and commitment processes as well as mindfulness and acceptance processes. The processes of mindfulness and acceptance also include defusion from thoughts and acceptance of one's experience. Commitment and behavior change processes also include clarifying values and behavioral action in accordance with those values. Theoretically, each of these core processes, working alone and together, facilitates psychological flexibility.

To be psychologically flexible means to broaden the behavioral repertoire, to respond to the present moment. So, to review, the treatment components are presented in part 2 of this book. These form a framework within which the six core processes are implemented. These core processes are flexible and can be targeted in any of the treatment components. They are each targeted with specific therapy tools (that is, exercises and metaphors) and homework. In order to decide which therapy process to target at which time, we recommend you ask yourself these questions:

- Which overarching therapy theme is needed right now: mindfulness and acceptance, or behavior change and committed action?

- Given the theme, which core process needs to be targeted?

- Referring to part 2 of this book, what component of treatment are you working within, and what tools (exercises) will be effective to target that core process?

To illustrate the theory and application of the six core processes, we provide a case example followed by a description of the theoretical basis of each core process and application to that case example.

■ Case Example: Dan

Dan is a twenty-year-old man who presents with body image dissatisfaction. You will be seeing him for twelve individual psychotherapy sessions using acceptance and commitment therapy. Dan considers himself short for a man—he's five foot five—and is unhappy with his height. He is also obese, weighing 230 pounds. Dan states that he has been upset at some level about his appearance since childhood. He believes that he is "chunky." He reports that his brothers took after his dad and are both over six feet tall and quite muscular, while he took after his mother, who also has a weight problem and is five feet tall. He states that he feels unattractive and believes that no one would ever want to date him because of his physical appearance. He states that he feels every part of his body is "bulky, but in a fat way—not in a muscular way."

Since adolescence, Dan has tried a variety of diets, including high protein, low fat, and fads such as carrot shakes. He has also tried working out by lifting weights at home, but he stays away from the gym because "I'm too ashamed to lift weights around the other guys because I'm fat and weak." He has lost a few pounds on the diets, but he eventually gains the weight back, plus a few extra pounds. He adds that anytime he begins to work out, he ends up eating more and putting on weight without developing the muscle he wants. He reports that he's never able to stick to a diet for more than a month. He has a pattern of trying a new diet, quitting when weight loss begins, and then trying another diet when he gains weight back. He reports that the few friends he has have made fun of him for being on a diet, saying that he's "eating like a girl." In an attempt to fit in socially, he ends up caving to peer pressure to drink beer and eat fattening foods with the other men in his college residence hall.

Dan describes his body image distress and disordered eating behaviors with positive affect, often using humor about his challenges with body image. He admits some embarrassment about having this problem, because, he says, "My brothers say this is a problem that women have. Men shouldn't get upset about their weight and size. They call me a 'big boy' and say I should be the 'happy fat guy.'" He describes this as a "lifetime" struggle, yet does not demonstrate any visible emotion in his report of self-hate. He remarks, "It's not like I have an eating disorder or anything. I know there are people much worse off than me—probably a lot of women who you see in here." When asked why he is seeking help for the problem, he quietly states, "I'm just tired of hating myself. I'm sick of not wanting to look in the mirror, and hating what I see when I do. I've tried the diets and I don't think I'm ever going to achieve that muscular, svelte look I'm going for, but I can't seem to let it go and just be happy."

In the case of Dan and other clients who present with body image dissatisfaction problems, it is important to rule out an eating disorder. Typically, enough information is gathered in an unstructured clinical interview to make a diagnosis. In Dan's case, he reveals that he binge eats occasionally (once every other week) and then subsequently restricts his diet for a day or two following the binge to compensate. He also sometimes engages in self-induced vomiting (once every couple of months) when he overeats. He does not exercise excessively. Although he acknowledged bingeing and purging, he does not engage in these behaviors frequently enough to meet the diagnostic criteria for bulimia, which would require that the binge episodes and compensatory behaviors occur at least twice per week for three months. If you need assistance making a diagnostic decision, you can administer a semistructured interview, such as the Eating Disorder Examination (EDE; Fairburn & Cooper, 1993) or the Eating Disorder Examination for Children (ChEDE; Bryant-Waugh, Cooper, Taylor, & Lask, 1996).

Understanding Your Client: The Use of Assessment Data

During the first session, you may find it useful to administer one or more ACT-relevant assessments to better understand the client's thoughts, feelings, and behaviors related to body image dissatisfaction. We have divided assessment measures into three sections: (1) those that are useful for determining weight dissatisfaction and assessing desired weight and body shape, (2) those that are useful for assessing body image dissatisfaction and disordered eating pathology, and (3) those that are helpful in assessing experiential avoidance and acceptance or psychological flexibility. These assessments can also be readministered during or after treatment to assess symptom change and progress. You do not need to administer all of the following assessments to every client, and you may choose to administer some not listed here instead. Use your clinical judgment to determine which measures would be most appropriate to help you evaluate each individual client.

Measures That Assess Weight Dissatisfaction and Desired Weight

Assessment of Body Weight Dissatisfaction. A practical method of assessing body image dissatisfaction is to obtain the client's actual body weight as well as the client's self-stated desired body weight. To determine how dissatisfied the client is with current body weight, subtract the client's self-stated ideal weight from the actual weight. The larger the discrepancy, the more intense the body weight dissatisfaction. For example, a client who weighs 212 pounds but desires to be 150 pounds has a weight dissatisfaction of 62 pounds.

Assessment of Desired Weight Using Body Mass Index (BMI). Self-stated body weight can also provide information regarding the client's drive for thinness and how realistic this desired weight may be. Once the client reports the desired weight, you can determine the body mass index associated with that desired body weight. BMI scores below 17.5 are considered underweight, 20 to 25 is normal, 26 to 29 is overweight, and 30 or above is obese. You can use an online BMI calculator. (An Internet search for BMI calculators will yield a variety of useful websites that will calculate BMI for you.) On the BMI calculator, enter the client's actual height and desired body weight. In the case of a six-foot-tall client who desires to weigh 100 pounds, the BMI would be 13.6, which indicates that the client desires to reach an extremely low and unhealthy weight.

Assessment by Body Silhouette Preference. Another variation of assessing body dissatisfaction is to present the client with drawings of silhouette figures that represent a continuum of body shapes and sizes for the client's gender. There are several different assessment tools involving the use of silhouettes to evaluate body image dissatisfaction with respect to the discrepancy between one's ideal shape and size and actual shape and size. The Body Image Assessment for Obesity (BIA-O; Williamson et al., 2000) is one example of a reliable and valid measure of body image dissatisfaction using silhouettes. The original Body Image Assessment (BIA), by Williamson, Davis, Bennett, Goreczny, and Gleaves (1989), also utilizes silhouettes to evaluate body image problems and is used with eating disorder populations. The BIA-O expands upon this measure for use with obese individuals, whereas other body image assessments utilizing silhouette drawings are limited to normal weight to thin samples, or are for those with eating disorders. Normative data has been collected for this measure with men and women with a broad range of body mass indexes (Williamson et al., 2000). Given that a high BMI (that is, being overweight) is the strongest predictor of body image dissatisfaction, the applicability of the BIA-O to obese individuals is particularly salient.

In this assessment, there are nine silhouette figures representing thin to very overweight body sizes on cards. In the assessment, clients make three card selections according the following requests: "Select the silhouette that most accurately depicts your body size as you perceive it to be." "Please select the silhouette that most accurately depicts the body size that you would most prefer." "Please select a silhouette that represents a body size that you believe is realistic for you to maintain over a long period of time" (Williamson et al., 2000). Each of these responses receives a number. Body image dissatisfaction is assessed by the discrepancy (in a numerical score assigned to the card choices) between the individual's perceived body shape or size and the ideal and realistic card choices. This type of assessment is a visually cued method of assessing clients' perception of their body image, as well as the degree to which their ideal shape and size are realistic.

Measures That Assess Body Image Dissatisfaction and Disordered Eating Pathology

Body Image Avoidance Questionnaire (BIAQ). This nineteen-item measure (Rosen, Srebnik, Saltzberg, & Wendt, 1991) assesses avoidance of situations that provoke body image concerns. Clients rate how often they engage in specific body image avoidance behavior, such as wearing darker clothing or avoiding physical intimacy.

Body Image Quality of Life Inventory (BIQLI). This inventory (Cash & Fleming, 2002) assesses how body image problems affect client quality of life and engagement in domains such as sense of self, social functioning, sexuality, emotional well-being, eating, exercise, grooming, and so on.

Eating Attitudes Test (EAT-26). The EAT-26 (Garner, Olmsted, Bohr, & Garfinkel, 1982) is a twenty-six-item self-report questionnaire assessing maladaptive eating attitudes and behaviors in both adolescent and adult populations, including bingeing, purging, calorie restriction, and disordered eating attitudes.

Eating Disorders Examination (EDE, 12th edition). The EDE (Fairburn & Cooper, 1993) is a semistructured clinical interview intended for diagnostic assessment of anorexia and bulimia.

Eating Disorders Inventory–III (EDI–III). The EDI-III (Garner, 2004) is a reliable and valid ninety-one-item self-report measure assessing symptomology and diagnostic criteria for anorexia and bulimia. Items are ranked on a scale of always, usually, often, sometimes, rarely, or never.

Forbidden Food Survey (FSS). This questionnaire (Ruggiero, Williamson, Davis, Schlundt, & Carey, 1988) lists forty-five specific foods and beverages, including nine items for each of the five food groups and foods with low, medium, and high calorie content. Clients rate how each food item makes them feel about themselves using a five-point scale, ranging from "I would feel very good about myself after eating this food" to "I would feel very badly about myself after eating this food."

Goldfarb Fear of Fat Scale (GFFS). This ten-item self-report (Goldfarb, Dykens, & Gerrard, 1985) measures the fear of being or becoming fat. Each item is rated from 1 (very untrue) to 10 (very true).

Mizes Anorectic Cognitions questionnaire (MAC). This thirty-three-item self-report questionnaire (Mizes & Klegses, 1989) assesses thoughts experienced by clients with anorexia and related problems. The MAC yields a total score and three subscale scores for fear of weight gain, control of eating or weight to maintain self-esteem, and body image as a basis for social approval. The original MAC was revised into a shorter twenty-four-item questionnaire (MAC-R; Mizes et al., 2000).

Obesity-Related Well-Being questionnaire (ORWELL 97). Use this questionnaire (Mannucci et al., 1999) to assess the extent to which obesity-related problems interfere with client quality of life.

Physical Appearance State and Trait Anxiety Scale–State Version (PASTAS-S). The PASTAS (Reed, Thompson, Brannick, & Sacco, 1991) is a reliable and valid fifteen-item self-report measure of body anxiety that specifies anxiety levels about certain body parts (hips, waist, legs, arms). Items are ranked on a five-point scale where 0 is not at all anxious and 4 is extremely anxious. The state version specifies how anxious clients feel "right now" with regard to their body.

Preoccupation with Eating, Weight, and Shape scale (PEWS). The PEWS (Niemeier, Craighead, Pung, & Elder, 2002) is an eight-item self-report scale that was developed to assess preoccupation with food and eating, weight, and shape. The PEWS has been used with female college students, women with binge-eating disorder, and women with bulimia nervosa, and has been shown to have high internal consistency, concurrent and discriminate validity, and sensitivity to change.

Situational Inventory of Body-Image Dysphoria (SIBID). The SIBID (Cash, 1994) measures the frequency and intensity of negative feelings related to body image across forty-eight situations, such as grooming, eating, intimacy, and physical activity. A short version (Cash, 2002) includes twenty items instead of forty-eight.

Thought Control Questionnaire (TCQ). The TCQ (Wells & Davies, 1994) is a thirty-item self-report questionnaire measuring individual differences in responses to unwanted thoughts. Responses to items are indicated on a four-point Likert scale of never to almost always.

Measures That Assess Experiential Avoidance and Acceptance or Psychological Flexibility

Acceptance and Action Questionnaire (AAQ). The AAQ (Hayes, Strosahl, Wilson, et al., 2004) has both a nine- and a sixteen-item version, both of which have been validated to measure experiential avoidance. The measure has subscales for willingness to experience difficult private events and the ability to act in the presence of difficult private events. The items are ranked on a seven-point Likert scale. Higher scores indicate greater experiential avoidance. The sixteen-item version has also been refactored where higher scores indicate greater levels of acceptance and willingness (Bond & Bunce, 2003).

Acceptance and Action Questionnaire (AAQ-2). The AAQ-2 (Bond et al., 2009) is a ten-item questionnaire that has an overall score for acceptance or willingness. Higher scores indicate greater psychological flexibility or acceptance. Lower scores indicate greater experiential avoidance. This version of the AAQ-2 has been shown to have high correlations with the AAQ (above).

Acceptance and Action Questionnaire for Weight-Related Difficulties (AAQ-W). The AAQ-W (Lillis & Hayes, 2008) is a twenty-two-item self-report questionnaire assessing willingness to connect with undesirable thoughts and feelings specifically in regard to weight and eating-related topics. It is designed for the purpose of assessment in the context of weight loss or weight maintenance.

Integrating ACT Core Processes and Assessment Data

As described in this section, data from questionnaires can be integrated into the delivery of treatment using the six ACT core processes. As with any treatment, case conceptualization is essential in helping you to determine the most appropriate treatment focus at any one point in time. Remember that as you learn more about the client, it may be useful to reassess the utility of your conceptualization and make adaptations to the treatment. In describing the core processes, we will use examples from the case of Dan to give a sense of how each area might be addressed in treatment. Here we just give an overview. In the following chapters, we will elaborate on exercises and specifics for each target area.

Mindfulness and Acceptance: Self-as-Context

All humans have a self-concept that is based on the thoughts we have about our self. We tell stories about this self-concept: "I'm a very loyal person" "I'm a procrastinator" "I have some good qualities and some bad ones." As described previously in this chapter, relational frame theory proposes that the experiences we have and the stories we form about those experiences create a sense of who we are. This sense of self is not a grounded one and shifts almost constantly based on both internal and external experiences. Based on our earlier example of "I'm a big girl," the goal would be to help the client to gain awareness that "I'm a big girl" is a thought about self that triggers certain emotions, but that thought is just a thought or description of the body. The meaning of "big" shifts depending on the context, and it need not control one's behavior. The goal of self-as-context is to develop flexibility rather than having a rigid view of the self or being tied to a certain "reality." The objective is to develop a sense of self that is the context for a range of thoughts, feelings, and experiences. There is a self that can "hold" all of the client's experiences rather than the client being defined by any one idea, emotion, or characteristic.

In ACT, an appreciation for self-as-context is built through mindfulness practice. (For more on mindfulness practice, see chapter 7). In Dan's case, the goal was for him to work on describing and noticing the thoughts that he had about his body image. Items that Dan endorsed on the questionnaire measures provided examples of the body image thoughts that he most frequently experienced, and he developed mindfulness skills to observe those thoughts as they happened.

Many different mindfulness exercises exist to observe thoughts, and we describe some in chapter 7 of this book. For Dan, it was helpful for him to imagine that his thoughts were snowflakes falling and melting as they hit the ground. He said that sometimes his mind felt "stormy" and this evoked the image of a blizzard with thoughts piling up in snowdrifts. Instead of attempting to shovel away all the snow (that is, attempting to get rid of the thoughts), he learned to notice the amount of "snow" that was falling on the ground in his mind daily.

Mindfulness and Acceptance: Defusion

Being fused to a certain thought as truth prohibits contact with the present moment and the ability to behave in accordance with the present moment. *Defusion* is the process that targets this problem. Instead of helping clients change their thoughts, ACT encourages them to notice their thoughts and reorient to the present moment. The difference between cognitive fusion and defusion can be demonstrated in the difference between saying, "I am fat" (cognitive fusion), and saying, "I am having the thought that I am fat." Cognitive defusion involves the ability to notice each thought as being a thought, rather than adhering to thoughts as facts. Becoming defused from thoughts allows clients to choose whether they respond to the thought behaviorally or not. In this way, it promotes behavioral flexibility.

In the case of Dan, defusion was developed when he was exposed to stressful body image situations that triggered negative thoughts. For example, data from the Body Image Avoidance Questionnaire indicated that wearing workout clothing triggered uncomfortable thoughts for Dan. In treatment, Dan wore shorts when he went to the gym with a friend. During his workout, Dan practiced his self-as-context skills by acknowledging that uncomfortable thoughts were occurring within his head, and he also practiced defusion by acknowledging that those thoughts were thoughts, and there was a difference between "Everyone is laughing at the fat on my body" and "I am having the thought that everyone is looking at my body." Defusing from the thoughts about being judged allowed Dan to participate in exercising at the gym with his friend even though he was having uncomfortable body image thoughts.

Mindfulness and /Acceptance: Acceptance

Acceptance is the turning point of giving up old behaviors that are not working. Acceptance is an active process, not a resignation. It is embracing reality as the individual experiences it. When we say "embracing," this does not mean liking. To accept a feeling, all that is needed is to experience it instead of avoiding it. You don't need to enjoy the experience; you only need to have it. To do this requires willingness. *Willingness* means being willing to be flexible.

Sometimes clients enter treatment with full awareness and acceptance that their behavior patterns are problematic. In Dan's case, he was able to identify the high costs of body dissatisfaction and know that it interferes with life. He stated, "Yes, I see how my desire for a better body interferes with my relationships, my health, my freedom." His responses to the Body Image Quality of Life Inventory confirmed that his body dissatisfaction limited his quality of life. His body size per se was not the problem; the problem was his struggle to escape from his body, which cost him time, emotional energy, and social relationships, which he avoided. After Dan accepted that a problem existed with his efforts to change his body, the next question he pondered was this: "Am I willing to try something different?" The different behavior involved willingness to accept his uncomfortable body image thoughts and feelings, and to give up avoidance behaviors.

Behavior Change and Committed Action: Contact with the Present Moment

Being in contact with the present moment is a constant focus in ACT. Even when reflecting on past experiences, the important aspect is how these experiences impact "the now." The past is not unimportant. The collective experiences of the past have shaped behavior and formed one's ideas about self and the world. However, given that the past is unchangeable, it matters most to promote acceptance of that, and of the thoughts and feelings the individual currently experiences. This is something we can work with to promote more vital and meaningful lives for our clients. In order to promote contact with the present moment, ACT targets reduction of experiential avoidance. Behaviors functioning as experiential avoidance interfere with contacting the present moment. In the mindfulness and acceptance components of treatment, skills are taught as means of being in contact with the present moment.

In Dan's case, it was necessary that he remain in contact with the present moment during values clarification exercises. In order to clarify what is meaningful in life, Dan had to be willing and able to participate in the present moment. When working with Dan on values clarification and committed action toward goals, there was continuous orientation to the present moment. As Dan began to explore the values most meaningful to him, he was sometimes pulled back by thoughts about the past or by fear of failure. At those times, it was helpful to reorient him to the present moment, reminding him that he can have a new experience now.

Behavior Change and Committed Action: Values

Hayes and Strosahl define *values* as "chosen qualities of purposive action" (2004, 10). In *values clarification*, clients are asked to identify what domains of life (such as family, health, good friends, romantic relationships, career, citizenship, spirituality, and so on) are most meaningful. Where do clients want to spend their energy? At this point in treatment, clients have identified that they don't want to spend energy on avoidance and associated behaviors. Values clarification offers alternatives about where to spend energy in life.

In Dan's case, he developed willingness to accept uncomfortable feelings that he previously spent energy attempting to avoid. Letting go of avoidance behaviors reduced the suffering that those behaviors produced. However, if reduced suffering was the only result, there probably wouldn't be much motivation to let go of old behaviors because those avoidance behaviors produced an immediate reduction in discomfort. Why should Dan let go of avoidance and feel anxious, sad, and the range of other emotions that might arise? ACT does not posit that clients let go of old behaviors "just because" they are unhealthy. Behavior change in ACT is in the service of an individual's values, what is truly meaningful to that person. In Dan's case, what was meaningful was also unclear. The goal of values clarification exercises is to identify core values and to engage in values-based behaviors. Living in the service of one's values means to move forward toward values-based goals along with the range of feelings that may arise in pursuit of those values and goals.

Behavior Change and Committed Action: Committed Action

This brings us to committed action. In ACT, *committed action* (or commitment) means either to follow through with a specific values-based goal or to practice mindfulness and acceptance in response to unchangeable situations. As we have discussed, acceptance is an active process, and therefore acceptance itself is a committed action. Goals that clients have developed that are consistent with their values are another area for committed action. ACT emphasizes workability. Therefore, in helping a client make a commitment to a set of behaviors, you should attend to whether the behavior is actually workable in your client's life or not.

Goals can be shifted to better match current resources, capabilities, or the life situation of clients while still fitting with their values. In Dan's case, he stated that he valued his relationship with his seven-year-old nephew and wanted to roller-skate with him, but Dan's obesity prevented him from safely participating in this activity. However, the underlying value of strengthening his relationship with his nephew was workable, and Dan was able to identify several workable goals to bond with his nephew. Data from the ORWELL questionnaire can identify other predictable barriers that may restrict obese clients from engaging in certain activities, but the key is to find a workable solution. Beyond obesity, other clients may have physical limitations, yet everyone can learn to adapt and discover a more vital life. *Barriers to values* is a component of treatment where the clinician should work with clients to predict factors that might get in the way of valued action. Barriers can be either practical or perceived obstacles, such as financial limitations or other practical factors. An analysis of these factors can focus on addressing practical problems. However, it may also be useful to address concerns that only appear to be real (i.e., "I could never change that.")

Moving toward one's values while experiencing a range of human emotions is not easy work. Some barriers to valued living are often only barriers to the extent that clients perceive them as such. The thought "I can't do this" and similar thoughts can exist as barriers if clients do not practice defusion when these arise. Feelings can be perceived as barriers, such as when clients believe if they feel depressed, they cannot function with the feeling of depression. In relation to committed action around acceptance, clients might think, "I can't ever accept this." Identifying the thoughts that may arise as barriers will allow clients to notice these and practice defusion and mindfulness in response. In this way, they can commit to moving forward on their specified values-based behavior, knowing that these thoughts and feelings may arise, and that they do not need to be barriers.

Conclusion

At this point, we have established that body image dissatisfaction is a problem that affects a wide range of individuals with a psychological impact that may include symptoms of depression, anxiety, and narrowing of life functioning. Because body image dissatisfaction impacts the quality of life of clients, ACT provides a novel and useful intervention. The treatment focuses on letting go of the overemphasis on the body and on broadening living through values-based living. In chapter 3, we provide an introduction to the application of ACT for body image dissatisfaction. The chapter includes clinical issues related to the application of ACT in general, including recommendations for clinicians on ACT training and consultation, the therapeutic relationship in ACT, and addressing potential treatment barriers in ACT. We also provide case examples for discussion, highlighting the use of ACT to treat body image dissatisfaction in various clinical settings.

CHAPTER 3

Using ACT to Treat Body Image Dissatisfaction

What would life be if we had no courage to attempt anything?
—Vincent Van Gogh

Taking the Leap: Learning to Use ACT

Teaching someone how to conduct acceptance and commitment therapy is a bit like teaching someone to ice-skate. You can explain *how* ice-skating works and the components of how to stay upright ("Bend your knees and feel your center of gravity"). You can explain how to push forward and how the edges of the blades hold the ice. That is what we have done in chapter 2, as we described the theory behind ACT and how it is applied. In this chapter, we continue to describe in words how to use this book to implement ACT. Again, using our skating example, this is like explaining how to do a jump on ice skates ("First you skate backward, and then you hit the toe of the skate into the ice and, bending your knees, you pull upward into a spin as you jump…"). The explanation feels inadequate, doesn't it?

Our point is that the verbal explanation of *how* to implement ACT may feel inadequate. Much like ice-skating, practicing ACT is best learned through a combination of instruction *and* experience. Therefore, we recommend that you take advantage of clinician training experiences such as workshops, clinical consultation groups, and supervision. If you've never practiced ACT, you may have some anxiety about doing it "right." You may want to find the "right" way to do it in this book. While we hope to offer a solid guide for you, ACT is not about being "right." ACT, practiced effectively, is about doing what works, and taking a risk that you may not be certain that it will work.

As you embark on this treatment, consider this metaphor: Imagine an ice-skater jumping and spinning fast in the air. (Do you have the image?) A skater learns to do this first on a harness that holds her body in the air and guides her down on the ice easily. It's a means of practice. As you read this book, we hope that it will serve as a framework to guide your work just as the harness guides the skater. However, at some point the harness is removed and the skater must perform the jump alone for the first time. In this situation, the skater can implement certain guidelines (hold her arms in, keep her head up, and so on). Similarly, we provide guidelines throughout this book for you to follow.

The most important factor for the skater to make that jump successful is to really go for it and follow through, letting her body fully complete that midair spin. This takes great courage, the unforgiving ice being below. Sometimes an uncertain skater will only follow through halfway with the jump. In this case, she will fall out of it midair. Quite literally, she falls short of finishing the midair rotation. The result is an ineffective jump at best, and a hard fall at worst.

This is quite like ACT. There will be a time where you are in a room alone with your client. There will be no supervisor, no consultation group, and no immediate rule to follow to ensure your therapy move is "right," since every client is different. Experience will need to be your guide. Our suggestion: Have the courage to follow through, really go for it, take that great leap, and, we believe, you will not fall short. If you do feel a therapy session or your work with a client falls short somehow, remember this: Ice-skaters practice those jumps thousands of times. They fall a lot, and they also get up quickly after falling, and try again and again. (Have you ever seen a skater sit on the ice?) As clinicians, we also practice our trade (be it psychotherapy, nursing, social work, or medicine) in the quest for improvement, effective follow-through, and a good ending. That being the case, we hope you enjoy your experience practicing ACT. When a therapeutic move works with a client, it is much like landing a jump on the narrow edge of a skate blade: it is a solid feeling of joy, accomplishment, and some relief. However, just as even experienced skaters fall, an experienced ACT therapist will have times where therapeutic work falls short of being effective for a client. For the skater, going back to the coach to gather feedback and improve skills is a necessity—even Olympic-level skaters have coaches watching from the sidelines. For the clinician, we recommend seeking clinical supervision, either formally via a supervisor or in a consultation group. Continuous support in your clinical work from others in the field is the best strategy for increased effectiveness.

Before embarking on the treatment section of this book, this chapter will prepare you to implement the information presented in each of the following chapters. We will focus on (1) tailoring the treatment to individual client needs, (2) developing a therapeutic relationship, and (3) developing competency to deliver ACT. We will end this chapter with case examples and subsequent questions for consideration and discussion.

Tailoring Treatment to Client Needs

Our goal in this book is to provide a flexible framework for you to implement ACT to treat body image problems across a wide variety of settings and populations. In chapter 2, we reviewed some assessment techniques and measures that you can use at your initial session to determine a client's needs and develop an individualized ACT treatment plan.

Length of Treatment

In this book, we do not prescribe a set length of treatment, nor do we provide a prescriptive, cookie-cutter approach to deliver ACT in a session-by-session format. Each client you treat will have different needs. Clients who present with comorbid problems in addition to body image (for example, substance abuse, depression, anxiety disorder, or eating disorder) may need more sessions than with other forms of psychopathology. You may either apply the treatment in a brief, five-session format or extend it over time. This treatment protocol has been applied in group format with college women struggling with body dissatisfaction at a university counseling center. In that setting, one hour was devoted to each treatment component. (We will cover the five treatment components, one per chapter, in the remainder of this book.) The research study by Pearson (2009) conducted this treatment protocol using an eight-hour workshop format, with a community sample of women experiencing body dissatisfaction. The treatment, when provided over an eight-hour day, was shown to be effective at two-week follow-up. A weight-loss study by Lillis and colleagues (2009) showed that a one-day ACT workshop increased psychological well-being and acceptance. Therefore, the briefest modality of this treatment could potentially be five-sessions, either group or individual therapy, with one hour devoted to each treatment component.

Alternatively, if you are not limited in number of sessions, each component of ACT is flexible in terms of length of time. The essence of ACT is to do what is effective, what is workable. In that sense, we encourage you to adjust the length of each component of this therapy to meet your client's individual needs. Some clients need more time devoted to creative hopelessness, while others are able to quickly see how their behaviors are not working. This book is designed as a guide for the clinician. Unless you are conducting a research study where adhering to a manual is necessary, we encourage you to remain flexible with your approach to length of treatment. ACT introduces clients to taking a new path in life, one of acceptance and valued living instead of avoidance. Because it is a new path and not a destination, clients may be introduced to the approach in a brief form of therapy or walk this path with a therapist for a more extended period of time. The question of when a client is ready to end therapy is also an individualized response. However, we do advocate continual evaluation of client progress in order to inform the treatment. Moreover, if the client does not improve or were to deteriorate, APA ethical guidelines would require the clinician to consider treatment alternatives, including referrals.

Frequency of Treatment

Just as we do not specify a length of treatment, neither do we specify the frequency of sessions. The standard frequency is one hour per week, but you can use your clinical judgment to recommend a frequency most appropriate to the client. Some clients may need to come every other week. Others, with more severe problems, may be seen two or three times per week. Although we do not provide a chapter on follow-up sessions, we recommend that you determine an appropriate follow-up plan to assess maintenance of treatment gains and to provide booster sessions. If necessary, focus your follow-ups on reviewing the components of ACT with which the clients struggle most in their aftercare.

Sequence of Treatment

We organized the chapters of this book in a way that is most effective for us to present ACT to you. This arrangement is also based upon the sequence of treatment components conducted in ACT research studies. However, we encourage you to decide the most effective way for you to present to your client based on your case conceptualization. When conducting psychotherapy with clients, as opposed to conducting a research study, flexibility with respect to sequence of treatment components is often effective. (Some practitioners have felt that the "rule" of rigid adherence to a treatment manual has decreased the adoption of newer therapy models.) Consider the example of a psychologist practicing in a primary care setting using a consultation-liaison model of care. In that situation, you might only meet with a client once or twice. In that case, we suggest that assessment of the client's specific needs guide which treatment component you use. A series of three sessions to teach the application of mindfulness might be most useful. Also, for some clients, beginning with values clarification (chapter 8) is more effective than beginning with creative hopelessness (chapter 5). Clinically we have found this to be the case when clients are not connecting with the direct cost of their behaviors. Sometimes clarification of what they would like in life, versus what they have lost, is a more effective beginning to treatment. By presenting values first, you can then help clients to connect their struggle with living a valued life to their maladaptive control strategies. As much as possible, we encourage you to use part 2 as a treatment guide, but we also urge you to remain flexible.

Termination of Treatment

A variety of factors always determines termination of therapy. Some of these factors are uncontrollable, such as requirements determined by managed care, the client's financial constraints, therapist availability, or other individual factors. Because skills such as mindfulness and acceptance are a path and not a destination, one could continue to develop these skills throughout a lifetime. Does that mean therapy continues forever? Well, of course not. The most effective outcome of ACT is generalization of acceptance and values-based living to various areas of life with the reduction of avoidance-based behaviors. Assessments of acceptance, such as the AAQ, and assessments of symptom frequency can guide treatment progress. Values-based assessments also may be a measurable indicator of generalization of ACT to life domains. You may find these standardized assessments to be useful as objective indicators of progress. It is important to conduct ongoing assessment of the client's personal values and goals as well as the reduction of unworkable behaviors. (For some suggestions on assessments of acceptance, values, body image dissatisfaction, and disordered eating attitudes, please refer to the assessment section in chapter 2. Also, visit www.contextualpsychology.org for a comprehensive review of ACT-specific assessments, including the newest ACT-related measures.)

Checking in with clients about their experience of life outside of therapy is another important indicator of progress. We recommend that you, to whatever extent possible, allow clients to guide when they are ready to terminate therapy based upon the degree to which they have experienced progress toward their personal goals.

Developing a Therapeutic Relationship

Although we describe ACT theory and strategies, we want to emphasize the importance of doing this work in the context of a strong therapeutic relationship. Therefore, it is important for you to deliver ACT in the context of a therapeutic relationship rather than mechanically adhering to ACT theory and strategies.

A classic meta-analytic study by Smith and Glass (1977) showed that, regardless of treatment approach or technique, 75 percent of psychotherapy clients showed more symptom improvement than untreated people. Smith and Glass suggested that the improvement did not result from specific techniques. Instead, improvement was attributed to relationship factors, such as empathy, genuineness, and warmth. In a related study, depressed clients who rated their therapist as low on empathy frequently failed to complete homework assignments, terminated early, and did not make significant progress (Burns & Nolen-Hoeksema, 1992).

In ACT, the use of self-disclosure can be an effective aspect of the therapeutic relationship. By being mindful of thoughts and feelings, and also by modeling nondefensive, nonavoidant behavior, you can be a powerful model of walking the talk. Although self-disclosure requires skill and clinical judgment, it can enhance the therapeutic alliance. Hanson (2005) investigated clients' perceptions of therapist self-disclosure and nondisclosure. Sixteen female and two male clients discussed their experience of times when a therapist disclosed, as well as times when a therapist failed to disclose, personal information. Out of 157 incidents, clients rated therapist self-disclosure more helpful than harmful, and rated reluctance to disclose as more harmful than helpful. Your self-disclosure need not be limited to sharing life events with your client; it can also include discussing the impact of your client's behaviors on you. Thus, strategic use of self-disclosure may be clinically useful.

Developing Competency in ACT: Scope of Treatment

While ACT is a behavioral therapy, we encourage clinicians of other theoretical orientations to explore the application of ACT in their clinical work. The tools inherent in ACT are often consistent with other therapeutic approaches and, in our experience, may be well matched to psychotherapists with diverse training backgrounds. Tools such as experiential exercises, mindfulness, and acceptance are not unique to ACT. However, as

ACT is a behaviorally based intervention, to adhere to this treatment necessarily requires orientation to behavioral principles. When working within a particular theoretical orientation, you operate out of a specific set of clinical assumptions. Decisions on how and when to use therapeutic tools in ACT are based on a functional-contextual conceptualization of behavior. Your clinical decisions should be contextually based, with consideration of a basic clinical analysis of the client's problem. If you are trained in a theoretical orientation that is not behavioral, then use of ACT will require a conscious shift in conceptualization of client behavior. The degree to which one can effectively shift between two different theoretical orientations at once is not known.

ACT contains tools that have been used in various orientations. Mindfulness, for example, isn't based in psychotherapy at all but in Eastern meditation traditions. Therefore, if you plan to use this book as an adjunct to therapy of another orientation, we encourage you to be aware of the context out of which you make specific therapy decisions: is your decision based from a behavioral conceptualization of a particular behavior paired with an appropriate intervention, or are you conceptualizing the client's behavior from a different therapeutic framework and providing an ACT-based intervention? We aren't suggesting that the latter intervention would be inappropriate or "wrong." However, in that case, it would no longer be ACT per se. This is important in the sense that we can't determine the potential effectiveness of the treatment outside the scope of the empirical evidence. So far, ACT studies have not combined therapeutic orientations in a given research study.

If you are an ACT therapist, we hope this book will enhance your work with individuals struggling with body dissatisfaction. As you'll notice, part 2 includes the components of ACT that we have tailored with body image dissatisfaction in mind. It's likely that you'll have other therapy targets that you'll also attend to. Therefore, the exercises specific to body image dissatisfaction or disordered eating that we offer may be integrated into your overall ACT work with a client. Likewise, if you use ACT for body image dissatisfaction with a client and notice that other issues arise, be flexible with the treatment and address any clinically relevant problems as they arise. While this book is not intended to treat other psychological disorders, the nature of ACT is such that you are not constrained to focus only on one content area. The content of clients' problems is theoretically less relevant than the functional class of their behaviors. Therefore, body image dissatisfaction may be one of many behaviors you target in therapy. If you use ACT as your primary therapeutic approach, we're confident that you will easily integrate this material into the larger context of therapeutic work.

Training and Use of ACT-Based Treatment

Clinical training is critical to the most successful implementation of this treatment. It involves attending workshops, meeting regularly with an ACT-trained colleague who can provide you with feedback and support, and/or joining an ACT Listserv or online discussion group (for example, at www.contextualpsychology.org). Therapists who receive intensive training on delivering the treatment protocol tend to produce better patient outcomes. In one research study, therapists were assigned to no training, self-instruction, or intensive training on how to implement treatment. Those therapists who received the intensive training had better patient outcomes, fewer dropouts, and lower patient recidivism (Burlingame, Fuhriman, Paul, & Ogles, 1989).

Here is a self-assessment to consider how much training or consultation you may need:

1.   Had you ever heard of ACT before you read this book?

2.   Have you ever used ACT to treat a psychological problem?

3.   Have you ever used ACT to treat body image dissatisfaction?

4.   How many years of experience do you have as a therapist?

5.   Have you ever used a behavioral or cognitive behavioral treatment protocol?

6.   Have you ever treated individuals with body image dissatisfaction?

If your answer to question 1 is no, then we recommend that you begin by attending an ACT experiential workshop. There are workshops for those clinicians new to ACT and also more advanced workshops for clinicians familiar with ACT. Workshops provide you with both clinical training in the treatment and personal experience. With this therapy, it is important that you have some practice applying creative hopelessness, mindfulness, and acceptance to your experience as a therapist or even in your own life. ACT workshops are held at various locations across the country. You can find one in your area by accessing www.contextualpsychology.org and going to the link "Training."

If you answered yes to question 1 but no to question 2, we recommend that you find an ACT consultation group led by a clinician trained in ACT. Discussing one case with a consultation group is an effective way to begin your work as an ACT therapist. Often ACT consultation groups will help you work through each component of treatment and provide recommendations for assessment for your client. In the group, you can access supervision related to the case and work through reactions you have to the therapy process. An ACT consultation group is also particularly beneficial to those therapists from different theoretical orientations who would like to integrate some ACT work into their practice.

If you answered yes to questions 1 and 2 but no to question 3, then this book may be the most effective training tool. Because ACT is based on the theory that behaviors may serve similar functions, the content of your work with clients is theoretically not as salient as understanding the underlying function of their behaviors. If you have practiced therapy using ACT and body image dissatisfaction is a new content area for you, it will be important to learn how to conceptualize that problem from an ACT approach. Chapters 4 through 9, devoted to the components of ACT treatment, will be useful in that regard. You may notice differences in clients who are preoccupied with their body image; we ask to you remember to pay attention to your own reactions (thoughts and feelings) to your clients, as well as any assumptions you may have. We always recommend continued consultation with other professionals. It's also important to consider and assess potential eating disorders and related behaviors with this population.

We hope that this book will be useful for students in graduate clinical programs as well as for master's-level psychotherapists, health care professionals, and psychologists. We recommend that, in supervision, you discuss treatment application as well as technical and theoretical issues. It's important for even experienced clinicians to seek consultation. If you are new to ACT but experienced as a therapist, we encourage you to approach this treatment as you would any new experience to produce effective outcomes: be open and flexible, and be teachable. By being open and flexible, you resist the urge to be "right" and therefore allow a broader range of conceptualizations and potential treatment decisions to be open for you and your client. By being teachable, you broaden your own clinical experience to learn a new approach. It may be one that you don't use again—perhaps one that you don't find effective. That's okay too! Learning ACT, practicing ACT, and receiving ACT as a treatment are all processes without final destinations.

Modeling the ACT relationship, Dr. Steven Hayes's clinical supervision is a collaborative one with his students, with openness to the different ideas about clinical decisions and treatment directions. The intent is to stay mindful about what would be most effective for particular clients in their particular situation at that time, instead of being fused to a specific therapist's thoughts about what was "right." To do this requires purposeful detachment from being the authority or the one with all the answers. This includes detaching from the belief that what you have always done as a clinician will work again with your new client. Arguably, new clinicians and students may be most effective at this detachment. Lack of experience is related to less confidence; this may produce more openness to feedback from the client and others toward what is effective for each client. More experience may actually result in the development of clinical patterns of decision making and the perception of greater confidence. With a more experienced clinician, there has been more time (and therefore more experience) to become fused to certain ideas about what is right. ACT is most effectively applied when the clinician suspends those ideas and instead uses mindfulness to make clinical judgments based on objective awareness. On the other hand, this may be more challenging for a new clinician who is more comfortable with a concrete guide about how to do therapy. An experienced clinician may be more effective at integrating flexibility into a treatment protocol and using objectivity and mindfulness in session. If you are a new clinician, or are new to mindfulness, learning to use objective awareness in session is a skill that requires practice.

We have provided some of our thoughts about the potential impact of experience on the application of ACT. However, these are only our thoughts, based on our experience as ACT clinicians. We encourage you to consider how your own experience may impact flexibility, openness, and mindfulness in session. If you find that you are more likely to think you have the right answers, mindfulness may be the most effective tool to use in session. If you are less confident and are uncomfortable with being flexible in your approach (that is, you'd like to follow this protocol word for word), we encourage you to actively remain flexible and sit with the discomfort of not always knowing what comes next. Bottom line: We encourage all therapists to be mindful and flexible when using ACT.

Potential Treatment Barriers

Theoretically, there may be as many treatment barriers as there are clients. We can't possibly capture every barrier that may exist in the implementation of this protocol. Many potential therapeutic barriers are common across psychotherapy in general. These may include attrition and therapy-interfering behaviors (such as missed sessions, substance abuse that interferes with treatment, or problems in the therapeutic relationship). Some potential therapy barriers are common in ACT and may also exist in other approaches. One of these is the novelty of addressing thoughts and feelings with an acceptance-based versus change-based approach. Our society is quite change focused, especially with respect to getting rid of unpleasant emotions. Turn on the television and you might soon see a commercial for the next "happy pill." The push to get out of negative emotion is prevalent in the media: drink this and be happy; buy this and be happy; take this class, attend this workshop, or read this book and be happy. Instead of getting rid of negative thoughts or spending energy changing negative thoughts to positive ones, ACT suggests that clients let the thoughts be there and experience the range of feelings humans experience.

Eliminating Resistance as a Barrier

As a clinician, you are likely to experience some resistance from your clients to this new way of approaching thoughts and feelings. Initial resistance may come up when addressing control as a problem. Any range of responses may occur, from a mild disbelief to an expression of feeling misunderstood ("You can't possibly be asking me to accept the feelings I experience—they're much too painful") to anger ("Wait! I came to therapy to get rid of this depression, and you're asking me to accept it!?). Approach these reactions by noticing and describing them to your clients. You might remark to your clients that you notice they are having some thoughts about this new approach, and ask that they hold these thoughts lightly instead of allowing them to be truth. Resistance may also show up through unwillingness to move in a valued direction. The reaction "I can't possibly meet that goal with all the anxiety I have. I have to get rid of the anxiety before I do that [valued behavior]," is common. Inherent in this reaction is the belief that anxiety, depression, or other unpleasant emotions need to be abolished before action is taken. With ACT, you suggest the opposite: that clients change their behavior while experiencing the uncomfortable emotions. Be anxious and socialize at the same time, carry sadness with you as you attend work or take care of your children, and so on. This idea is likely to be new to clients who have been waiting for the emotions to go away before fully living their lives. With regard to body image dissatisfaction, folks may have been waiting until a certain weight loss occurs before participating in valued activities. "I can't possibly go to the gym and be around other people until I lose the weight" might be a common response. Suggesting that if, in fact, exercising is a valued activity there is no need to wait for weight loss may evoke anxiety and subsequent resistance.

Conceptualize the resistance as a series of thoughts and reactions for the client and you to notice. You also may have resistance as a clinician to the approach. Those in the helping professions generally want people to feel better. You may notice the pull to want your client to have a reduction in symptoms, to not feel anxious in certain settings where there is no actual threat. Notice these reactions in yourself, as representations of your own belief system. There is no need to spend energy attempting to change these reactions or beliefs. Instead put your clinical energy into helping your client sit with those thoughts and reactions as you do the same. While sitting with the discomfort, put your clinical energy into the aspects of therapy that you value: perhaps improving the therapeutic relationship with your client, providing empathy to your client about the discomfort you both are experiencing, and remembering to focus on values-guided behavior for your client and yourself as a clinician. In these ways, resistance does not need to be a therapeutic barrier.

Other Barriers to Treatment

ACT encourages the pursuit of workability. If for any reason the treatment itself is not working for the client, do an assessment to determine the cause. Perhaps the focus on body image dissatisfaction is not the most salient problem for your client and you need to shift your treatment focus. You can always return to this as a treatment focus once other problems are addressed. ACT is a rather client-centered therapy. Allow your client to provide feedback about the relative importance of different therapeutic goals. You can assess whether moving away from body image dissatisfaction or other therapy targets is functioning as avoidance, or whether a shift in focus would be effective.

A certain behavior only becomes a treatment barrier when and if it interferes with treatment effectiveness. Potential treatment barriers such as missed sessions, chronic lateness to sessions, or other interfering factors, including dangerous behaviors (such as suicidality, substance abuse, self-injury, or eating disorders), do not necessarily prevent continuation of this treatment. Depending on the degree of severity of life interference, the individual may need a high level of care in treatment (for example, increased session frequency or even a different treatment modality such as inpatient treatment versus outpatient treatment). Otherwise, provide ACT-consistent interventions to address reduction in these behaviors, or use your own treatment modality to address interfering behaviors in session. We have found it helpful from an ACT approach to address such behaviors openly and directly with clients from the perspective of how the behavior prevents the client from moving in a valued direction: "Is this what you want to be about? Has your experience been that this behavior has worked for you? What do you notice about the impact of the behavior in your relationships—for example, in our therapy relationship?" These suggested questions may begin a good discussion about the workability of any potential therapy barrier.

Case Examples for Discussion

In order to best illustrate how ACT can be applied to different clients in varied settings, we provide three case examples below, each with a different client and a different therapist. Case 1 is an individual psychotherapy client who has recently started treatment at an outpatient mental health center with a master's-level clinical social worker who is new to ACT. Case 2 is a long-term psychotherapy case in which treatment includes dealing with body image dissatisfaction within the broader context of therapy. The therapist is a clinical psychologist in private practice with over ten years of psychotherapy experience. Case 3 is a patient in a primary care physician's office who is referred for assessment and brief psychotherapy to the nurse practitioner, a psychiatric nurse who also has a master's degree in marriage and family therapy. As you read these cases, using the recommendations we provide from an ACT perspective, consider the following factors: assessment, treatment length, scope of treatment, therapist training, and potential treatment barriers. At the end of each case example, we provide some questions to guide discussion. If you are new to ACT, read through the case examples and questions, and then return to the questions after you have finished reading this book.

■ Case Example 1: Renee, client

The client is a thirty-year-old Caucasian female named Renee, who is living with her boy-friend of two years. She has stated that she would like individual psychotherapy to work on issues related to childhood sexual and physical abuse perpetrated by an adult male neighbor. Renee reports that the abuse occurred between the ages of eleven and thirteen. During that time she became suicidal and made an attempt by overdosing on over-the-counter medication. She reported the abuse to her mother, who called authorities. The perpetrator was subsequently arrested, and a court case ensued. Renee testified against him and he received a prison sentence. Renee states that during the trial, she coped with stress by eating and also began purging and abusing laxatives. She subsequently developed a serious case of bulimia, which extended into her early twenties. She received inpatient treatment for bulimia at a residential treatment program and has not binged or purged in eight years.

The intake revealed that since moving in with her boyfriend six months ago, Renee has experienced increased anxiety and nightmares related to the childhood trauma. She admits that she has also started bingeing and purging again in the past six months, and that she has an enduring dislike of her body. She reports hating to look in the mirror because she views her body as an object that men take advantage of. She reports having disliked her body since puberty, when she began gaining weight and maturing physically. Renee states that she feels she never "got over" the abuse and has always viewed her body as the "enemy." She states that, although she understands she didn't cause the abuse, she can't help but hate her body for being attractive to men. This resentment has impacted her relationship with her boyfriend as well. She reports that every time he looks at her body or compliments her, she becomes angry and scared and has an increase in judgmental thoughts about her body.

■ Case Example 1: C. J., clinician

C. J. is a licensed clinical social worker at a local outpatient mental health agency. She has five years of postgraduate experience conducting individual and group psychotherapy at the outpatient agency. C. J. has experience working with a wide range of clients, but her primary interest and experience has been PTSD treatment and women's issues. Her theoretical orientation is psychodynamic with a focus on family systems.

Due to the limitations on number of psychotherapy sessions at the outpatient clinic, C. J. has been interested in learning and applying brief psychotherapy. She initially was introduced to ACT at the outpatient mental health center by a psychology practicum student who was trained in ACT. Following their discussions, C. J. attended a weekend ACT workshop for clinicians for continuing education units. Subsequently she purchased a couple of ACT self-help books, including Get Out of Your Mind and Into Your Life *(Hayes & Smith, 2005),* ACT for Anorexia *(Heffner & Eifert, 2004) and* Life Beyond Trauma *(Follette & Pistorello,*

2007). She has been using these books with her clients as an adjunct to psychotherapy. Her experience with ACT so far feels consistent with her clinical style, given the experiential nature of the therapy. However, she worries about implementing an ACT therapy protocol given that she has never conducted ACT with a client as the primary psychotherapy.

Questions for Discussion and Consideration

1. What training might C. J. need to work effectively with Renee?

2. What potential barriers might Renee bring to the therapy situation, and how might C. J. address those with her?

3. What potential barriers might exist based on factors related to C. J. as the therapist or the therapy setting? What are some possible solutions to reduce these barriers?

4. Considering Renee's history and symptoms, what types of assessments would be useful for initial evaluation?

5. What measures would be useful for ongoing evaluation of progress in therapy?

■ *Case Example 2: Alisha, client*

Alisha is a fifty-five-year-old African American woman who has been engaged in long-term psychotherapy with Dr. J., a clinical psychologist. Originally Alisha entered therapy for bulimia, which she admittedly had struggled with for over fifteen years. At times, her symptoms would remit for several months, only to return. The frequency of bingeing and purging would escalate to several times a day during her most challenging times. Her first year of treatment resulted in cessation of bingeing and purging. The past two years of treatment have been focused on developing and maintaining close relationships. Alisha describes intense social anxiety when around coworkers in social situations. She does not have any close friends and has not had a romantic relationship in over ten years. She reports the reason for her lack of relationships to be dissatisfaction with her body. She describes a dislike of her body so extreme that she feels other people will be repulsed by her and will not want to be seen with her. Information about her history of relationships reveals a childhood and adolescence filled with losses of friends due to her family frequently moving to different cities. She states that she was never able to keep a friend because as soon as she'd develop the relationship, she would move. In addition, her family of origin included several losses, including the tragic and accidental death of her younger sister and the divorce of her parents when Alisha was fourteen.

■ *Case Example 2: Dr. J., clinician*

Dr. J. is a clinical psychologist in private practice with twenty years of postgraduate experience. His initial training was psychodynamic in orientation. However, following graduate school, he gained postdoctoral training in cognitive behavioral therapy. He has continued to actively seek training in various therapeutic approaches over the years, and he views his work as "eclectic" in theoretical orientation. He is known for stating that he uses "what works" with each client instead of adhering to only one school of therapy. His practice has historically included clients with a diversity of ages and clinical presentations. Over the past five years, Dr. J. gained some interest in learning acceptance and commitment therapy. He has read the original ACT book (Hayes et al., 1999) book to gain an understanding of the theoretical underpinnings of ACT, and he also attended a two-day clinician workshop. Following this, Dr. J. felt a connection specifically with the experiential quality of ACT. On his caseload are three individuals with long-standing body image distress. He is hopeful that ACT will help his clients gain greater acceptance of their body where other therapies have focused on attempting to change their existing beliefs about their image.

One of these clients is Alisha. Dr. J. decides he would like to use this book to integrate ACT into her existing therapy. Alisha has been seeing Dr. J. for three years. During this time, Dr. J. has implemented a cognitive behavioral approach to therapy, which did result in decreased bingeing and purging episodes. He also has continued to use a humanistic approach to provide supportive therapy regarding relationship issues. He would like to integrate this ACT protocol into the humanistic and psychodynamic approaches to treat her existing body image problems.

Questions for Discussion and Consideration

1. How might Dr. J.'s experience or theoretical orientation impact his effectiveness in use of the ACT treatment protocol?

2. What benefits could Dr. J. bring to Alisha by treating her with ACT?

3. What considerations should be made with respect to integrating ACT into Alisha's current treatment?

■ Case Example 3: Eric, client

Eric is a thirty-eight-year-old Caucasian male who is a patient in a primary care clinic. He is medically obese and experiences depression symptoms. Despite recommendations from his physician to adhere to a low-calorie diet for the purpose of weight loss, Eric gained another ten pounds by his next biannual clinic visit. He reacts with despair over the weight gain, commenting that he feels he doesn't deserve to lose weight because he is "so ugly anyway, it wouldn't matter." He expresses that his weight is a hopeless situation and that the weight has interfered in nearly every part of his life. He reports that no matter how hard he tries to adhere to a lower-calorie diet, he ends up binge eating. He tells the physician, "When I look in the mirror, I see a hopeless situation. I feel helpless and I eat." The physician refers Eric to P. D., the consulting mental health professional in the medical practice. The physician hopes that P. D. can provide a brief intervention to motivate Eric to participate in a weight-loss program. Upon meeting with P. D., Eric admits he has always felt poorly about his physical appearance. He reports that he dislikes nearly everything about his body, including his face, his height, and, of course, his weight. Eric states that there are so many things about his body that he feels are out of control that he loses motivation for weight loss.

Case Example 3: P. D., clinician

P. D., practiced for fifteen years as a psychiatric nurse practitioner before returning to school and obtaining her MFT. She then had five years of experience working in private practice with a psychiatrist, providing individual and couples counseling as an adjunct to their psychiatric treatment. She transferred to a family medicine practice where she provides psychological consultation and brief therapy interventions (maximum five sessions). Her experience with ACT began with her own individual psychotherapy, which she received from an ACT therapist while in her MFT program. Following this therapy, which she found helpful, she has actively sought ACT training. She has read empirical articles where ACT has been used with medical populations. She has a special interest in the effectiveness of ACT as a treatment for chronic pain. On Thursday evenings, she conducts an ACT group for patients in the medicine practice who struggle with chronic pain. For this, she has been using Acceptance and Commitment Therapy for Chronic Pain, *by Dahl, Wilson, Luciano, and Hayes (2005). In addition to practicing ACT therapy, she has attended two workshops for professionals and also attended an ACT world conference. She is hopeful that use of ACT for body image dissatisfaction over three to five sessions will help end Eric's suffering due to body dissatisfaction and motivate him to engage in a weight-loss program.*

Questions for Discussion and Consideration

1.   What components of ACT might be most useful to Eric in this brief period of time to decrease body image dissatisfaction and enhance motivation for change?

2.   Considering that Eric is obese and in medical need of weight loss, how can P. D. use ACT to both encourage weight loss and help Eric decrease his preoccupation with his body dissatisfaction?

3.   Theoretically, why would decreasing Eric's preoccupation with his body image increase his motivation for behavior change regarding weight loss?

Conclusion

As the case examples above show, the treatment protocol contained in this book can be used in a variety of settings by a diverse group of mental health practitioners, and it can be applied to numerous clinical presentations of body dissatisfaction. The wide applicability of this protocol is one of its benefits. The flexibility of length of treatment (that is, either brief or long-term) is another. ACT is not content driven but rather process driven. The nature of the presenting problem is not as relevant as the function it serves for the individual. For you as the clinician, attention to your own personal processes during sessions is equally important as attention to those of the client. Your own mindfulness of thoughts and feelings during and outside of session will help you to model and teach this to your client. Noticing these processes over the course of therapy will allow you to provide a more effective application of this treatment. With this present-moment focus, you may more quickly notice and intervene upon potential treatment barriers. Attention to what is effective at the present moment for your specific client is the most useful approach to drive clinical decision making in ACT.

We hope that you find this therapy useful to your clients with body image dissatisfaction. If you decide to seek further training or consultation in ACT as you work with your clients, we hope that this therapeutic approach broadens your own life as well as that of your clients. In the following chapters, we offer not what we as clinicians believe is the right way to conduct therapy, but rather a path of living that we sincerely hope will decrease human suffering.

PART 2

Applying ACT to Body Image Dissatisfaction

CHAPTER 4

Introducing ACT to Your Client

There is a basin in the mind where words float around on thought and thought on sound and sight. Then there is a depth of thought untouched by words, and deeper still a gulf of formless feeling untouched by thought.

—Zora Neal Hurston

The Problem: Control, Not Body Image

As humans, we often live in the "basin of the mind," as Ms. Hurston states (1991, p. 31), where words dominate behavior. With ACT, you help your clients to be aware of their experience versus what they think about their experience (that is, "the depth of thought untouched by words"). An important part of this is encouraging emotional experiencing. That "gulf of formless feeling untouched by thought" that Hurston refers to is exactly the place that your work can take you with your clients. In order to do this, control strategies that keep clients at the level of thought, away from feeling, must be identified. It's likely that your clients have not encountered an approach like this before: letting go of strategies that block them from feelings, both pleasant and unpleasant. Given that this book is dedicated to clients struggling with body image dissatisfaction, a discussion about this struggle is an effective place to begin treatment. In your initial sessions of implementing ACT for body image dissatisfaction, discussing your clients' struggles and orienting them to how ACT may help address those struggles will be important. In this way, clients will make an initial connection to the pain associated with their specific body image dissatisfaction and learn of a possible alternative through this treatment.

This chapter serves as an orientation to ACT for clients in the initial phase of treatment. Some basic tenets of ACT, such as the conceptualization of control strategies being problematic, the universality of human pain, and the difference between emotional experiencing versus avoiding may be introduced at the beginning of treatment. Gaining an initial commitment from clients regarding this treatment is also important. Suggestions on how to provide a rationale to your clients about the use of ACT to treat body image dissatisfaction is reviewed in this chapter. In short, we devote this chapter to how you as the clinician can introduce ACT to your client as an option for treatment of body image dissatisfaction. Whether you are beginning treatment with clients or are introducing ACT as a new approach in your existing treatment plan, we suggest the approach outlines below as a way to begin the treatment of body image dissatisfaction using ACT.

After obtaining informed consent, your first task with clients is to connect them with their specific struggle related to body image. While clients have likely already identified a body image or weight-related concern, it is important that they connect with the emotions associated with this struggle. Complaining about not liking one's body or stating dissatisfaction about weight or shape is, in many circumstances, a socially acceptable topic of discussion. Your clients may be in good company, feeling similar to friends who also struggle with weight and body image dissatisfaction. A quick appraisal of our societal obsession with weight loss and appearance provides evidence that not liking the body is socially validated. The general concept is, "If you don't like it, change it." Accordingly your clients may have tried many strategies to change their appearance, weight, or shape. Along the way, these efforts may have been reinforced by family and friends. As you elicit this topic in treatment, you'll want to focus less on the content (or specific nature of the dissatisfaction) and more on the experience of clients as they walk the world feeling uncomfortable in their own skin.

In addition to tapping into client experience with body image dissatisfaction, ACT looks deeper—into why these clients are so preoccupied with their bodies. Identifying other life issues that clients may be attempting to avoid or control via an overemphasis on body image issues will be necessary in order to thoroughly assess if a preoccupation with weight and shape serves the function of avoiding other difficult life problems. Theoretically, there may be other, seemingly less controllable issues (other people or certain situations) that are uncomfortable for clients to deal with. While they are likely quite aware of experiencing negative thoughts and uncomfortable feelings about their body, they are likely not aware that efforts to control their body image have become part of the struggle. In efforts to control, or to change thoughts about the body and associated feelings of discomfort, clients may have engaged in a variety of behaviors: dieting, exercise programs, preoccupation with weight and weight loss, reassurance-seeking from others about appearance, or avoidance of social activities. We refer to all of these as *control strategies*. None of these behaviors is "bad" or ineffective in its own right. The problem arises when the control strategy doesn't produce the desired outcome and causes additional suffering.

For example, if a client fears negative evaluation and is socially anxious, she may avoid social situations and use her body image dissatisfaction as her rationale for not interacting with others. She may explain her fear of close relationships as being due to her weight or shape (for example, "No one wants to be seen with the 'fat girl.' I can't go out with anyone until I lose twenty pounds."). This type of belief is likely to have a number of antecedents. Perhaps as far back as childhood, she may have used her weight as rationale for long-standing social isolation. And to be honest, this may have been reinforced by the societal stigma related to obesity, which may have been emphasized in adolescence. As an adult, this client may have had experiences of rejection that she believes were based on her appearance. This belief and the fear of future rejections may have then promoted social avoidance. In addition, given how early this pattern occurred, the client may have not developed effective social skills. At this point, when she sees you, her explanation is that she's unlovable because she is unattractive; by her experience, she is unlikable and undesirable because she is heavy. And so she has tried everything to lose the weight, and it has not worked. She reports that she ends up "relapsing on food" and regains any weight lost.

She believes her problem is her weight. However, from an ACT point of view, the root of her problem is fear of negative evaluation or rejection by others. She simultaneously desires and fears connection with another human being. The unfortunate truth is that rejection by others due to weight may be a reality for some people, given societal stigma. It is important to validate these experiences with your clients. Therefore, the fear of rejection may be experientially based, and may also be quite valid. While validating this point, it is important to also emphasize the primary fear that is being avoided. In this case, it is the fear of connection with another human being. So both are true: she fears being close to people, and by being overweight, she may experience some stigma in the form of rejection or judgment by people she attempts to be close to.

In this case, it would be important to assess what exactly she fears about being close to people. If fear of rejection is one reason, validating any experiences she's had with rejection due to weight-related stigma is important. However, moving beyond this, it will be important to assess what else she fears about being close with another human being. It will also be important to discuss the ambiguity that exists in the possibility of rejection. Focusing on her weight as her reason for socially isolating herself, she avoids the more uncontrollable truth that she'll never have a guarantee of acceptance by others. The possibility of rejection, no matter what weight or shape she is, always will exist. Experiencing the pain of long-standing loneliness and the fear of rejection by others is part of the work to be done. Eventually, when this client realizes that she can choose to socially engage no matter what her body weight or shape, the control strategy of weight maintenance and preoccupation with weight will not be necessary. If she indeed values building relationships to alleviate loneliness, moving in that direction, with the fear and reality of potential rejection, will be the hard work that she faces ahead.

Telling the Story, Facing the Pain

Allowing clients to describe their struggle with body dissatisfaction is one way to facilitate an initial connection to the pain that exists when people are uncomfortable in their own body. Doing this is also useful for you to gain an initial assessment of the various control strategies clients have tried. You'll see how they attempted to change their body in hopes of changing their body image and potentially all the different areas of their life that they perceive as having been impacted by their appearance. This data helps you to gain a better understanding of the specific areas of life that have been impacted by their self-perceptions (for example, relationships, leisure activities, or work) and also to validate the distress level they have experienced. With this in mind, consider the case example below.

■ Case Example: Annie

Annie, a forty-year-old married mother of two, has been attending individual psychotherapy for symptoms of depression. After several sessions, it becomes apparent that Annie relates many of her depression symptoms directly to disliking her body weight and shape. She has stated that she believes weight loss would improve her marriage, her social life, and overall quality of life and reduce her depression symptoms. Despite other variables in her life that may be contributing to her depressed mood, she keeps coming back to the theme of body dissatisfaction. She is convinced that if she could lose weight, her entire life would be different and better. Without the weight loss, she believes nothing else can change. She feels stuck. Annie believes, very strongly, that a "better body" is her cure.

At this juncture in ACT, you'd want to first let Annie describe to you a history of how her body image has impacted various areas of her life—that is, how she believes that her body or weight has created pain in her life. Already, from the brief description above, it is evident that she believes her body controls the quality of her marriage and her relationships with others. This is likely not the first time Annie has believed that. As long as she continues to buy into these thoughts as truth, she will struggle to change her body in order to change everything in her life, including her interpersonal relationships. (As an aside, cosmetic surgeons routinely assess around patients' expectations related to the outcome and impact of surgery. Many consider it a red flag when patients expect life transformation as opposed to specific enhancements in appearance.)

The initial goal in ACT is to create awareness of the struggle clients engage in when trying various tactics (dieting or focusing on achieving the "perfect" body) to create happiness. Annie has likely made several attempts to change her body shape or weight. It is important to assess the impact of these efforts on various areas of her life. You might ask, for example, "Did your relationships improve when you lost ten pounds? How so?" Clients may believe that things really did improve when their weight was lower. While it is quite possible that certain factors related to health do improve with medically necessary weight loss, you are looking for long-standing themes in the client's life that she hopes a change in body image will create. Beyond the medical benefits, what beliefs does your client have about changes in appearance that perpetuate her preoccupation with weight loss?

Ask your clients to tell you their story about their body. The exercises presented a bit later in this chapter (Mind-to-Body and Body-to-Mind Letters and How Long Have You Been Struggling?) provide examples of techniques you can use to help clients tell their body image story. During these exercises, your goal is to hear their struggle as a story that they tell themselves. As you listen to them tell about their body image distress and their history of dieting and related behaviors, you can trust that they have listened to this dialogue many times. Much of the story they will tell you is like an internal tape they listen to frequently. By hearing this story, you will have an opportunity to identify various control strategies within the struggle.

As clients describe their story, it may be useful to write down some control strategies that you notice. Control strategies may be behaviors or beliefs that have become rules that guide their behaviors. The following section illustrates some common control strategies.

I've always felt like I have rounded and soft features, even though I've never been over-weight. This has always made me feel less masculine. Over the past three years, I decided to really commit to become more built. So I tried a high-protein diet last year and added weight lifting into my exercise program to build muscle. I gained twenty pounds but didn't add much muscle. I got frustrated and I went off of that diet and tried another type of sup-plement that's advertised to build muscles. If I could just find the right combination of food and exercise that would bulk me up more, I'd feel more confident and more masculine.

Control Strategy: Trying special diets

Belief: The diet will produce muscles that will create feelings of confidence and masculinity.

If I could find a workout program that I could stick with, then I could lose the weight. My husband would feel closer to me then. But he doesn't think we can afford a gym member-ship, so what am I supposed to do? If I can't lose the weight, our relationship will never improve. If I can't work out, I'll never lose the weight. It's hopeless.

Control Strategy: Focusing on weight loss instead of the relationship itself

Belief: It's only through weight loss that relationships will improve; otherwise improving the relationship will be impossible.

I've tried everything to be the "thin girl." Ever since junior high I've been dieting. First I tried not eating lunch for a year. Then I started bingeing and purging in high school. All the while, I hated my body. Even when I lost thirty pounds in college, I still hated my body. It was like I could never be the right shape or weight to be happy. I was always dissatisfied.

Control Strategy: Trying different weight-loss methods

Belief: Being the "right" weight or shape will produce happiness.

I say a mantra to myself every morning: "I am beautiful." It doesn't stick very long and I have to repeat it all day, especially when I feel insecure. When that doesn't work, I ask other people for reassurance about how I look. But even when they tell me I look good, I don't believe them. I tell myself I'm too anxious to ask men on dates or to go to the pool in the summer. There's no way I can do that until I lose at least twenty pounds.

Control Strategies: Positive self-talk; reassurance seeking; avoidance

Beliefs: I must believe I look good. Other people must think I look good. Otherwise I must lose weight.

I count calories of everything I eat, and I've always had good foods and bad foods. No matter what, I always feel fat and unattractive after eating a bad food. It's gotten so bad that I avoid going to dinner with friends.

Control Strategies: Eating only certain foods; avoidance of going out with friends

Beliefs: There are good foods and bad foods. Foods have an immediate impact on attractiveness.

All my pants have to be a certain size. If I wear over a size 8, then I won't purchase the clothing as a punishment. I feel like an unworthy person if my clothing size is a double digit.

Control Strategy: Avoiding purchasing clothes unless the body is a certain size

Belief: There is an acceptable size that determines one's worthiness.

I can't look in mirrors anymore. Every time I look in the mirror, I have such horrible thoughts about my body. I avoid looking at myself in the shower or when I get dressed in the morning. I feel so unattractive that I'm embarrassed to socialize with people.

Control Strategies: Avoiding mirrors; avoiding socialization

Belief: I am not worthy of socializing with others if I perceive myself as unattractive.

I've tried everything to lose weight. Sometimes I'll lose ten pounds, but I'll gain it right back. I don't know why, but I feel like I don't deserve to be at a healthy weight. I feel uncomfortable with my body no matter what. When I do lose weight, men look at me differently and it makes me uncomfortable. Yet when I'm heavy, people look at me with judgment. I just can't win!

Control Strategies: The inability to lose weight or keep weight off (that is, purposeful weight gain or maintenance of an unhealthy weight)

Belief: Men are threatening to me physically (perhaps this has been part of the client's experience). If I remain heavy, I won't receive male attention.

EXERCISE: Mind-to-Body and Body-to-Mind Letters

One way of supporting clients in telling their story is to invite them to write two letters to describe the content of their internal tapes. One letter will be written from the perspective of their mind to their body, and the other from the perspective of their body to their mind.

The following is a sample mind-to-body letter from Annie, the case example described above. Notice that Annie's mind-to-body letter describes the thoughts, feelings, and suffering typically associated with body dissatisfaction.

Dear Body,

I hate you! You cause me so much pain. If you were not so disgusting, I'd be happier. You prevent me from having friends. When people meet me, they do not see me as the beautiful person that I am in my heart. Instead they see a fat, unlovable pig that they want to get away from.

Next, have your clients write a letter from their body to their mind. Ask them to include any thoughts or feelings that their body has about their mind. The following is a sample body-to-mind letter from Annie.

Dear Mind,

I hate you too. You give me no peace. You think you can control me, but I control you. When you set a goal to run a mile at the gym, I give out on you. I make you too weak to reach that goal. I will destroy you and your life, and there is nothing you can do to stop me.

The mind-to-body and body-to-mind letters are a technique to explore the client's body image story. The letters allow clients to describe the struggle and the conflict between the body (weight or shape) and the mind (thoughts and feelings). The letters can reveal important themes in the mind-body relationship. Annie's mind-to-body letter, for example, reveals how her body image interferes with having meaningful relationships with people. Her body-to-mind letter reflects the problem of control and how her attempts to control her weight by exercise tend to fail and lead to more intense and negative body image thoughts and feelings.

EXERCISE: How Long Have You Been Struggling?

To facilitate connection with the pain of body dissatisfaction, this experiential exercise may be useful. In this exercise, you'll guide your clients in a brief visualization where they imagine themselves at the age they first noticed becoming uncomfortable with their body. Ask your clients to imagine details about their body, size, clothes, and appearance at that age. Ask them to remember what was going on at that time in their life. Ask if they remember the exact time when they became uncomfortable or judgmental about their appearance. You may use the following script as a guide for the exercise.

Go ahead and find a comfortable position in your chair and either close your eyes or find a neutral point to focus on in the room. Now remember the age at which you first became uncomfortable with your appearance or your body weight or shape. This may have been recent, or it may have been very early in your life. Go ahead and take a moment to identify the age that you were at that time.

Once you've identified that age, remember what year it was and what you were doing in your life at that time. Where were you living? Alone? With a partner? With your parents? What was happening in your life at that age? Were you in school? Working? Take yourself back to that time in your mind. Really be there.

And now, bring your attention to your memory of your body at that age. Remember, if you can, some item of clothing you wore then. Or, if you cannot remember a specific outfit or item of clothing, remember, if you can, what your general way of dressing was at that age. Do you remember what size you wore at that time? Do you remember how much you weighed? Remember now as much as possible about your physical appearance at that age when you first began to dislike your body.

What do you remember that brought your attention to first disliking your body? Was there a specific event at that age in your life? Did you reach a certain weight? Did something difficult happen that changed your perception of your body image? Recall this and the feelings you had along with it. What did you feel like at that age when you first realized you did not like your body? How did it feel to suddenly be dissatisfied when you looked in the mirror?

Notice now that you are carrying that same dissatisfaction that you recalled at an earlier age. This is pain that has been with you for a period of time. Has is gotten better or worse? Notice, as you slowly bring your attention back to the room, that you are the same person who you just imagined at an earlier age. You have walked for a period of time with this pain of disliking your body.

After completing the visualization, use the questions below to guide you and your clients in a discussion about their struggle. The purpose of this discussion is to facilitate for your clients a connection with their feelings about body dissatisfaction and associated problems that they believe body weight and shape have caused. As we mentioned above, one of the first steps in ACT is to recognize the emotional pain that has been long-standing in the client's life and to identify the behaviors that the client engages in to avoid or suppress the emotional pain. Experiential exercises often are useful for taking clients beyond the descriptive level of their problem in order to become more aware of their pain. Below are some suggested exercises that may facilitate connection to feelings, drawing upon the material evoked in the visualization:

- "Draw, write, or describe a timeline of events (from birth to present) that depicts significant body image events that occurred in your life. Events may include incidents such as teasing by peers, first diet, family comments about food or weight, memories of Mom dieting, early onset of menarche, and so on."

- "Can you think of another struggle that you have experienced that's gone on as long as your struggle with body image and eating? If you can, I'm sure you've tried to solve that struggle as well in different ways."

- "Have you tried in different ways to solve the struggle with body image and eating? Tell me some of the things you've tried."

- "It makes sense that you would try to get out of or end that struggle. If you were in a relationship with someone who created a struggle for you or caused you pain, wouldn't you also try to fix that or get out of that relationship?"

- "This struggle is very similar to a struggle with a difficult relationship. You have a relationship with yourself, with your body. And my guess is that you've been trying to get out of or escape this for as long as it has been with you. Why don't we talk about some of the ways you have avoided emotional discomfort over the years?"

Following this discussion, bring to clients' attention the various control strategies you noticed in the stories they shared about their struggle. The purpose of drawing attention to these strategies is to validate that they have tried many ways to improve their relationship with their body and reduce their distress. Normalization of control strategies is useful at this time; everyone tries to control things that are unpleasant, including thoughts, feelings, and external problems. When beginning ACT with your clients, simply having clients begin to notice the various ways they have tried to control their body weight and shape and lessen their distress is the goal.

Does It Work? The Key Concept of Workability

A key concept in ACT is an experiential connection to behavior as being workable versus unworkable, or ineffective versus effective to living a vital life. We call this *workability*.

It can be helpful to discuss workability using a metaphor of a beach ball, which was described by a very creative ACT client who could relate to the concept of experiential avoidance. To present this metaphor, ask the client to imagine being in a swimming pool with a beach ball that represents all of his unwanted thoughts and feelings. He does not want to have this ball of distress with him in the pool, and his body image dissatisfaction behavior is a way for him to shove that ball under the water. Unfortunately, the air-filled ball cannot be held underwater forever because it naturally pushes up and rises to the surface. The struggle to hold the ball under water is exhausting, and despite the client's best efforts, the ball will eventually blast out past the surface, becoming more noticeable and more intense than if he had just let it float in the pool with him. We have found that clients understand this metaphor very well, and especially connect to it when they learn that a fellow client created it.

You may point out that the strategies are not "bad" or "good," but perhaps have not been the solution for ending the struggle with eating and weight. The bottom-line message conveyed in this discussion of workability is that, while some of these strategies have worked temporarily, they haven't worked in the long run to bring about the result the client seeks. Again, be aware that strategies work in some ways. For example, being a workaholic could make you successful. However, it may not produce a balanced life or a very fun life.

Earlier in the chapter, we listed examples of control strategies; these control strategies are also examples of unworkable solutions. Yo-yo dieting, in which weight is lost and then regained, is another control strategy that is also an unworkable solution. Likewise, avoidance of social situations prevents negative body image thoughts from emerging but also prevents clients from engaging in meaningful social activities. As an alternative solution, ACT encourages clients to identify and abandon unworkable strategies that provide short-term relief but result in long-term suffering. More workable strategies for body image problems involve acceptance and willingness to experience body image thoughts while maintaining commitment to valued life directions and goals. Unworkable solutions focus on creating a more likable body, whereas workable solutions involve creating a meaningful life, even if difficult body image thoughts occur.

We will discuss effective versus ineffective behaviors and the relative workability of various control strategies in greater depth when we explore creative hopelessness in chapter 5 and control as the problem in chapter 6. The preliminary discussion of ACT with your client outlined in this chapter provides a foundation for elaborating on the core components of ACT discussed in detail in chapters 5 through 9.

Pain vs. Suffering: Understanding the Difference

ACT distinguishes between pain and suffering, terms that are often used interchangeably in everyday language. "Pain" is defined as a reaction to naturally uncomfortable experiences. "Suffering" is defined as prolonged discomfort that results from our struggle to avoid feeling pain. In a sense, suffering is a function of our efforts to avoid pain. Consider the following case example of pain versus suffering.

■ *Case Example: John*

John is a twenty-nine-year-old single Caucasian male who works full-time as a nurse at a local hospital. He is medically obese (five foot eight and 280 pounds) and has been obese since childhood. John is self-referred to see you for individual therapy because he has been feeling depressed about a lack of relationships in his life, and also because he started binge eating. While at first the bingeing was infrequent, recently it has become more frequent (up to four times a week), which he admits concerns him. John reports believing he is a failure because he is currently not married and has never had a long-term romantic relationship. He attributes this to his weight, stating that no one could ever be attracted to him.

John describes a history during childhood of peers making fun of his weight. He reports being repeatedly physically accosted by a group of boys in junior high school who would push him on the ground outside his school and kick him. In addition, John related experiencing many years of stigma from peers and extended family who admonished him for being over-weight and not in better physical shape. Due to these experiences, John reports that his parents were often involved with the school officials, helping John stay safe while attending school, but his parents did not advocate for him when extended family made punishing remarks about his weight. John states he felt loved by his parents but never felt fully accepted as a member of his family. After high school, John reports that college was less threatening. However, he reports that he felt traumatized by years of teasing and social isolation in elementary, junior high, and high school, and he felt isolated during college. He states that he did not make very many friends in college; he would simply go to class and then return to his residence hall. On the weekends, he reports he would go home to his parents.

Throughout his childhood and adolescence, John's parents tried a variety of different diets and exercise programs, none of which resulted in weight loss for him. Food was John's method of self-soothing the painful emotions evoked by the taunting and abuse he endured at school. He also resented that no one seemed to accept him for himself. Acceptance always seemed dependent upon weight loss, even from his family.

Following college, where he received his bachelor's degree in nursing, John was hired at a local hospital. Living alone and working nights, John's loneliness increased. He desired close relationships, but did not have any experience with successfully making friends. He feared social rejection and punishment. Anxiety, he reports, was present for him even in work-related social interactions. Living alone, John decided to rebel against the whole of society, which he felt had an agenda for him to lose weight and appear muscular and trim. Therefore he ate anything he wanted to, reporting that he began binge eating during times of emotional or work stress. John reported feeling angry during his binges, feeling that he was retaliating against anyone who ever told him to diet.

At the same time, John believed that his weight was keeping him separate from people. He remembered the multiple voices from peers telling him that no one wanted to be seen with a "fatty" (as he was often called). As his weight crept up even more, fear finally took over, and John reported that he desperately tried to stop binge eating about two years ago. However, overeating was a control strategy and a means of self-soothing. It was a long-standing pattern for John. Desperately wanting to stop gaining weight, he came to see you for help with a process he describes as being "totally out of control."

John's Pain

John clearly has experienced a significant amount of emotional pain resulting from the rejection and abuse of other people. He missed out on social interaction throughout his life and did not learn typical social skills. As an adult, he realized this. In this case, you would want to validate the loneliness, neglect, and emotional pain that John experienced throughout most of his life. Explain to him that other people's behavior is not within our personal control. Despite John's parents' efforts to intervene, no one was there to save him from the abuse of his peers. Currently he continues to experience loneliness and fear of rejection.

John's Suffering

In John's attempts to soothe and alleviate painful emotions of loneliness, he has a lifelong pattern of overeating. Following college, he began binge eating as a means of "getting back" at people who historically made attempts to control his diet. His control strategy is food, which has created additional suffering both emotionally and physically with the consequences of long-term obesity. Because John has returned to food when-ever uncomfortable emotions arise, he has never processed grief, anger, sadness, or other emotions. As time has passed, suppression of those emotions has resulted in an increase in their strength, and new experiences with loneliness and rejection have added to the overall pain he has not allowed himself to experience. His eating (as a control strategy) has increased in relationship to an increase in unprocessed emotional material. His belief that his body image is the direct cause of his loneliness and lack of connection to others eventually led to frantic efforts to control his eating through purging. Thus, when one control strategy became out of control, he developed another control strategy to further attempt to solve the problem. The impact of this is additional suffering, with overeating and purging on top of the unprocessed emotional pain.

When working with your clients, it is important to distinguish pain they have experienced or are experiencing from suffering. Suffering includes any process that is induced by control strategies aimed at alleviating pain. In attempts to alleviate pain or avoid pain, additional suffering is often created. Clarify for your clients that, while emotional pain is quite unavoidable in human experience, suffering is optional. Specifically, elicit examples of the strategies creating additional suffering (such as the social consequences of not eating at restaurants for fear of calories; the health consequences of bingeing or purging; or the misery of subjecting oneself to a very restrictive diet). Eliminating these avoidance behaviors in order to decrease suffering is something your client can have control over. Letting go of control strategies aimed at reducing emotional pain in order to reduce additional suffering may seem a perplexing process for your client. "You mean I must experience emotional pain in order to suffer less?" one client asked. From an ACT perspective, this is our theoretical and clinical experience.

At this point, it is useful to identify what other areas of life feel out of control to your clients—specifically, are there aspects of their life that include emotional pain that they attempt to avoid? Identifying these problems will be important, as the preoccupation with body image may serve as distraction or as avoidance of pain in these uncontrollable areas of life.

After discussing some control strategies directly related to weight and body image, normalize that there are many things in life that we human beings would like to control that are not within our control. Using the exercise below, ask clients to generate a few examples of other life situations, not directly related to eating or weight, that they would like to control or change but that are not within their direct control.

EXERCISE: Things You'd Like to Control and Cannot Control

Ask clients to list, as shown in the following example, five aspects of their life that are important or meaningful to them and that they have little or no control over. Here's John's list:

Things I'd like to control and cannot control:

- *My mother is very ill and I can't do anything to make her better.*

- *I wish I had a committed romantic relationship.*

- *My sister hasn't talked to me in four years because she's addicted to drugs and our family doesn't know where she is.*

- *I always wanted to go into acting, but my parents told me it was a silly career. So I became a nurse instead. I enjoy it, but I feel like I've lost my dream of being a performer because I never pursued it.*

- *I have confusion about spirituality and religious beliefs and often feel lost.*

The purpose of this exercise is for you to gather an initial impression of what other life issues clients may be attempting to avoid or control with their overemphasis on body image issues; for example, "I can't control my husband's long hours at work. He's never home." This same person may be obsessed with losing weight, holding the belief that weight loss would yield a closer relationship with her husband. At your discretion, you may suggest that it's seemingly easier to attempt to control body image through dieting than it is to attempt to control other life issues. However, the functional relationship between an overemphasis on body image as an attempt to control another life problem is best discussed with the client at a later time. This exercise is an opportunity to gather initial information for both the client and the therapist.

The Therapeutic Relationship: Commitment and Alliance Building

The therapeutic relationship in ACT combines commitment and alliance building by both you and your clients. While therapeutic relationships have an inherent power differential that is always present between therapists and clients, taking a collaborative stance is important in ACT. Committing to "stand with" clients in an accepting manner with the full range of emotions and experiences they may share during your work is key to building a strong alliance with them. Deferring to them regarding their experiences, thoughts, feelings, and values instead of being the "expert" in the room is important for building an egalitarian relationship with clients. In this section, we provide further guidance on the important features of the therapeutic relationship in ACT and how to facilitate a workable partnership for treatment.

Commitment to a Vital Life

Talking with your clients about the commitment necessary to engage in ACT is a useful conversation to have early in treatment. You may share with them that the overall goal of using ACT to treat body image dissatisfaction is to help them let go of preoccupation with body weight and shape and move in the direction of their values, thereby developing a more enriched, balanced, and vital life. It's important to convey that weight-loss behavior is not wrong or bad; weight loss and efforts at maintaining appearance can be physically healthy and represent self-care. The problem occurs when preoccupation with appearance and underlying beliefs about appearance create suffering and function as a way to avoid painful emotions about other life difficulties. Letting go of any behavior pattern is difficult and requires commitment to move forward toward values in the face of difficult emotions. Committing to letting go of old behavior patterns or avoidance related to body image dissatisfaction will allow for a broader range of behavioral responses in life. Instead of responding in the same ways to the same thoughts and feelings, commitment to letting go of what isn't working (and what is causing suffering) is the first step toward creating a more vital life.

The Difficult and Meaningful Work of Therapy

Share with your clients that they may enjoy this treatment at times, and they may experience it as difficult at times. It is often useful to make the point at the start of treatment that clients are choosing to embark on some difficult and meaningful work. Clients may have thoughts about not continuing the work at times, as you may be asking them to make difficult changes or experience painful emotions. A new way of living life is being suggested, and clients may find it a challenge to adapt to it. However, the work entailed is in the service of improving their quality of life, creating meaningful and vital living with less preoccupation with weight and appearance.

Acceptance and Nonjudgment

As with most psychotherapies, warmth and a nonjudgmental stance by the clinician from the beginning of treatment are vital. The following guidelines may help you facilitate an ACT-consistent therapeutic stance:

- Lean in (physically and emotionally) to your clients' sharing of emotion and experience.

- Express to your clients the impact they have on you as a human being, emotionally and interpersonally, when you feel authenticity from them.

- Be authentic and egalitarian with your client.

- Ask permission to push your clients when you see an opportunity for emotional experiencing.

- When there is pain, respond first with compassion as a human being.

ACT is not an instructional therapy. It is an experiential therapy, based on being authentic and behaving in accordance with your values even when this is difficult.

Since acceptance and commitment therapy is an acceptance-based treatment, it is important that you do not present the goal of therapy as being to change client eating behavior, weight, thoughts, or feelings. Instead you need to convey an overall message of acceptance and nonjudgment. Recognize that these clients seek treatment because of difficulty surrounding eating and body image, and that treatment aims to help them gain a new perspective in these areas of life and to better understand how their eating behavior impacts their life. The universal nature of human pain and the desire to control or lessen that pain may be a point of alliance building with your clients.

Accept, Choose, Take Action: The Basics of ACT

As you introduce ACT to your clients, provide these two statements for them to consider: "It is normal to be happy" and "We need to think and feel better to be able to behave better." Discuss these with your clients. Let's take a little closer look at what you might touch on in that discussion.

It is normal to be happy. Does your client believe this statement? Many people do believe this, as we live in a society that emphasizes pleasure seeking and quick solutions to relieve pain. Emphasize to your clients that while it is quite understandable to want to be happy, happiness is only one of many human emotions. There is no identifiable normal or abnormal emotion.

We need to think and feel better to be able to behave better. Although our feelings and thoughts are undeniably strong at times, our behavior is always a choice (unless we are under the influence of a drug or in another state of consciousness). Many people believe that it is necessary to change thoughts and feelings before changing behavior. Some therapeutic techniques spend considerable time and energy changing thoughts in order to change behavior. ACT approaches thoughts and feelings differently; it approaches behavior change without focusing on changing thoughts or feelings. If your clients don't buy this and believe that thoughts and feelings must be changed in order to change behavior, you may ask them if they believe they can open the door just by thinking it open. When they say no, say the following:

What if a fire started in this room and you knew you had to get out quickly, but I told you that there were two requirements to get out of the room: First, you needed to calm down, even with the fire burning and smoke enveloping the room. Second, you first needed to believe that you could open the door with your mind before your could get out of your chair to open it. No matter what, you couldn't open the door unless you first changed your belief about the power of your mind.

Clearly, whatever you believed wouldn't matter much; and it wouldn't matter if you were upset or calm. You'd get up and open the door. If you've been requiring that your thinking or feeling change before taking action in your life, you may have noticed that some of those actions haven't happened yet because it's nearly impossible to change thoughts and feelings. In ACT, we're not going to spend energy doing that. We just want to help you take the action—to open the door.

You may want to write down the acronym ACT—accept, choose, take action—and give it to your clients. It can be a useful, brief description to remind your clients of the basic tenets of the therapy they're embarking on. Or you may want to give your clients the following handout, which describes some primary goals of acceptance and commitment therapy. The handout may help in the initial orientation to treatment.

ACCEPTANCE AND COMMITMENT THERAPY

Three primary components of acceptance and commitment therapy (ACT) are accept, choose, and take action. Here's an easy way to remember this:

A – Accept

C – Choose

T – Take action

Accept

This involves accepting your thoughts and feelings about yourself, which are essentially not controllable. The idea is to accept what you already have anyway, and end the struggle with unwanted thoughts and feelings by not attempting to change them, not acting upon them, and ultimately letting them go.

Choose

Choosing a direction in your life involves identifying what you value in life and what you want your life to stand for. This is about finding out what is truly important to you.

Take Action

This involves taking steps toward realizing your valued life goals. It is about making a commitment to action and changing what you can change. This step involves learning to behave in a way that moves you forward in the direction of your chosen values.

Adapted from Michelle Heffner and Georg H. Eifert, *The Anorexia Workbook: How to Accept Yourself, Heal Your Suffering, and Reclaim Your Life* (Oakland, CA: New Harbinger Publications, 2004).

Conclusion

This chapter provided guidance on introducing clients to ACT with respect to the basic tenets of the therapy. When beginning to use ACT to treat body image dissatisfaction, we suggest eliciting a description from clients about their body image struggle. Describing how problems of control—not problems with their body—are what treatment will address is important in the initial phase of treatment. In the beginning, it is important that clients learn how control strategies tend to produce unworkable solutions and add suffering to existing human pain. Following this introduction to the treatment, we move to the treatment component of creative hopelessness, to which chapter 5 is devoted.

CHAPTER 5

Creative Hopelessness: Openness to Trying Something Different

Insanity is doing the same thing over and over again and expecting different results.

—Albert Einstein

When Control Doesn't Work: Introducing Creative Hopelessness

After you and your clients have identified control strategies and discussed the relative effectiveness of those control strategies, you will be ready to help your clients identify ways that control strategies have actually not worked to create a desired outcome. Becoming aware of the behaviors that haven't worked to produce a desired outcome and being open to trying a new approach to living life are the two essential components of creative hopelessness. Creative hopelessness means letting go of the false hope that unworkable control strategies will eventually work.

In the context of this book, creative hopelessness focuses on how attempts to control thoughts and feelings about body image are futile. Experiential avoidance, which means engaging in behaviors to change or avoid feeling bad about one's body, is a common function underlying the class of behaviors related to weight control and body image.

When clients have reached a point of creative hopelessness, they have reached an experiential understanding of three things: (1) the specific behaviors or strategies that they have tried in order to attain what they want, (2) that their past attempts to attain what they want have not worked, and (3) that openness to redefining what they want in life and pursuing that through different means may be necessary.

■ Case Example: Jessica

Jessica, a thirty-year-old Caucasian single female has been referred to you by her primary care physician. She is a survivor of breast cancer and has been cancer free for two years. Her primary care physician became concerned about Jessica's psychological well-being in a recent annual checkup after Jessica reported quitting her job due to stress (she worked throughout her illness), increased alcohol consumption (at least three drinks every night), and some thoughts of suicide. At her initial visit with you, Jessica reported feeling depressed about her appearance. She stated she gained thirty pounds during cancer treatment, and that she has not been able to lose the weight. Jessica reported decreased socialization and decreased contact with family members in the past two years, stating, "My friends and family don't want to be seen with me because I look sick and unattractive."

In addition to disliking her weight gain, Jessica also reported feeling unattractive due to changes in the shape of different parts of her body, changes in her skin tone and color, and changes to the quality of her hair following regrowth after chemotherapy. She stated, "Overall, I just hate myself when I look in the mirror. I'm not the same person I was before this disease. I didn't survive cancer; cancer killed the person I was."

Jessica reported that although she worked throughout her illness, she recently quit her job and is receiving unemployment. She described spending her days inside her home, rarely going outdoors, and spending a lot of time on the Internet. She described feeling guilty that she isn't more grateful for surviving cancer, saying, "This disease left a shell of the person I was. I feel empty inside. I wish it had killed me, because sometimes I don't want to live anymore."

Jessica's current distress focuses on her appearance and how her appearance is representative of cancer, which she feels defines her life at this point. She defines herself currently by the external features of her body and has used this as a measuring stick of strength. Even though she physically survived the cancer, Jessica feels dead because she cannot identify a sense of self beyond what she sees in the mirror, which has been changed by the disease. If Jessica were your client and if you were using ACT, you would have spent the first session gathering data on some of the control strategies she has used historically, as well as those that she currently uses to cope with uncomfortable emotions and thoughts. As you read Jessica's story in her own words below, consider what those strategies are and how these attempts at control have left Jessica feeling that she did not survive cancer.

Jessica: From the point that I was diagnosed, I tried everything to pretend this [cancer] wasn't happening to me. I worked with a beauty consultant who advised me on makeup that would enhance my appearance. I spent hundreds of dollars on different wigs after losing my hair. When I noticed I started to gain some weight because I was too tired to work out, I tried several diets to maintain my weight and look just like I did before cancer. I was eating healthier than ever, determined to be the best-looking, healthiest cancer patient that my doctor had ever treated. This worked at first. People complimented me on my appearance. One friend even said I looked better than before my diagnosis! I felt I was beating cancer inside my body and on the outside too!

When treatment ended and I was declared cancer free, somehow I didn't feel as great as I'd fantasized I would. I wasn't sure why, but I didn't feel like I'd beat cancer. On the inside, I felt like it had beaten me down. I started having panic attacks at work for no apparent reason. Nothing seemed to make me happy anymore. I started drinking wine every night because I couldn't sleep. I'd lay in bed afraid the cancer was back, and I'd start crying for no apparent reason. The weight gain had continued, and I couldn't wear my old "precancer" clothes anymore. I'd spend hours trying on clothes from my closet that I wore before the diagnosis. I'd look at old pictures to compare my appearance. I was sure that I looked different now. I felt like I was looking at a different person in those pictures. At that point, I felt like it was useless to try to maintain my appearance anymore, because I'd never look like I did before this disease. That's when I started to feel really hopeless and depressed.

Friends and family would get frustrated with me because I would complain about how I looked. They'd say, "At least you're alive!" But I didn't feel that way; I don't feel that way. So I stopped returning their phone calls. They only see me as a cancer survivor, not as their friend or family member, not as who I was before this disease. I look in the mirror, and I see the effects of cancer. I see it in my body, in my weight, in my face. I feel like other people must look at me and see the same thing.

When you listen to Jessica's story, you likely realize that the weight is not Jessica's problem, nor is her appearance. When she was first diagnosed, Jessica focused on maintaining her appearance in order to avoid the fear and vulnerability associated with cancer and her treatment. Later, when these efforts failed, Jessica began to see the effects of the disease in her physical appearance. She has connected with the emotions of disliking how the cancer changed her physical appearance, but she has not fully connected with how cancer impacted her life and her relationships, or the fears that having a serious disease evoked about her future. Jessica is only partly aware of that. She understands cancer has changed her, but she still focuses on the external component of the change. This is one of her control strategies. From the point of diagnosis, Jessica tried several strategies to hide her illness and, more importantly, to suppress the feelings that having the illness naturally evoked. She never allowed herself to experience the fear, loss, anger, or other feelings that naturally occur in a life-threatening illness. Her overemphasis on appearance functioned well at first because it was an aspect of her life she could change. This worked temporarily. Eventually, however, because she couldn't successfully hide all the physical effects of the illness, this control strategy began to break down. Attempts to suppress feelings evoked by the experience with her illness stopped working.

In working with your own clients, as with Jessica, you'll want to help them connect with the impact of the control strategies in which they've been engaged. For Jessica, her various attempts to hide her vulnerability and focus on physical strength as her measure of health resulted in her feeling a loss of self and feeling dead. A useful way to learn about the impacts of avoidance of feelings and control strategies aimed at avoiding experiencing life is to ask clients what they have noticed is missing from their life.

- Do they feel that their life is vital or meaningful while engaging in the control strategies? (For example, do they feel that life is meaningful and vital when preoccupied with thoughts about their appearance?)

- What is lost in their efforts to not feel what is present?

- What is the cost for them?

Control Strategies and Experiential Avoidance

Remind your clients again how being overly focused on body image and eating may serve as avoidance of more painful, uncontrollable life events. Assess what feelings would arise if the client were to let go of worrying about weight or body image. Here are some questions to consider:

- "If you let go of your specific control strategy with food, what feelings might come up?"

- "What life topics might you focus on instead?"

- "Would this be difficult? More painful?"

If you've had your clients complete the exercise Things You'd Like to Control and Cannot Control (see chapter 4), you may find it useful at this time to consider the issues clients provided in that exercise. These issues might be more present for clients if they let go of being overly focused on body image.

To illustrate how to approach creative hopelessness, let's return to the case of Jessica as an example. This is your second meeting with Jessica, and you may begin something like this:

Therapist: From what I can tell, Jessica, you worked very hard to fight the cancer, to make it go away.

Jessica: Yes, and it did go away.

Therapist: Yes, the cancer as a disease is gone. But I get the feeling that you feel it's still with you in certain ways.

Jessica: Yes. I see it when I look in the mirror. If I looked the same as I did before treatment, then I don't think I'd have a problem feeling like a survivor.

Therapist:	I'm noticing that you've had a very strong belief, from the beginning of your diagnosis, that if you looked healthy, then the cancer couldn't hurt you. Is that right?
Jessica:	Absolutely.
Therapist:	So you tried all kinds of things to keep your body feeling and looking the same as it did before the diagnosis. You worked really hard at that. But eventually those strategies stopped working.
Jessica:	Yes. I gained weight and couldn't get it off. And my skin never returned to its original color, and my hair is a totally different texture and color than before chemo.
Therapist:	So you've noticed some physical changes that you've tried hard to change but cannot change. And it also sounds like your efforts to not feel sick or different also stopped working in other ways.
Jessica:	What do you mean?
Therapist:	I'm talking about suppressing feelings about having cancer that don't relate directly to your physical appearance. My guess is that some of those feelings started to come back when all the makeup and diets and wigs couldn't take away the reality of your disease. At some point, you realized that you couldn't make your feelings disappear, even when the cancer did.

Here you point out the ineffectiveness of suppressing feelings through external means, such as weight control. In order to explain the futility of attempting to suppress feelings and thoughts, you may discuss the _abstinence violation model_ with clients as a metaphor for thought suppression—that is, all eating disorders begin with a diet that is a purposeful suppression or restriction of calories. If the restriction is extreme, no one can do this for very long without violating the restriction. It is simply biologically impossible. Most clients will be able to connect with the experience of either purposeful or nonpurposeful calorie restriction, followed by hunger and then subsequent overeating. You can draw a parallel for your clients that just as they are more likely to think a thought that they try to push away, they are also more likely to binge eat after a period of restricted eating. If they have compensatory behaviors (such as purging or laxative use), this would then come next in the chain of behaviors. The abstinence violation model may also be applied to body image distress. The more clients focus on trying to change or minimize a part of the body they are uncomfortable with, the more apparent that body part will become and the more subsequent attention they will pay to that body part. This same principle can be applied to thoughts and feelings. The stronger the attempt to not have or suppress the thought or feeling, the stronger it will be.

Ask your clients if there are thoughts that they often try to push away or try to not think about. Then ask them to give you an example of one of these thoughts and have them say the thought out loud (for example, "I try not to think about the boyfriend who left me last year"). Ask your clients what their experience has been with trying not to think that particular thought or thoughts related to it. Even as you talk about this with them, stop and ask, "What if, after just bringing this thought up in session, I asked you to stop thinking about it this instant? Do you think you could do that? How difficult would that be?" Next, challenge your clients to a brief period of thought suppression, asking them to try to not think about that particular topic or thoughts related to it. Ask them what their experience is with this. Is it easy? Ask them how they attempt to suppress thoughts. Do they try thinking of other things? This information will be useful to you as a clinician as you work with your clients on defusing (that is, distancing) from thoughts later in treatment.

Relating thought suppression to eating, weight, and body image issues, you may use the abstinence violation model of dieting to illustrate the ineffectiveness of suppression with a more concrete example. You may, for example, ask your clients these questions: "How many times have you tried to not eat a certain food, tried to eliminate it from your diet? Has this worked in the long run?" "If you try to not think about food all day [which the client may have done], what typically happens?)"

As an assessment of thought suppression, you may provide the White Bear Suppression Inventory to clients, a useful fifteen-item self-report measure of the tendency to suppress unwanted thoughts (Wegner & Zanakos, 1994). Clients rate, from 1 to 5, how much they agree with statements such as "I have thoughts that I cannot stop" and "I often do things to distract myself from my thoughts." Higher scores indicate that the client tends to suppress, rather than accept, unwanted thoughts. Administration of this questionnaire can provide useful feedback to the client and stimulate discussion of the client's use of thought suppression as a coping strategy.

You can use data from this inventory when discussing thought suppression with your clients. You may give the White Bear Suppression Inventory as a repeated measure over the course of treatment for assessment purposes. In this way, you can target thought suppression relative to the client's individual needs in this area.

Individuals with body image dissatisfaction may have engaged in a variety of eating and weight-control behaviors in attempts to reduce direct distress about their body image. And, as we mentioned earlier, the overemphasis on body image as being of primary importance to life satisfaction may also function as avoidance of more difficult or uncontrollable topics. While you may choose not to use the term "experiential avoidance" with your clients to describe their behaviors, you'll find that a general explanation of how behaviors may be intended to decrease distress will be useful.

Disordered Eating as Experiential Avoidance

Below we offer theoretical conceptualizations of how disordered eating behaviors may function as experiential avoidance. From an ACT conceptualization, the manifestations of disordered eating behaviors may appear quite different yet function similarly. Specifically, food and eating behaviors may become either positively reinforcing or negatively reinforcing with respect to physiological sensations or emotions. Food may soothe, creating positive feelings and positive physiological responses in order to escape more negative emotions. Likewise, the restriction of food or the purging of food may also serve to distract from uncomfortable emotions with the physical sensation of hunger or to alleviate uncomfortable emotions via purging. Let's take a closer look now at experiential avoidance as a common function of disordered eating and body image dissatisfaction.

Binge eating. Some clients engage in *objective binge eating*, which means they consume an abnormally large amount of food in a discrete time period. Others may engage in *subjective binge eating*, which means consumption of a small amount of a "forbidden" food. Binge eating has been conceptualized as a means of escaping from unpleasant thoughts and feelings (Arnow, Kenardy, & Agras, 1992; Heatherton & Baumeister, 1991; Webber, 1994). Clients often report experiencing some sort of negative mood (anxiety, depression, and so on) immediately before a binge-eating episode, and that the binge produces an immediate reduction in the negative mood (Elmore & de Castro, 1990). Binge eating can function as an experiential avoidance strategy because the binge eating provides an escape from negative mood.

Purging. Aversive states often arise after binge eating. These aversive states may include guilt, shame, frustration, fear of weight gain, physical bloating or gastrointestinal distress, and so on. Purging can function as an experiential avoidance strategy because the purges allow one to escape from these negative feelings.

Excessive dieting. In the most severe cases, excessive dieting may lead to anorexia nervosa. Interviews of anorectic women indicated that restriction allows them to temporarily escape from unwanted emotions (Cockell, Geller, & Linden, 2002). They reported that when they feel "bad," they restrict and the "bad feelings" are replaced with feelings of being powerful and in control over food.

Body dissatisfaction. The excessive focus on weight, body image, and body shape can function as an experiential avoidance strategy to escape from dealing with more difficult life topics, such as relationships, work, and other life stressors.

The Role of Experiential Avoidance in Body Image Dissatisfaction

Schmidt and Treasure (2006) provide a literature review that documents how disordered eating behaviors are avoidance-based coping strategies that allow one to suppress "negative" emotions. Although these behaviors allow a temporary escape, the long-term consequences create additional problems that impact the person's quality of life, such as infertility, fatigue, and continued emotional distress. However, immediate consequences are more effective than delayed consequences at controlling behavior. Thus, the immediate relief associated with experiential avoidance is more powerful than the delayed harmful consequence. Therefore, your job as therapist is to illustrate why and how experiential avoidance has not been workable in the ways the client has hoped. A good place to start with this task is to illustrate for the client that avoidance strategies aimed at decreasing thoughts and emotions generally do not work the long run and generally lead to increased suffering. For example, a man feeling sad over the loss of a romantic relationship may shift the focus of his thoughts and feelings to perceived inadequacies in his body (such as obsessing that he has insufficient muscle tone or too much fat). Instead of grieving the loss of the relationship, he may perceive more control over his physical imperfections and may spend hours analyzing or attempting to change these. He may even conclude that imperfections in his body were the reason for ending the relationship. Consequently he has created another area of struggle on top of the existing sadness and loss related to the relationship ending.

Clearly the process of reinforcement is not simple with disordered eating. However, most often when people engage in ineffective or destructive behaviors, there is an immediate reward (consider drugs or alcohol) that has become a stronger reinforcement than the costs of the destructive behavior. With body image preoccupation, an immediate reward may be social connection for discussing a topic that is common to many. Clients may gain some immediate relief from anxiety or other uncomfortable feelings by shifting focus to the body, exercise, or food; other immediate reinforcing factors may be a sense of success or accomplishment in following self-imposed rules related to image maintenance. Our example of the man obsessed with physical imperfections may find he is in good company in discussing this at the gym. Because clients may perceive that the behavior has worked as a coping strategy, your job is to balance this viewpoint by illustrating why and how the behavior has not been workable in the ways clients have hoped. A good place to start with this task is to illustrate for your clients that avoidance strategies aimed at decreasing thoughts and emotions generally do not work. Let's continue with our example of the man avoiding grief by focusing on physical imperfections. He may not immediately experience negative consequences of not processing the feelings associated with losing his relationship. However, over time, his shift in focus to his perceived physical inadequacies may impact his social functioning. Unprocessed grief related to the lost relationship may interfere with the development of new relationships. The focus on physical imperfections may begin to result in anxiety and depression (as the literature shows) and with persistent thoughts about not being "good enough" physically.

Facilitating Creative Hopelessness

Creative hopelessness involves acknowledging that the client's usual experiential avoidance strategies have not worked and often lead to additional suffering. As you work with your clients through the process of creative hopelessness, the questions below may be helpful to consider. At this point in treatment, these questions may be a work in progress for you, as clients may reveal new areas of avoidance or share other ways in which they realize their life is impacted by being overly focused on body image. In order to facilitate the process of creative hopelessness with your clients, gaining an initial understanding of each of these three questions as the therapist will be important. Your clients may also share an understanding of these points, and you can feel free to discuss these questions with them.

1. How does being overly focused on body image function as avoidance in the client's life—that is, what larger issue, feeling, or situation does it function to avoid?

2. What specific behaviors or thoughts is the client actively engaged in that function as experiential avoidance of difficult or painful emotions?

3. What areas of the client's life are being impacted by this struggle—that is, how is the current overemphasis on body image or weight becoming ineffective or unworkable?

To illustrate assessment of these three points, we continue our conversation with Jessica and her therapist.

Jessica: So you're saying I'm suppressing feelings about cancer? I know how I felt about cancer. It sucked! It was the most awful thing I've ever experienced.

Therapist: Tell me about how it was awful.

Jessica: Where do I start?

Therapist: You said you've been having some panic attacks lately, and also some tears.

Jessica: Yes. I cry sometimes now when I look in the mirror and see someone I don't know, and then I get panicky when I think about the cancer coming back.

Therapist: What do you feel when you look in mirror, or when you think about the cancer returning?

Jessica: I feel scared. My appearance scares me, because it's so different. I see what the disease did to me. I'm not sure I could survive it again.

Therapist: It sounds like you feel vulnerable.

Jessica: I do. I hate to admit that, because I wanted to be strong so the cancer couldn't beat me. But I feel totally scared of getting hurt, of other people hurting me because they don't understand what I went through—what I'm going through.

Therapist: So you've been feeling really alone and pretty scared for a long time.

Jessica: Yes. I felt alone from the moment I was diagnosed. I felt like no one understood the fear I felt, or how a diagnosis like that totally changes your life. I'm not sure who I am anymore. One thing's for sure: I'm not who I used to be.

Therapist: So it sounds like you've tried all these things to not change from the person you were before the diagnosis. That makes sense, because you felt connected to people before you were diagnosed. Afterward you felt alone and scared, so you tried everything possible to maintain familiarity in your appearance because you felt like you were losing yourself.

Jessica:	Yes, I did. Now I've started drinking and that doesn't help either. It just makes me feel horrible. I'm lonely, without work, and I don't even know who I am anymore.
Therapist:	What if you stopped trying to find that person you used to be and started from here, as you are now.
Jessica:	What do you mean? My life is horrible.
Therapist:	Well, it sounds like everything you've tried to escape the cancer hasn't worked: You've tried to hold onto your prediagnosed self, and you've realized that's not possible. You've tried to not feel the fear of the disease or its return. That hasn't worked, as you're still having the panic attacks. So it feels to me like you're stuck. You need a different way out.

At this point, Jessica begins to discuss some of the feelings she has been avoiding. She is coming into experiential contact with the struggle she has been engaged in: trying to get rid of the feelings, thoughts, and experiences related to having a serious illness.

She has tried to get rid of these by, first, focusing on control of the external to avoid feelings associated with the disease. Second, she blames the uncontrollable changes in her appearance for the feelings she cannot ultimately control. However, she is beginning to understand that her feelings have been only partly related to her external appearance and are more related to human experiences of isolation and vulnerability. She has struggled against those feelings and other feelings associated with the experience of having cancer—feelings that she has experienced since the first day of her diagnosis.

Experiencing Creative Hopelessness

When your clients begin to understand the true nature of their struggle, an experiential exercise using a metaphor may help elucidate the process of the struggle (see below). How will you know that your clients have begun to understand the cost of the preoccupation with weight and shape? Typically they will likely express some emotion with regard to the loss involved in having placed excess energy into body image–related activities or avoidance (such as relationships that have been neglected). Your clients may also express emotion related to the realization that their efforts to be happy by attempting to "look good" have not worked (for example, despite years of various attempts, the client continues to suffer). Metaphors are often used in ACT in order to identify psychological processes (such as suppressing thoughts and emotions) in order to help clients view the problem objectively. Understanding the impact of thought suppression and observing themselves engage in this is often a new process for clients. It can be a challenging process, especially when clients are stuck in the very process (that is, fighting with thoughts) that they are trying to observe. The following metaphor is useful in providing clients with a way to conceptualize the futility of battle against thoughts and emotions.

Adapted from Hayes et al. (1999)

Ask your clients to find a comfortable sitting position with their eyes closed. Let them know that you'll be guiding them in a visualization exercise.

Imagine first that you are at a time in your life when you were carefree and did not have the concerns you have now with your body image. This may take you back to the age of a young child. Imagine yourself at that age, when you were not coping with the struggle you currently have. You are carefree, walking through a field. Imagine the field you are in. What do your surroundings look like? Imagine now that you're walking or running through the field, and all of a sudden you fall into a hole. You're quite stunned but not injured.

You look around, and as far as you can tell, you have no way to get out of the hole. There's no ladder, no stairs. It's very deep, and it's dark. At this point, you realize you are no longer carefree. You have a mountainous problem on your hands. You begin to feel quite scared and overwhelmed. Then you look down and realize there's a shovel at your feet. Excited at the prospect of getting out of the hole, you pick up the shovel and begin to dig.

You dig furiously, scooping up dirt from the sides of the hole and the bottom of the hole. You're trying to use the shovel to get you out of this hole, to help you escape this mess you've found yourself in. You dig and dig until you're completely exhausted. You look around and realize that you've only dug a deeper hole, and that piles of dirt around you are making the space inside the hole smaller and smaller. Your efforts at digging are useless.

Now as you look at yourself in the hole, you realize you've grown up to the age you are now. You've been in this same hole for that many years. You look at your arms and legs and see that you're an adult person now, yet you still don't have a workable solution for getting out of this place. The shovel is so heavy in your hands, and the efforts of your work have not gotten you anywhere but deeper and deeper in this hole. What can you do now?

Ask clients to open their eyes and come back to the room. Take a moment now to allow clients to share their experience of the metaphor. You may offer questions like these:

- ■ "Do you feel stuck in your life now in a way similar to how you were trapped in the hole?"

- ■ "What ways do you see you've been digging?"

- ■ "How have these methods not worked for you? How have the control strategies dug your hole deeper?"

- ■ "What might be a different solution?"

The alternate solution to digging is, of course, putting down the shovel. If clients do not suggest this alternative, you may suggest it and ask how that translates into doing something different in their life.

Clients will often be perplexed at the thought of putting down the shovel. They may ask, "Doesn't that mean giving up? I am not a quitter." They may even be offended because they think that you are suggesting that they resign themselves to living in a hole. In that case, it may be helpful to discuss that clients are not quitting. Instead, they are acknowledging that they are in a situation that they cannot control and are letting go of a struggle they cannot win. They may even consider the possibility of being more comfortable in their hole. What is familiar is often comfortable, even if it is a destructive behavior or a behavior that causes suffering. The process of accepting emotional pain that comes with letting go of old, familiar coping strategies is difficult. Those who are willing to let go of old ways of coping are courageous in facing the reality of existing emotional pain.

At this time, clients may realize that they are being asked to consider giving up their long-held control strategies. Given that this book is about body image dissatisfaction rather than serious eating disorders, one problem you may encounter is a lack of personal cost that clients have experienced from being overly focused on body image. Why not hold on to it? Why not keep focusing on losing the last ten pounds or finding the "right" diet? The answer to this lies in the distress that the struggle evokes. It may be useful to remind your clients of the age at which they first began the struggle with body image or disordered eating patterns. Eliciting from clients the number of diets, hours per day, or energy given to this area of their life is also a useful tool to show unworkability. Further, having clients describe the situations in which they have used this as a strategy to avoid dating, social engagements, interpersonal relationships, sports, or wearing certain clothing, or generally how often they have felt uncomfortable in their own body is also useful.

In other cases, clients will challenge the notion that letting go is a viable alternative. The Polygraph Metaphor (below) is helpful in working with client resistance.

EXERCISE: Polygraph Metaphor— Struggling with Resistance

Adapted from Hayes et al. (1999)

Sometimes you will need to roll with client resistance. We recommend that you use this exercise when clients struggle with resistance in session. This dialogue is an example of how you can use the Polygraph Metaphor.

Client: I see what you're saying, but I don't know if it makes sense. Obviously there are times that you can control your emotions, and it helps. I learned relaxation, and I do it every morning, and it works well to relieve my stress.

Therapist: You bring up a really good point. I'm glad you mentioned relaxation, and I want to encourage you to continue telling me when something does not make sense. It really helps us to work together when you speak up. So you have learned relaxation, and it works?

Client: Yes. I've been doing it for five years.

Therapist: Okay. Well, let's imagine that I hooked you up to a polygraph machine to measure your anxiety levels. We start out with a baseline measure of your anxiety as it is right now. Then you start the relaxation, and your anxiety level goes down. We're thinking, "Wow! This relaxation really works to control anxiety." Then I take out a gun and put it to your head, and I say, "You must stay relaxed. If your anxiety level increases at all, I will shoot you—dead." How well do you think the relaxation is going to work now?

Client: I think I'd be in trouble.

Therapist: Yes. Relaxation might seem like a good way to control your anxiety, but there are just some situations in which anxiety naturally occurs. If there were at gun to your head, anxiety would happen, whether you wanted it to or not. The ironic thing is that if you didn't want that anxiety and really tried to get rid of feeling scared, all that pressure to relax would only increase the anxiety. You're right: you would be in trouble.

When you discuss creative hopelessness with your clients, it is important to note that the situation is not literally hopeless. There is a difference between what clients cannot control (thoughts and feelings) and what they can change and control (behavior). Creative hopelessness may be conceptualized as a turning point, a point of departure, or a chance to take a new path. The client is able to see, perhaps for the first time, what behavioral strategies have not worked in life; in this way, creative hopelessness is a period of increased awareness. The client will begin to see that a different path is needed. One client treated with ACT asked why it is not possible to reprogram her mind to think differently.

Client: I went to another therapist once, and she asked me if I ever moved the garbage can in my home. We talked about how I initially kept going back to the old location, but I eventually reprogrammed my mind to go to the new location. That made sense to me, so I'm really confused that you are saying something different.

Therapist : Thank you for noticing that you feel confused. So far, we've been talking about thoughts and feelings and how thoughts and feelings are difficult, sometimes harmful, to change. You mention going to the garbage can, but that is not a thought or feeling. Going to the garbage can is a behavior, and I absolutely agree with your other therapist that you can change your behavior. Her example demonstrates that behavior change is not easy, and when you first try to do something different, it does not feel natural. You may go back to the old behavior a few times before the new behavior is established. You actually have a lot of power to control your behavior, and we will work on helping you to choose values-based behaviors each day. In the meantime, you will also learn to let go of the struggle to control your thoughts and feelings, which are much more difficult to change than behavior.

The Polygraph Metaphor and the Man in the Hole Metaphor are intended to convey how it is that a particular avoidance strategy has not been working for clients. If your clients appear to connect with one of the metaphors, it may be useful to carry it throughout therapy, returning to it in order to identify future attempts to control or avoid emotion. For example, the term "digging" in the Man in the Hole Metaphor may be used if you notice clients talking about a behavior that functions as avoidance in session. You may ask, "Is this another means of digging?" Clients may also be able to identify their own behavior with use of metaphors, which is indicative of some ability to detach and observe their own behavior.

Achieving Creative Hopelessness

You may be thinking, "How will I know that my client has reached a point of creative hopelessness in the ACT work?" The answer: You may not know. The not knowing if the treatment is working at this point is part of your journey in acceptance and willingness. Statements from clients may indicate a connection to the unworkability of their behaviors: "I'm never going to be able to change how I feel, am I?" "I've never really been happy doing this [behavior]." "What if I can't stop doing what I've been doing?" Comments like these may indicate that your client has come to some realization of the ineffectiveness of prior behavior and attempts at controlling emotions and thoughts. However, clinically relevant behaviors such as change in affect during this realization of unworkability may be more reliable. When clients realize that their old way of living is not workable, this is usually not emotionally easy. Tears, anger, or other intense emotions often come up during this realization.

An important note: Allow your clients to have whatever emotions come up without making your own attempt to soothe or decrease those emotions. During creative hopelessness, you may feel a pull to soothe clients or reassure them that they will find a way "out of the hole." While certainly done out of good intention, this only serves to reinforce clients' long-held ideas that they cannot tolerate the difficult emotions that are present in the absence of the control behavior. Letting clients leave a session feeling scared or unsure is reasonable as long as you emphasize the need for self-care during that time.

Conclusion

In the early stages of using ACT to treat body image dissatisfaction, you have helped your clients identify the control strategies aimed at suppressing or avoiding painful emotions. By now, they have gained an initial understanding, from an experiential standpoint, or how the control strategies have been ineffective in reducing their pain and have actually produced additional suffering. Identification of control strategies aimed at experiential avoidance is a process that will continue to unfold, perhaps throughout the client's life. At this point, the client has developed a sense of creative hopelessness, acknowledging that continued use of experiential avoidance strategies will lead to the same maladaptive results.

Humans will inevitably try to find new ways of avoiding pain. By using metaphors, you can help your clients view their struggle to control emotions objectively. It's easy to get stuck in the process of engaging in yet another control strategy and not even recognize it. As the clinician, you can point this out to your clients and, using a metaphor (such as the Man in the Hole), point out the process in an objective manner ("I can see you're digging again"). Because identification of control strategies is a process, we devote our next chapter to learning to recognize when a particular behavior is becoming problematic by creating additional suffering. In addition to discussing control as the problem, we introduce acceptance and discuss again the concept of willingness in facilitating acceptance as an alternate way of approaching life experiences. Now that your client recognizes that avoidance of emotions doesn't work in the long run, the concept of being willing to experience the emotions instead of looking for a new control strategy is the process through which acceptance is achieved.

CHAPTER 6

Control as the Problem, Acceptance as the Solution

For after all, the best thing one can do when it's raining is to let it rain.

—Henry Wadsworth Longfellow

Seeking an Alternative to Old Coping Strategies

So far the goal of therapy has been to teach your clients the basic principle of experiential avoidance and how focusing on body image dissatisfaction is a means of avoiding uncomfortable emotions related to other life issues. In creative hopelessness, your clients came in contact with the ineffectiveness of their control strategies and experienced these strategies as ineffective long-term solutions. Now they stand at a point of departure from their old coping strategies, and they seek a new alternative to those strategies. Our purpose in this chapter is to continue to reinforce that control strategies are ineffective ways of escaping pain, and to present acceptance and willingness as alternate approaches to managing life's problems.

Before we look more closely at the treatment process, we think you'll find a brief review of research showing the effectiveness of ACT in treating clients with body image and related problems helpful. For example, some overweight clients with body image problems may be binge eaters. Binge eaters tend to report that negative mood precipitates a binge-eating episode and the binge eating produces an immediate reduction in feelings of anxiety and depression (Elmore & de Castro, 1990). In this case, binge eating functions as an experiential avoidance strategy because the consumption of food allows the client to escape from an uncomfortable mood, but the long-term effect of binge eating can lead to weight gain. Such clients can benefit from identifying binge eating as an unworkable experiential avoidance strategy and begin to consider acceptance of negative mood as a more viable solution.

Recent laboratory and clinical research supports the approach that control is the problem and acceptance is the solution for binge eating. In one analog research study, undergraduates were randomly assigned to either no intervention, control intervention (distraction and cognitive restructuring), or acceptance intervention, then given chocolate candy to keep, without eating, for forty-eight hours (Forman et al., 2007). Results indicate that acceptance was more effective than control among participants with high susceptibility to the presence of food.

In another study (Rasmussen-Hall, 2007), female undergraduates with a history of self-harm or binge-purge behavior, compared to matched controls, had higher scores on measures of *alexithymia* (difficulty recognizing and describing emotions) and greater experiential avoidance, as measured by termination of a stressful laboratory task.

A randomized control trial (Lillis et al., 2009) involved randomly assigning obese patients in a weight-loss program to either a one-day ACT workshop or a no-treatment control. Results showed a reduction in experiential avoidance among the ACT workshop participants, who also achieved greater weight-loss maintenance, improved blood pressure, less psychological distress, less stigma, enhanced quality of life, and less binge eating at three-month follow-up.

More recently the treatment approach in this book was applied to a sample of women with body image dissatisfaction in a one-day workshop format (Pearson, 2009). When compared to a wait-list control condition, the treatment group showed significant reductions in eating disorder pathology, anxiety related to body image, and frequency of thoughts related to weight and body image, and significant increases in acceptance. In addition, acceptance was also shown to mediate these changes during treatment. As research in the area of acceptance-based interventions unfolds, we are seeing consistent results with increases in psychological flexibility and reductions in distress across a variety of psychological problems.

New Control Strategies

As you proceed with treatment, it is important to recognize if your clients initiate new control strategies, viewing these as the new way, the answer, or the way out of emotional pain. Your clients may even arrive at a session with an announcement of their new answer, strategy, or solution. Sometimes, after they realize fully that what they have been trying is not workable, this is a method of finding a quick fix. Also, they may be attempting to please you by being the "good client" and finding a solution. If so, these therapist-pleasing behaviors are often control strategies that allow clients to avoid feeling like "bad" or "dumb" clients. Gently point out to your clients how their newly proposed solution is merely a new means of controlling an unwanted thought or feeling, similar to their old, ineffective ways of coping. Consider the following case example.

■ Case Example: Jennie

Jennie, who has obsessive thoughts about weight and body image, spends her weekends at home alone researching diet programs, calculating her daily caloric intake, and trying on various items of clothing while obsessing about her body in the mirror. During the creative hopelessness sessions, she realized that attempting to control her body image distress through diets, calorie counting, and hypervigilance has not been effective. She arrives at the next session and tells you that she threw away her scale and chose to "keep busy" last weekend by taking work home with her. She did not engage in her typical diet research, calorie counting, or other behaviors. She states, "I barely thought about my weight at all!" While this is not "bad" or a "wrong" way to attempt to feel better, the function of staying busy with work is likely the same as obsessing about weight and shape: to numb or avoid some uncomfortable emotion.

In this situation, your first step is to identify all the purposes that Jennie served by staying busy. Allow Jennie to clarify the feelings, thoughts, and behaviors she experienced. You may ask Jennie to identify what thoughts and feelings she experiences as a weekend approaches. What thoughts and emotions arise when she has unoccupied time alone? When she is in social situations, does she experience anxiety related to her body image or other fears of judgment?

The new control strategies that clients choose are as varied as individuals themselves. The important aspect to attend to therapeutically is the function of the activity: does your client show a willingness to experience feelings that the old coping strategy functioned to reduce? Conducting an assessment of new coping behaviors can be tricky. Clients may expound on the positive benefits of the new strategy because their new behavior has led to immediate relief; however, they have not engaged in the new behavior long enough to have experienced the effects of long-term suffering that might be caused by the new strategy.

Clients often make numerous new attempts to find a solution, and each new attempt functions to keep them from feeling the difficult emotion they want to avoid. Experiential learning is a process, not an event. Each new "solution" clients produce offers an opportunity for learning about the relative workability of avoiding unpleasant emotions. During their trials of new control strategies, ask questions like these:

- "What feelings did you have while you were doing the new behavior?"

- "How did you feel afterward?"

- "Did you ultimately engage in the old behavior later (that is, the one you are trying to stop)?"

- "What if you had been unable to use that new control strategy? What would you have ended up feeling then?"

- "Do you see any similarities between this new strategy you're trying and the old behavior you've stopped?"

- "Besides not engaging in the behavior you want to stop, what else do you like about this new activity?"

These questions may help clients to see the similarity in function between their new and old control strategies. It is most effective for clients to experience their new control strategy as being unworkable, instead of you telling them that the strategy is unworkable. However, while experience is the best teacher, it also takes time. Your clients may hold on to a control behavior even as treatment progresses. It is important to emphasize that letting go of various control strategies is a process. The first step to this process is learning to recognize a control strategy for what it is. As the clinician, point out control strategies to your clients when you recognize them; alternately, you may prompt them client by asking, "Does [this behavior] feel familiar to you? Does it seem similar to something you have tried in the past?" Questions such as these may help your clients recognize similar functions to their behaviors.

THE ABCs OF BEHAVIOR WORKSHEET

The worksheet below walks clients through the process of identifying how their behavior functions to reduce, eliminate, or control unwanted emotions. Their ability to identify this process is important because it may help to prevent clients from slipping into avoidance-driven behaviors in the future; preventing avoidance-driven behaviors will help them to maintain effective living.

You may find it useful to give this worksheet to clients as a homework assignment. Walk them through a salient example (perhaps one they've shared in session) to illustrate how to complete the columns on the worksheet.

The first column (A = Antecedent) is to identify the antecedent event that triggers an unwanted internal experience. In the second column (Experience), the client is to specify the unwanted internal experience, which may include a combination of physiological, emotional, and cognitive reactions. In the third column (B = Behavior), the client is to identify the behavior engaged in to manage those internal experiences. In the final column (C = Consequences), the client identifies the positive and negative consequences of that behavior. It's likely that both positive and negative consequences exist. For example, a client may identify a positive consequence related to immediate relief of an uncomfortable emotional state, but it is also important to help the client identify any potential area of additional suffering or longer-term ineffectiveness the behavior produces.

THE ABCs OF BEHAVIOR WORKSHEET

Antecedent	Experience			Behavior	Consequences	
	Emotion	Physical Sensation	Thought		Positive	Negative

Acceptance & Commitment Therapy for Body Image Dissatisfaction

Here is how Jennie, our case example, might complete the worksheet:

THE ABCs OF BEHAVIOR WORKSHEET

Antecedent	Experience			Behavior	Consequences	
	Emotion	Physical Sensation	Thought		Positive	Negative
People at work invite me to a party on Friday night.	Fear	Upset stomach	I'm too fat to go. No one will want to be seen around me.	Avoided going to the party; went to the gym and worked out by myself.	Felt immediate relief because I didn't have to face everyone. Felt proud about working out.	Felt lonely and depressed because of being alone at the gym.

Short-Term vs. Long-Term Consequences of Behavior

You will find it helpful to identify if the new behavior is maintained by negative or positive reinforcement. In *negative reinforcement*, a behavior is maintained because the consequence of that behavior allows for avoidance of an aversive stimulus. For example, avoiding social interaction when one is socially anxious reduces anxiety. In this way, avoidance is reinforced because the anxiety is reduced by the avoidance of the aversive stimulus. Anxiety is reduced and the avoidance behavior increases.

In *positive reinforcement*, a behavior is increased because a stimulus is added as a consequence of the behavior (for example, feeling proud following a workout at the gym).

Behaviors are often maintained by a combination of positive and negative reinforcement. In Jennie's case, the behavior of staying busy may be negatively reinforced because it alleviates her disturbing thoughts about her body and positively reinforced because it increases her feelings of competence and success. However, she also ends up experiencing increased depression and loneliness through her avoidance behavior. This added suffering is a consequence of her choice to avoid contact with people.

Remember that behaviors increase because of their immediate positive or negative reinforcing consequences. If a client justifies behaviors by focusing on the immediate positive consequences (what she gets) or negative consequences (what she gets away from), you should help her to explore the long-term effects of those behaviors and whether they have worked in the long run as well as they have worked in the short run.

Avoidance-Driven vs. Values-Driven Behavior

Another step is to identify if the new behavior is avoidance driven or values driven. If the strategy is driven primarily by the desire to avoid uncomfortable emotions, then it will eventually become unworkable. Remember that Jennie struggles with feeling alone. Feelings of isolation and depression are the cost of her avoidance of socialization and her preoccupation with her body appearance. If the strategy is values driven, then it moves the client toward a more vital life. Values are client-identified meaningful life directions. Some examples of valued life domains may be family, friendships, leisure, career, health, and well-being. Values clarification will be discussed later in this book, but it is helpful to begin considering whether clients' behavior moves them toward any of these core areas. Let's look again at Jennie's situation.

Jennie now reports that a friend invited her to a class at a local gym. She reports that she attended the exercise class with her friend and, at first, felt even more anxious and judgmental about her body. However, she reports that she attended the class on Friday night because she was sick and tired of sitting at home worrying about her appearance and counting calories.

As a clinician, ask yourself important questions like these: Is Jennie escalating her control strategies (for example, engaging in exercise as a compensatory behavior to rid her body of calories)? What is her goal for participating in this weekly class? Imagine that in this case Jennie tells you that as the exercise class continued, she began to feel less self-conscious and noticed that she was enjoying spending time with her friend. She reports that after the class, her friend suggested they grab a bite to eat at a local restaurant. Jennie comments that she ate dinner with another person for the first time in months and also noticed that she didn't pay attention to the caloric content of the food. She states that she never imagined that an activity focused on the body (such as the exercise class) would have the impact of reducing her social anxiety, which had always been prompted by her body image distress. The experience of feeling social enjoyment and closeness reduced her obsessive thoughts about her body, reduced her isolation, and ultimately reduced her social anxiety. In this example, we see several potential values. One of those, connecting with another person, suggests that Jennie's participation in the exercise class was associated with her values, rather than avoidance-driven behavior. Jennie's example presents a great opportunity to introduce willingness as an alternative to control. Jennie was willing to experience her initial discomfort and anxiety in the service of connecting with her friend.

Willingness

As soon as clients begin to understand why controlling feelings and thoughts is problematic and ultimately not effective, the time has come to introduce willingness. From an ACT perspective, willingness means to have an approach toward life of nonresistance and openness to what is most effective or what is valued, even if that means experiencing some painful emotions. Being willing to experience what is emotionally true in the moment, without actively attempting to suppress it, is the alternative to control. In creative hopelessness and the identification of control strategies as problematic, the client may ask, "What can I do when I feel bad feelings or uncomfortable emotions?" Or, instead of asking that question, the client may arrive with an alternate control strategy as described above. The first step after realizing that control strategies haven't worked is simply to be willing to feel the feelings that exist. The concept of willingness can be difficult to grasp at first, and it's definitely okay if the client doesn't understand it right away. Doing an exercise about willingness, like the one using the Tug-of-War Metaphor, which we offer later in this chapter, is often useful. To illustrate the concept of willingness and how it becomes important in the process of moving beyond ineffective control strategies, we have provided a case example.

■ Case Example: Jaime

Jaime is a forty-five-year-old Hispanic married male who is seeing you for outpatient individual psychotherapy. He presents for therapy with symptoms of depression and anxiety, and meets diagnostic criteria for major depressive disorder and social anxiety disorder. Jaime works as a laboratory technician and does not have much contact with people on his job. His primary contact at home is his wife. He reports that his depression and social anxiety stem from his belief that other people see him as a "freak" because of weight gain and his lack of ability to participate in activities he used to enjoy.

Jaime reports that he survived a severe motor vehicle accident five years ago. He explains that his wife was driving when a truck attempting to cross four lanes of traffic hit the passenger's side of their car, crushing the door on his body. His wife survived relatively unharmed, with only minor injuries. However, Jaime suffered multiple broken bones in his legs and arms, and multiple severe lacerations to his face. He also suffered burns over 30 percent of his body (primarily to his face, neck, arms, and hands) when gas from the truck ignited an explosion before he was removed from the crushed car.

He states that he received months of rehabilitation and two reconstructive surgeries to his face. However, he believes his face is "hideous," stating that he was never pleased with the results of the surgeries. Additionally, he underwent skin grafts on his arms and hands for burns, the appearance of which he is also dissatisfied with. Since the accident occurred, he states that he has not been able to resume physical activities, such as jogging and biking, that he used to enjoy, due to chronic pain. As a result of limited physical activity, he has gained 40 pounds. At five foot six and 210 pounds, he is overweight and reports being uncomfortable with his size. Jaime states that he still feels like an "accident victim" when he looks in the mirror and sees the physical impact on his face and neck. He reports he believes he is unable to lose weight or gain muscle mass because of the long-term effects of physical injury to his legs and arms, as well as chronic pain.

You take some history on the impact of the accident on Jaime's life. He reports that his life was "stolen" by the accident because he took a leave of absence from his job during the period of hospitalization and rehabilitation afterward. Following this leave, he returned to work but was laid off shortly after, due to cuts in the company budget. However, he believes that he was laid off because of other employees' discomfort with his physical appearance. He states, "People who used to talk to me and hang out with me at work stopped talking to me when I returned. They seemed uncomfortable with the scars and my difficulty walking. I don't think they knew what to say."

He reports that his marriage has suffered also since the accident. He admits that he has been too uncomfortable with his body to have sexual relations with his wife since the accident. He states that they have only had sex two times in the past year. During those times, he reports that anxiety interfered with sexual performance because "I hated that my wife had to look at all the damage to my body. I felt embarrassed and unattractive." He also reports decreased socialization due to anxiety about being around people. Where he and his wife used to socialize regularly with mutual friends, he now stays home while she goes out with their friends. He reports feeling "awkward" in public. At times, he states, he'll get ready to go on a social outing and "fall apart" when he isn't satisfied with how he looks. "I can't imagine that anyone would want to be seen with me," he states.

Over the past several months, he has started to experience more symptoms of depression. He states, "I realized I have been ruled by shame about how I looked and anxiety about other people's judgments. I have avoided living life at all costs. In the past few months, I've become really depressed because I realized that I feel this accident has stolen my life from me. I'm forty-five years old and I realize I've lost the past five years of my life. I've neglected my wife and our friends. I've lost friends, and now I'm afraid I'm going to lose my marriage! I've neglected myself too. But it's like I can't overcome feeling so uncomfortable with the changes in my body. It's like I feel trapped inside the weight gain and the scars and the chronic pain. I feel like a prisoner."

Over the course of treatment with Jaime, he easily identifies several values he has. In fact, he has spent a great deal of time alone, thinking about what he would really like out of life. Over the past few years, his values have become more painfully clear to him: getting another job, reconnecting with old friends, and saving his marriage. And as those values have become clearer, he has felt more and more trapped by the beliefs that he cannot pursue these because of his appearance. Being quite fused with stories in his mind that he is physically unappealing to his wife and that others wouldn't want to be seen with him, he continues to respond to life with avoidance.

The problem: He has not been willing to make the necessary changes to pursue what he wants out of life. His belief is that his life can't ever be the same as before the accident because of his physical appearance. He believes that the accident stole his life by "disfiguring" his body. Your work with him would emphasize that his life can be more vital if he is willing to approach anxiety-provoking situations in the service of his values. But first, he needs to let go of the fight between himself and his mind, which tells him various stories about how he is too ugly or not masculine enough to function in the world. You decide to use the Tug-of-War Metaphor, using the script in the exercise below.

EXERCISE: Tug-of-War Metaphor

Adapted from Hayes et al. (1999)

Instruct your clients to find a physically comfortable position and close their eyes or focus on a neutral point in the room. Ask them to imagine themselves at the age when theys first encountered the struggle with eating and weight issues. You may use the following script as a guide for this exercise.

Imagine you are the age you were when you first became uncomfortable with your body. I'd like you to really have a clear image of yourself at that time: what you were wearing, the size you were, what exactly you looked like. Once you have that image, now imagine that person is holding tightly to a rope. On the other end of that rope is a very large, frightening monster. Take a moment to imagine what this monster looks like—in detail. Once you have a clear image of the monster, imagine that the monster pulls hard on the other end of the rope. The monster tries to pull you into a large, deep, dark pit that lies between the two of you. You pull on the rope with all your strength to keep from being pulled into the pit.

You've been playing tug-of-war with this monster since you were the age that you first decided you were unhappy with your body. All this time you've been trying to beat the monster at this game. But it's not a fun game of tug-of-war. This is quite a dangerous game, because you've been trying hard to not fall into that pit in between you and the monster. It's deep, and you fear you'd die if you fell in. You've been pulled closer and closer to the pit, and at this point in life, you're very tired of fighting to stay out of it. Your hands are burned from pulling on the rope. Your arms ache from fatigue. Your feet slip on the ground as you edge closer and closer to the hole. You're starting to realize that tugging on the rope is not winning this battle; it's only making you tired and scared.

Ask clients to open their eyes. First, allow clients to provide initial responses to the exercise. Then ask how those responses relate the exercise to the struggle with body image. Returning to the case of Jaime, consider the following questions:

■ What does the monster represent?

■ What does pulling on the rope represent?

■ What does falling into the hole represent?

While there are no right answers, you may suggest that the monster represents the difficult feelings your client attempts to avoid. In Jaime's case, this would be the thoughts he has about his body and the anxiety that results when he is faced with interacting with others. Pulling on the rope may represent all the energy and attention he gives to his appearance, body, weight, or shape; it is the amount of avoiding he does in reaction to his beliefs about his body being repulsive or unappealing to others. It's a tiring process, and he may feel as if he's on the losing end of this battle, which increases his feelings of depression. Letting go of the rope is willingness to stop fighting the feared feelings. For example, it may be the willingness to feel the sadness about not having relationships, the fear of judgment from others, or the fear of failing when he pursues what he wants in life. It may be the anger about changes in his body over which he has had no control. The point is to understand that the fight with the monster cannot be won and doesn't need to be won.

The hole may represent the fear that he will disappear, die, go insane—that catastrophe will happen if he loses the battle with the monster. With respect to losing the battle, Jaime stated, "I feel sometimes like the monster is the car accident and that I'm still fighting it. I feel like it's all the feelings and thoughts and trauma that the accident did to me, and I'm still fighting it." Actually, the monster is only as scary as the energy he puts into fighting it. With Jaime, the injuries from the accident are no longer actually threatening his life, but his thoughts about how these injuries impacted his body still affect his behavior in life. The more he tries to avoid the monster (the harder he pulls), the scarier the monster gets. The more he avoids difficult feelings, the stronger the belief is that he is unable to tolerate them.

You may ask Jaime, "What do you think it would be like to be willing to drop the rope?" He may share fears about experiencing sadness, anger, or other unpleasant emotions. He may share fears of what might happen if the focus on body image is lessened. For example, Jaime might say, "If I didn't think about how other people might judge my appearance and I started getting out more, then I'd have to actually try to have relationships with people again and become intimate with my wife again. I feel like I've forgotten how to do that! I might totally fail at these things, and then I couldn't blame the accident or my body for an inability to reconnect with others. I'd have to hold myself responsible. That's really scary!" In situations like this, we suggest that you sit quietly with the client's feared outcomes (such as Jaime's fear of failing to achieve what he wants)—without reassurance. Validate that dropping the rope would be a new approach, and that new approaches in life are often scary; this validation is often useful. Reminding him that his previous control strategies were not effective at making feelings go away may also be an effective response to the fear of willingness. The monster never disappeared anyway; the harder Jaime fought the monster, the stronger the monster became. And so it is with feelings. As Steven C. Hayes, the developer of ACT, puts it, "If you aren't willing to have it, you've got it." (Hayes & Strosahl, 2004, p. 281).

In-Session Willingness

When you work with clients like Jaime and Jennie, whom you met above, you will have opportunities to encourage willingness during your sessions with them. Using the ABCs of Behavior Worksheet, which we presented earlier in this chapter, can be helpful with this. Before we discuss how you can use the worksheet for in-session willingness, take a quick look at the worksheet now to refresh your memory of it.

After clients complete a couple of examples on the ABCs of Behavior Worksheet, ask them what it would be like to experience some of the emotions in the Antecedent column. Ask them to choose one of the examples and share in more detail about when and where the emotion they avoid is triggered and what it is like for them to experience that emotion (or what they imagine it would be like).

At times, you may discuss a situation with your client and evoke a difficult emotion within the context of the discussion. This allows for an experiential opportunity. Ask if the client is willing to have that emotion (anger, fear, sadness, or whatever) in the room in session. If you notice a client experiencing a difficult emotion, consider making comments like these:

- "It seems like you're feeling _____ right now as you're telling me about that circumstance. Am I right?"

- "Would you be willing, right now, in this room, to sit with this emotion?"

- "Would you be willing to feel _____ right now, with me, without doing anything to make it go away?"

- "What is it like to feel _____ right now without escaping that feeling?"

Asking these questions may prompt additional discomfort, which provides additional opportunity for experiencing emotion in a safe place with you. Silence during emotional experiencing is also useful; it can provide a context of acceptance that enhances rather than diminishes the emotional experience. Silence often increases a client's anxiety, which gives an opportunity to be willing—willing to sit silently with discomfort and to discuss the questions listed above and below. Silence will often be uncomfortable for you too, which will allow you to model being both uncomfortable with the silence and willing to experience that discomfort during the session. Eye contact with silence during client emotion allows your client to experience being "seen" during a vulnerable time. Sitting compassionately, with eye contact, may facilitate feelings of support and acceptance between you and your client.

If your client reacts to an invitation to experience emotion by distracting or distancing from the emotion, this offers an opportunity to notice avoidance. Here are some responses you might make:

- "When I mentioned that you seemed to be feeling _____, I noticed that you moved away from that feeling."

- "It seemed you were feeling _____ while you were telling that story, and then you changed the topic. Was it difficult for you to have that feeling here, now?"

- "Right now, I'm noticing you are moving away from the emotion you were just experiencing. Can I ask you to stop for a minute and invite you to move back into that emotion?"

Invitations to experience an emotion in session are wonderful opportunities to illustrate the process of willingness. If clients are able to do this in session, even if only for a brief period of time, thanking them for this effort is very important. Here are some suggestions:

- "Thank you for sharing this difficult experience with me and for being authentic as you experienced your feelings."

- "Thank you for being willing to share your feelings with me today. I feel like I understand your experience even better now."

- "I know this must have been difficult and new. And I want to thank you for sharing a piece of yourself today instead of trying so hard to avoid being real."

Above all, if clients are able to experience a difficult emotion in the room with you, let them know that this has been possible because they were willing. Willingness is a challenging concept to understand, and arguably it can be best understood experientially rather than intellectually.

Conclusion

At this point, you and your clients have identified how attempts to control or suppress thoughts and feelings have been unsuccessful, and your clients have identified the specific strategies that they use to suppress or avoid their thoughts and feelings. In this chapter, we've continued to reinforce that control is the problem and acceptance is the solution. In light of that, you learned to recognize and manage new control strategies that clients may present during the course of treatment. You also learned to distinguish between avoidance-driven and values-driven behavior, and to help clients understand the function of their behaviors. Willingness was introduced as a means of letting go of avoidance-driven behaviors and moving toward values-driven behaviors.

Once clients have some willingness to experience difficult emotions, they may wonder how to tolerate those emotions without slipping back into control strategies to avoid them. In our next chapter, we introduce mindfulness as a way to become more aware of thoughts and emotions, and as a way to experience them—that is, experience them in a mindful way. Exercises aimed at experiencing thoughts and emotions mindfully will be described, with attention to how this process ultimately facilitates acceptance.

CHAPTER 7

Mindful Acceptance of Thoughts, Emotions, and Physical Sensations

We are here to awaken from the illusion of our separateness.

—Thich Nhat Hanh

Mindfulness and Acceptance as Therapeutic Interventions

Mindfulness originated in ancient Eastern cultures as a spiritual and philosophical practice. While the development of mindfulness-based interventions began much earlier, since the mid-1990s, mindfulness has been integrated into several psychotherapy interventions, with preliminary evidence showing effective outcomes. Some interventions with a mindfulness component include mindfulness-based cognitive behavioral therapy for depression (Teasdale et al., 2002), dialectical behavior therapy (DBT) for borderline personality disorder (Linehan, 1993), and Vipassana meditation for substance-use disorders (Bowen et al., 2006) among others.

Defining Mindfulness

Creating an operational definition of mindfulness is a work in progress, as the construct has several definitions historically. Mindfulness has been conceptualized as a state of increased attention brought about through meditation (Hanh, 1976). Several other definitions have been proposed in the philosophical, spiritual, and psychological literatures. At this time, there is not one operational definition of mindfulness that is universally agreed upon. However, Bishop and colleagues (2004) have proposed an operational definition for use in evidence-based psychotherapy research, including two components: self-regulation of attention and orientation to experience. These two components are quite closely matched to the concept and use of mindfulness in acceptance and commitment therapy. Mindfulness, as a practice applied in ACT, means increasing attention to the present moment (one's experience) while letting go of judgments (thoughts).

In acceptance and commitment therapy, mindfulness may be best conceptualized as one of the "hows" of acceptance. It is a tool that facilitates a stance of acceptance toward emotions through increased awareness of feelings and through a distancing from the literality of thoughts, which we call *cognitive defusion*. Basically, cognitive defusion means noticing a thought as a thought instead of as an accurate representation of one's experience. For example, a client may have the thought "I am fat." In defusing from the thought, the client mindfully observes and describes, "I am having the thought that I am fat." This is very different from believing or fusing with the thought as a literal truth. By taking the perspective of an observer, the client is less likely to obsess about a particular thought or catastrophize when the thought occurs. Through mindfulness practice, the number and type of thoughts is noticed as part of one's experience, but not as representing the truth of one's experience.

As conceptualized by Thich Nhat Hanh (1976), mindfulness practice brings increased awareness to one's experience, including thoughts, emotions, and physical sensations, while actively letting go of the tendency to evaluate those experiences as good or bad. Evaluative thoughts certainly occur during mindfulness practice. Thoughts such as "I can't do this" or "This isn't working" are useful material to notice; however, we focus on a process of actively letting go of the thoughts. Actively letting go means allowing the thought to occur without suppressing or evaluating the thought. It is in the letting go that attention can be brought to one's broader experience. The experience of thoughts, feelings, and sensations is the focus of mindfulness practice; after all, it is this experience that is the focal point of acceptance.

While practicing mindfulness, clients are likely to notice some feelings or thoughts that are intense or unpleasant. There will probably be times when fear shows up, or thoughts about the past or future may occur. For example, when thinking about eating, a client may be overcome with fear of what the food will do to her. She may even experience a panic reaction (such as her heart racing, her hands shaking, and so on). These interactions of thoughts, emotions, and bodily sensations surrounding food are reactions that she can mindfully observe. Many clients ask, "How can I get acceptance?" Of course, acceptance is not a destination. It is a process, attained in part by the experiencing of what is. Acceptance is neither liking nor disliking, nor is it resignation. Noticing and experiencing what is occurring is, by definition, an acceptance of what is occurring. Discussing willingness to have emotions may be a good place to begin facilitating the process of mindful experiencing and acceptance with your clients.

Introducing Mindfulness to Your Client

The concept of becoming more mindful or aware of painful emotions may seem counterintuitive to your client. Generally, clients seek help in hopes of reducing distress and getting rid of negative thoughts. This is not a surprising occurrence in that our culture and many forms of psychotherapy actively encourage getting rid of "bad stuff." However, ACT takes a different tack. Through the process of creative hopelessness, you and your clients have discussed the ineffectiveness of avoidance, and you've introduced the concept of willingness with regard to approaching difficult emotions. To teach mindfulness, Hanh (1976) recommends beginning with being mindful of the experience of breathing. Attention to the breath is an effective starting point for teaching mindfulness practice, because breathing is an experience we carry with us at all times. In any situation, bringing the attention back to the breath is an effective method of maintaining experiential attention. The breath is also a neutral point of focus with which to begin mindfulness practice. We will explore mindfulness of breath more fully later in this chapter.

Why Mindfulness?

In describing to your clients the reasons for learning mindfulness skills, focus on these as a way of experiencing thoughts, feelings, and physical sensations versus a way of controlling or avoiding unpleasant experiences. In creative hopelessness, your clients have already identified certain control strategies that are not working to suppress thoughts and feelings. As discussed earlier, you have introduced the idea that there may be another path, other than the path of avoidance. You can remind your clients of this idea through phrases such as "putting down the shovel" or "dropping the rope," metaphors for letting go of control strategies. At this point, your clients may wonder how to cope with uncomfortable emotions, given that their old strategies aren't working; however, they probably do not see the next step. Hopefully your clients are willing to try something new, and they are ready to look at new options. If so, using mindfulness as a tool to facilitate the experiencing and increased awareness of emotions may be described as one part of their new path. Here are a few key points to emphasize when describing the utility of mindfulness to your clients:

1. Mindfulness is a tool for experiencing your thoughts, feelings, and physical sensations instead of avoiding them.

2. Mindfulness skills are practiced as a way of living life, not as a goal to achieve or a task to complete.

3. Being mindful means increasing awareness of your experience while letting go of judgments (thoughts) that arise.

4. Mindfulness is the "how" of creating acceptance in your life. By practicing mindfulness, acceptance will often increase.

5. Being mindful does not necessarily mean enjoying your experience or feeling at peace with your experience. It simply means becoming aware of your experience.

Mindfulness of Breath

As we mentioned above, attention to the breath provides a good starting point for mindfulness practice. Focus on the breath is one time-tested way of coming back to the present moment. When your clients are overwhelmed by thoughts and feelings that seem insurmountable, reminding them to breathe can be a simple way to help them let go of the turmoil inside and return to a more peaceful place.

EXERCISE: Mindfulness of Breath

In order to guide your clients in an initial mindful breathing exercise, first ask them to find a comfortable sitting position. Ask that they close their eyes or use a soft gaze in which they look at a neutral point in the room, such as the floor or a point on the wall. We suggest that you use the following script (or something similar) to guide your clients in a mindful breathing exercise.

First, bring your attention to the rhythm of your breath, the speed at which you inhale and exhale. Notice also where your breath is coming from. Are you breathing from your stomach or your chest? To find out, notice what part of your body moves as you breathe. If you need to put a hand on your stomach to help you feel the breath, do so now. You don't need to try to change your breathing, just notice how fast you inhale and exhale, and where the breath comes from. [Allow a few moments to pass for your client to focus on the breath.]

Now I'll ask you to follow your breath as it makes a path through your body and out again. Starting with the air entering your nose or mouth, notice the temperature of the inhale. Can you feel the air in your nose or mouth? Really focus on the inhale. [Allow a few moments to pass for your client to focus on the inhalation.]

If thoughts come into your mind, simply bring your attention back to your breath. If you notice sounds in or outside of this room, please gently bring your attention back to your breathing. If you need to do this one hundred times or one thousand times, that's okay. Again and again, bring your attention to your breath, focusing on the feeling of inhaling air through your nose or mouth.

Can you notice where you stop feeling the air on your inhale? Can you feel it in your throat? Notice now where your inhale stops, particularly at what place in your chest your breath stops. Notice this, and now imagine a circle marking that place in your chest where your inhale stops. [Allow a few moments to pass for your client to focus on this circle.]

As you visualize that circle, notice the air leaving that place as you exhale. Bring your attention to the feeling of your breath leaving your body from that place in your chest. Can you notice where you begin to feel the breath leaving your body? Can you feel the breath in your throat? [Allow a few moments to pass for your client to gain awareness of the exhalation.]

Now take a few moments to just notice the breath entering and leaving your body, paying attention to where you feel it. If you notice thoughts entering your mind, just notice those and gently bring your attention back to your breath. [Allow two to three minutes for the client to practice this part of the exercise.]

When you are ready, slowly bring your attention back to the room.

After this exercise, check in with your clients to process their reactions to it. Clients' reactions to mindfulness exercises vary. Some report feeling relaxed. Others, especially those who struggle with feelings of dissatisfaction about the size of their stomach, may report feeling intense anxiety or discomfort from the diaphragmatic breathing and increased attention to the inward and outward movement of the stomach area. Their verbal feedback is a wonderful opportunity to apply the principle of defusion from thoughts and acceptance of experience. In this way, reactions to mindfulness exercises practiced in session can be a practical example of applying acceptance to experience. The example below of a client-therapist dialogue following a mindful breathing exercise illustrates some common reactions and ACT-consistent responses.

Therapist: Tell me about what the breathing exercise was like for you. Do you have any initial reactions?

Client: Well, I didn't like it. It made me anxious to focus that much on my breath.

Therapist: I'm glad you could notice the anxiety, and that you completed the exercise anyway! Tell me how you knew you were experiencing anxiety. What did it feel like?

Client: Well, my throat started to feel tight, especially when you told me to notice feeling my breath in my throat. And then when I imagined the circle, my heart started racing because my breathing stopped right around where my heart is. I started to imagine the circle around my heart, and I felt all panicky.

Therapist: Wow! You were very connected to how you were feeling during this exercise. What happened after you noticed the anxiety in your throat and chest? Did it lessen or increase as the exercise continued?

Client: The anxiety happened at the beginning of the exercise. I just started thinking of other things and it ended up going away. I couldn't focus on my breathing the entire time.

Therapist: Okay, so it sounds like you ended up distracting yourself with the thoughts you were having. Did that work?

Client: It did work to reduce the anxiety from the breathing—except I ended up thinking negative thoughts about the exercise, so I actually ended up feeling worse after the exercise than I did beforehand.

Therapist: Thank you for being so honest about your experience with this. It's really common to struggle with this type of exercise at first. Thoughts will take everyone away from their experience, and you can expect that thoughts will happen during this type of exercise. It sounds like, though, that distracting yourself with the thoughts didn't really improve your experience in the end.

Client: No, not really.

Therapist: Is that true for you at other times? Do you sometimes distract yourself to cope with anxiety, only to have a bunch of judgmental thoughts?

Client: Yes. Sometimes distraction by thinking about other things works for a while, but I usually end of worrying about something. Or, in this case, I was judging myself for not being able to do the exercise.

Therapist: What if you had stayed with the anxiety in your throat and chest? What you do expect might have happened?

Client: I don't know. I might have had a panic attack.

Therapist: Is it possible that you carry the anxiety with you most of the time, and this exercise brought your attention to it?

Client: Maybe.

Therapist: It's something you could choose to explore if you practice this exercise again. If the anxiety comes up, another way to approach it would be to notice the feeling and bring your attention back to the feeling of your breath—the rate of your breathing, the temperature of your breath—and allow the anxiety to be there with the breath.

Client: That would be difficult.

Therapist: Yes, probably so. My question for you is, are you willing?

We recommend to clients that they begin a mindfulness practice with mindfulness of the breath. Practice can be as brief as ten minutes per day. The following handout may be given to clients as a guide for practicing mindfulness of breath at home.

MINDFULNESS OF BREATH

One of the most basic and simple ways to be a mindful observer is to sit down and focus on your breath. Here are some specific instructions on how to do this:

1. Go to the location you selected, choose a comfortable sitting posture, and then just quietly notice yourself in your space. The place should be quiet and comfortable. Turn off your cell phone and do what you can to ensure that you will not be interrupted. Ideally you would identify a space away from life's many distractions that can be a small oasis of peace for you.

2. Close your eyes and focus on your breathing.

3. Bring your attention to your breath, gently rising and falling in your chest and belly. Like ocean waves coming in and out, your breath is always there. Notice each breath. Focus on each inhale and exhale. As you inhale, observe the cool air passing through your nose. Feel your stomach expand. Imagine your lungs filling like a balloon. Listen to the sound of your exhale. Stay focused on your breathing—how you inhale and exhale.

4. If you notice your mind wandering and thinking all sorts of thoughts, accept it as a natural process. Then gently bring your attention back to your breath. Again, focus on the rising and falling of your breath in your chest and belly. Let your breath anchor you in the present moment.

5. If you find yourself becoming distracted by bodily sensations and feelings, notice them and acknowledge their presence. Do not try to hold on to them or make them go away. Allow them to be, watch them dissipate, and gently bring your attention back to your breath.

6. A good way to deal with feelings is to name them as you notice them. For instance, if you notice you are worrying, silently say to yourself, "Worry, worry, worry—there is worry." You can do the same thing with other thoughts and feelings; just name them as you notice them. This will help you notice the difference between yourself and your thoughts. You have thoughts and feelings, but you are not what those thoughts and feelings say, no matter how persistent or intense they may be.

Each time you do the mindful breathing exercise, complete the following record form and bring it to our next session to discuss your experience with practicing mindfulness.

Date	Thoughts, Emotions, and Physical Sensations
_____	_____
_____	_____
_____	_____

Attending to Experience: Mindfulness of Thoughts, Emotions, and Physical Sensations

A fundamental premise of ACT is the importance of willingness to be open to really experiencing all aspects of both internal and external experiences. The ability to be mindful or aware is essential for living a vital life. However, when we examine many aspects of modern life, there seems to be a strong emphasis on distraction and avoidance. Life is about staying busy and moving forward. Think how often you have seen someone walking with a friend on a beautiful day and talking on her cell phone. It seems we have forgotten how to just be with someone in the moment. Thus, being mindful or awake involves being present for both the joys and the pains associated with a vital life.

When we encourage our clients to attend to their experience, that includes events, thoughts, emotions, and physical sensations. For example, a car accident is an event in which a person experiences numerous physical sensations and emotions as the event occurs. Following the car accident, thoughts may occur that evaluate the event: "I should have taken a different road. It's totally my fault. People who drive red cars are always reckless drivers." These thoughts may or may not be accurate. Let's say the driver ran a red light, drove into a busy intersection, and hit an unsuspecting driver. The thought It's totally my fault might have legal accuracy in that situation.

However, instead of focusing on identifying the accuracy of each thought or attempting to change the thoughts to reflect "truth," mindfulness encourages noticing the thoughts and then noticing the emotional experience. For example, the driver having those thoughts—"It's totally my fault," and so on—may also feel sad, regretful, scared, or angry. He also may have physical experiences following an accident such as pain, fatigue, shock, and so on.

The purpose of mindful practices is to increase awareness of all of our experiences in order to be in contact with all aspects of life. This awareness provides the foundation for gaining acceptance of the present moment. Although some thoughts and feelings may be uncomfortable to experience, emotions and physical sensations provide useful information for the individual. Practicing mindful experiencing of emotions and physical sensations following a stressful event such as a car accident would theoretically facilitate acceptance of those experiences instead of avoidance of them. Acceptance, or active experiencing, of emotion can be a first step in changing your clients' relationship to their emotions, helping them to see their emotions as just one part of their experience. Thus, emotions represent one part of the internal landscape that does not have to be changed in order to move in valued life directions. Being mindful is not a simple process. If it were, people would not spend a lifetime practicing mindful meditation. In a sense, being mindful is a valued direction that can become a guiding principle. Rather than asking your clients to just be mindful, you can address different aspects of mindfulness including awareness of thoughts, emotions, and physical sensations. Below, we provide some specific guidance on mindful practices.

Thoughts—and Beliefs about Thoughts

In the mindfulness of breath exercise, your clients likely were pulled away from the experience of breathing by thoughts they experienced. In that exercise, your clients were instructed to notice the thoughts and bring attention back to their breath. Thoughts can hold a tremendous amount of power for human beings. Examining clients' beliefs about their thoughts and their reactions based on thoughts alone illustrates the relative importance placed on thinking versus experience. Your clients may believe that thoughts hold important power over the future. For example, they may believe that worrying prevents future negative events or that thoughts should be trusted as truth. Instead of contesting these beliefs, you may use some examples to illustrate a thought's relative lack of power. You might, for example, ask a client what would happen if she thought really hard about opening the door to the room you are in. If there were a fire in the room and she only had her thoughts to open the door, would she be able to escape? The obvious answer is no. This question, therefore, helps to illustrate that thoughts alone cannot change one's external experience; behavior is required to change experience. As has been mentioned before, your relationship with your client is critical at this point. You must be clear that you are not mocking your client. Emphasize that we are all stuck in a world where words have been given great power and that the goal is for you and your client to step back and observe the power of words from a new perspective. You can disclose your own sense of being stuck in words. For example, you may have thought you could never possibly finish your dissertation. The project may have seemed impossible for a variety of reasons, and yet the next step was very simply to sit down and write. You can describe a thought of not having an important idea or that your advisor would never agree to a project like yours. You can tell your client that at times most students just think they may not be smart enough to do a dissertation. And if a student begins to see that thought as a literal truth, it becomes almost impossible to sit down and write a proposal. After sharing your example, you can begin to use defusion with your client. Defusion is a very powerful tool for changing the client's relationship to thoughts.

Mindfulness of Thoughts

Defusion from thoughts actually becomes the process of being mindful of thoughts. By noticing a thought as a thought (and not a literal truth) and bringing attention back to experience (emotion, physical sensation, and so on), the client has become mindful of the process of having thoughts.

For example, defusing from the thought "It is now noon, so it's time for lunch" allows clients to make a choice about eating that is experientially motivated—that is, noticing feelings of hunger as a cue to eat rather than simply eating at a particular time. The process of defusing from this thought—"It's time for lunch"—begins with noticing it as a thought. Use of a metaphor—for example, the mind as a tape recorder with several tapes running or a computer with old programs—can help facilitate the process of defusion. You may say something like this to your client:

Your mind has hundreds of tapes running. Some of these tapes are from your past, some from your present. They aren't bad tapes, and probably some of them have been very helpful to you. The problem with listening to the tapes and following their directions is that they may or may not accurately reflect your current experience. You may be listening to an old tape and reacting to that instead of reacting to the present moment. The task is not to judge the tapes, turn off the tapes, or even change the tapes. You may have tried to do those things already. Being mindful simply means to notice the tapes in your mind as being taped messages, not as truth—even though some days they may play really loudly!

Another approach is to use an exercise that can rather dramatically demonstrate how words can lose their literal meaning when we get some distance from them. The Milk, Milk, Milk exercise may seem a little silly, but we have found over and over again that it helps clients to experientially understand this concept of defusion. Moreover, it is always good for a bit of a shared laugh between you and your client.

EXERCISE: Milk, Milk, Milk

Adapted from Hayes et al. (1999)

Ask your clients to repeat the word "milk" many times in a row: "milk, milk, milk, milk…" While doing this, the word begins to lose meaning because it lacks context. After illustrating this example with one word, try a sentence with your clients that is personally relevant to their body image problems.

Ask your clients if there is a thought they often have about their body. For example, a female client might have the thought "My thighs are fat," or a male client might have the thought "My biceps are too small." Ask your client to repeat the sentence several times without stopping. You may want to do this first to show how it sounds coming from someone else.

Sandy, a client who struggled with body image issues despite being rather thin, repeated the thought "My thighs are fat, my thighs are fat…" After doing this exercise, her first response was to laugh. After a bit of silence, she burst into tears. Here's the discussion with her therapist that followed the exercise:

Therapist: So it seems like this exercise brought up a lot of feelings for you. Can you tell me what is going on with you right now?

Sandy: Well, I see how in one way all of this is just words. I sort of get it in my head. But my mom always told me that my thighs were too big and I had to be careful not to wear shorts or clothes that would show them. This was even when I was a little kid. But I felt like there was something wrong with my body, even way back then.

Therapist: That sounds like it was very painful, and you have been suffering around that for a long time. Language is used a lot of times to make judgments and that can lock us into a cycle of suffering. Can you think of this idea that your thighs are too big as just a very old script that keeps getting played in your head?

Sandy: Well, I can think that, but the thought is still there.

Therapist: One way to think of this is looking at it like a computer pop-up. You know how, when you are searching certain websites, you keep getting computer pop-ups. You might be looking for a book on relationships and all kinds of things might pop up. There could be dating sites, advice for singles, and even some sites that look like they might be pornography. When that happens, you can notice the pop-up and just close it. Seeing the message does not make it true or necessary for you. Can you take that perspective with this thought—just notice it popping up? You can say, "Wow, there is that thought again," and simply move on.

Sandy: I could try.

Therapist: Well, see what happens with that thought this week. It is a very old one and tied to a lot of pain for you, so don't expect it to just disappear. Just notice it being at a bit of a distance from you and letting it go.

It is important that you remain mindful of the difficulty involved in letting go of old scripts that clients have been carrying around for years. It may seem obvious to you that a client who has a very successful career is not the failure his father told him he was. But those types of thoughts can be very persistent, and you should not be surprised when some of these thought cycles persist over time. Processing the emotions tied to these thoughts is an important part of the treatment.

Mindfulness of Emotions

In order to facilitate the teaching of mindfulness of emotions with your clients, we recommend utilizing a real situation attached to a difficult emotion in session. The exercise below, Approaching Difficult Situations, brings up several situations that may evoke uncomfortable emotional or physical states for your clients. You can use these to help your clients to notice how to be mindful in these situations that are particularly difficult emotionally (or physically) for them.

Help your clients to identify a hierarchy of difficult situations. The script below offers one way to elicit your client's most difficult situations:

Which situations distress you the most? Make a list of those situations. As you make your list, try to identify situations that you experience on a regular basis. For example, a death in the family is very distressing, but it is not a good choice for our purposes here because (hopefully) a family death is a rare event; it does not happen on a regular basis. I want you to identify situations that occur relatively frequently so that you will have many opportunities to practice experiencing them.

After the situations have been identified, you and your client can sort through the list to create a hierarchy of situations, from least stressful to most stressful. You may find the following Identifying Difficult Situations Worksheet helpful; it can be completed in session or given as homework.

IDENTIFYING DIFFICULT SITUATIONS WORKSHEET

Think about situations that are difficult for you emotionally or physically—situations that have to do with food, eating, or body image, as well as difficult situations that don't directly involve food, eating, or body image. List five difficult situations in each category below and place them in order of their difficulty (1 = most difficult; 5 = least difficult).

Difficult situations that revolve around food or eating:

1. _____

2. _____

3. _____

4. _____

5. _____

Difficult situations that revolve around body image:

1. _____

2. _____

3. _____

4. _____

5. _____

Difficult situations not directly related to food, eating, or body image:

1. _____

2. _____

3. _____

4. _____

5. _____

After your clients have identified their difficult situations, encourage them to practice mindfulness in each situation, starting with the least difficult and working up to the most difficult. You can refer to the Mindful Mirror exercise (below) for a sample of how to guide your client through difficult situations that many body image clients will list.

EXERCISE: The Mindful Mirror

(Materials needed: 1 full-length mirror, paper, and pen)

This exercise combines noticing thoughts and emotions, and facilitates body acceptance through experiencing and letting go of judgmental thoughts and difficult emotions. Looking in the mirror can be a very difficult situation for many people, particularly those with body image problems. In fact, normalizing that looking in mirrors is difficult may be useful in letting your clients know that they are not alone with this aspect of their struggle. For some, the mirror has become the enemy. When facilitating a workshop using this treatment with women experiencing body image distress, many of our participants had actively avoided looking in a full-length mirror for years. This exercise allowed the participants to become more aware of thoughts about their body as "just thought" versus "truth," thus facilitating defusion from thoughts about the body. Likewise, it will help you guide your clients in looking at their body in a mindful way with less attachment to judgments about their body. Here's a suggested script and instructions.

I'm going to ask you to do a mindfulness exercise related to thoughts you have about your body. The purpose of doing this exercise is to notice some common thoughts you have about your body, some of which may be judgmental. These thoughts may be the ones that you feel quite attached to as being true. What I'll ask you to do is look at yourself in a full-length mirror for three to five minutes. I'll ask you to notice thoughts and feelings that arise as you look at your body. Now, please stand in front of the mirror so you can see your entire body, head to toe.

Part 1: Silent Observing and Standing with the Emotion

When your clients stand in front of the full-length mirror, ask them to first notice (without talking) any immediate feelings that come up for them upon looking in the mirror. Ask them to literally "stand with themselves" as they have the feelings. Also ask them to notice any thoughts that immediately come up, and ask them to notice the thoughts, and to bring their attention back to their image in the mirror. Ask your clients to focus on their eyes in the mirror and notice where in their body they are experiencing emotion. For now, both you and your clients should stay silent, allowing the clients' experience to prevail in this part of the exercise. If your clients begin to verbalize reactions, gently suggest that they bring their attention back to their eyes in the mirror and the feelings in their body. Acknowledge that they may be having several thoughts, and ask them to do their best to let those go.

Part 2: Tell Me What You See

After three to five minutes, tell your clients that you are interested in what they see in the mirror. Ask them to look past the externals such as clothing, shoes, and jewelry. This is a chance to just notice their body in a new way. Beginning with their feet and moving upward on their body to the head, ask them to say aloud statements, judgments, or reactions they have to each area of their body. As your clients say these judgments and statements aloud, you'll be writing the statements on a piece of paper. Remind clients to defuse from thoughts by saying, "I am having the thought that _____." When your clients have completed the exercise, check in about feelings they experienced during the exercise, in both parts 1 and 2. Thank your clients for sharing their thoughts and emotions, and for participating in the exercise.

Part 3: Processing the Exercise

Now ask clients to sit across from you. Read the statements they made about their body. Then ask them to read the statements. By noticing the thoughts that occurred and then deliteralizing those thoughts by putting them on paper, the relative power of the thoughts has perhaps decreased. In processing the exercise, focus on your clients' emotional reactions, reminding them that this is pain they are carrying, much of which is based on reactions to thoughts. Looking in the mirror brought up painful thoughts, which felt real enough to evoke strong emotion. Noticing and letting go of those thoughts may result in the thoughts now feeling less real or perhaps less true.

Processing clients' emotional reactions to their statements is an important component to this exercise and is also important throughout ACT, at any time emotion arises. Processing emotional reactions simply means experiencing them in a safe place (such as your office) without avoidance. You may quietly sit with your clients, making with eye contact as they experience sadness in session and become tearful. Or, as you notice your clients' anxiety rising, you may first ask them to label the anxiety (for example, "I'm wondering if you can tell me what you're feeling right now?"), and then ask if they are willing to have that feeling with you in the room ("Are you willing to sit with this anxiety, with me, right now?"). As clients experience emotions in session, ACT would suggest that you don't rescue them with interventions to lessen the emotional valence. Instead, ACT suggests that you convey a stance of acceptance of the emotions. Silence with eye contact is one way of facilitating this. Encouraging clients to sit with the emotion is another. When you notice the emotion lessening in the room, you may find it useful to remark on that from a stance of gratitude ("I'm glad you felt safe to have that feeling here with me" or "Thank you for being willing to notice and experience your emotion today with me"). With respect to mindfulness, asking clients to describe the emotional experience without judgment is also important. If you notice your clients making judgmental statements (such as "I'm such a baby for crying"), you can point this out as a thought to be mindful of. You may say, "Can you notice that thought as a judgment and let it go?" Remind your clients that thoughts about their body are a good example of the tapes in their head.

Listening to those tapes and believing that they are true can lead to feelings of sadness. As the therapist, echoing your own emotional reaction to hearing your clients' negative self-judgments can also be useful. Your empathic connection to the nature of client experience can model the development of compassion for oneself. You may say, "I felt sad when I heard the thoughts about your body that you tell yourself. It must be hard to hear those tapes all the time." Encourage clients by telling them that, through mindfulness practice, the tapes may begin to hold less power or play less loudly.

At times, your clients may have something positive to say about their body, but watch for the links to negative judgment. For example, the often repeated phrase "You have such a pretty face..." is often tied to the unspoken "if only you were not so fat." Fusion with "good" thoughts can be as risky as the negative judgments—the process is all about letting go of judgment. The two sides of a coin are always linked and to hold on to one perspective will always tie clients to the opposite point of view.

Mindfulness of Physical Sensations

Another benefit of mindful experiencing is that it provides data for self-care with respect to physical sensations and emotions. Having an increased awareness of personal needs—for example, am I hungry, lonely, angry, sad?—will give clients the opportunity for making a personal choice to meet those needs. Mindfulness of physical sensations, such as fatigue, pain, thirst, and hunger, increases self-awareness and may promote self-care behaviors. For clients with body image dissatisfaction, disordered eating is a common problem. If your clients overeat, diet excessively, or have other disordered eating behaviors, getting in touch with hunger and fullness may promote more mindful eating. Avoidance of feeling full may be problematic for clients who restrict their food intake, or for those clients who purge or engage in other compensatory behaviors after binge eating. Avoidance of feeling hungry may be an issue for clients who overeat.

Mindful eating based on physiological cues has been utilized in various psychological interventions (Dicker & Craighead, 2004). In appetite awareness training (Craighead, 2008), clients are told to monitor hunger on a seven-point scale and to eat at the point when they become moderately hungry, and to stop eating when they become moderately full. This type of intervention requires increased attention to physiological cues regarding when one's stomach feels like when it becomes full versus empty. Other experiences involved in hunger (such as headache or light-headedness) and those that must be discriminated from hunger (for example, anxiety or fatigue) are also attended to. A client may report eating for various reasons, many of which are not attached to or motivated by the physiological experience of hunger (for example, social cues, the time of day, or the availability of food). These are not bad reasons for eating. Depending on the client's personal eating issues, eating for reasons other than hunger may sometimes be ineffective if the individual is eating when not hungry or perhaps not eating when hungry. The following case example illustrates how mindfulness of physical sensations can enhance self-care and provide a broader range of choices related to eating.

■ Case Example: Jim

Jim is a twenty-year-old college sophomore who has been referred to you at a university counseling center by his track-and-field coach. The coach is concerned because Jim spends far too much time working out with weights and is not attending to other important issues, particularly schoolwork. Jim has told the coach that he needs to focus on changing his muscle tone because his legs and arms are scrawny and just "ugly." Jim is becoming more withdrawn and seems preoccupied with checking on aspects of his appearance. He checks for changes in the size of his arms and legs on a daily basis. He also has experienced knee injuries that a sports medicine doctor determined were related to overtraining. The coach has placed Jim on a "no-train" suspension to allow his injuries to heal and won't allow Jim to return until he is cleared by the team doctor. After initial assessment, you learn that Jim is continuing to train with weights and believes that people do not understand how ugly his arms and legs really are. Jim is within a healthy weight range, and the size of his arms and legs is consistent with the overall dimensions of his body. However, he is unable to accept this view and is sure that his arms and legs are disproportionate to the rest of his body. Jim reports feeling depressed that he is injured and feels unable to stop working out even though he knows doing so hurts his body physically and jeopardizes his return to the track-and-field team. After working with Jim for two sessions, you feel he is well connected with the ineffectiveness of his continued exercising and that he realizes he continues to do this to avoid the anxiety he experiences when he looks at or thinks about his arm muscles. The anxiety is related to various topics, including a focus on parts of his body that he dislikes and how he appears when clothing, particularly T-shirts on his arms and track shorts on his legs, feels baggy. In addition, he reports feeling overwhelmed about other issues related to college life, such as schoolwork and social relationships, and he uses working out as a coping strategy for all life stress.

You have decided to use mindfulness to help Jim approach his anxiety with acceptance rather than avoidance. In your first mindfulness-focused session, you taught Jim exercises related to mindfulness of breath, thought, and emotion. Your focus in this session is mindfulness of physical sensations. Your target is helping Jim to respond to his body's cues rather than respond to thoughts he has about what he should or should not be doing. The following dialogue provides an example of the rationale for physiological mindfulness and acceptance:

Therapist: Jim, how have you been physically feeling with all the working out lately?

Jim: I'm okay. I did cut back from two hours a day before to only one hour a day this past week.

Therapist: What motivated you to cut back the time?

Jim: Well, because you, the doctor, and the coach want me to. And I have to if I want to return to the team.

Therapist: So you cut back on lifting weights because you feel there's a rule to do that.

Jim: There is a rule I have to do that.

Therapist: Well, there's a rule that you need to be physically healed from your injuries before you return to the team. That's true. And the doctor has told you that you'll need to take a break from working with weights for a few weeks in order for the injuries to heal, is that right?

Jim: That's right.

Therapist: And this is pretty hard for you, I know. Because when you cut back or stop lifting weights, what happens?

Jim: I feel really anxious about everything.

Therapist: Yes. And we have worked on some strategies for noticing the anxiety and letting yourself experience it. This will obviously take some work. I'd like to offer you another tool to help you to accept the current limitations your body has.

Jim: I can't ever accept that my body has limitations.

Therapist: That sounds like another thought to me. Can you notice it and let it go for now?

Jim: Okay. Okay.

Therapist: Thanks for being willing. So what if, instead of paying attention to the rules, you attended to your body, to the cues your body gives you? For example, what would it be like to eat food when you're hungry, drink water when you're thirsty, and stop exercising when you're in physical pain from an injury?

Jim: (Laughs.) That's like, the total opposite of what all my athletic training has taught me. Haven't you ever heard of "no pain, no gain"?

Therapist: Well, actually, that phrase is really perfect for this. The pain you have is the feelings that exist when you don't follow your own rules about eating and working with weights to change a part of your body. In your efforts to avoid that pain, you've upped your lifting and injured your body. The result of that is that you've been asked to take a break from the team. All of that is creating additional suffering, isn't it?

Jim: Yes, I'm suffering. But I don't see how stopping my weight lifting is going to produce anything good.

Therapist: Wouldn't you agree that taking care of your body is important to your athletic performance? That in the state you're in now, injured from

	overtraining, you're unable to do what you really value, which is to compete with the team?
Jim:	Yes, I guess my body just broke down.
Therapist:	It did. Your body said, "Enough!" I know how important the track team, your friends on the team, and your performance are to you—and I want you to have that back. So, I'm thinking, what if you started really listening to your body? You could use this experience as an opportunity to start practicing a different way of making decisions about your eating and your training. Instead of following rules that you create, you may be best served by making decisions based on what your body needs. This will require two things: mindfulness, or increased attention to your body cues, while also letting go of the judgment that will occur, and acceptance of some changes you may notice, like not lifting as much when you work with weights. Are you willing to try this?
Jim:	So basically you want me to pay more attention to what my body tells me versus what my mind tells me? So should I use the mindfulness of thought stuff we worked on last week and bring more attention to my body?
Therapist:	Exactly. We'll start with something you'd be willing to start paying more attention to. What do you think that would be?
Jim:	Well, right now, I already cut back on the weight lifting. I think I'd be willing to cut back a little more for the sake of healing the injury and getting back to the team.
Therapist:	Okay, great! Mindfulness, then, would focus on the discomfort or level of pain you feel in the injury. What I'd like you to do this week is to begin rating the pain on a ten-point scale, with 10 being the most intense pain you can imagine and 1 being no pain. This rating may take some getting used to. But, off the top of your head, what level of pain, on average, did you have when you worked out last week?
Jim:	Well, if I wrap the knee like I'm supposed to, I can lift weights that work on my thighs for about thirty minutes before I start feeling any pain. Then it's about a 5 almost immediately and goes way up pretty quickly after that. When I get back home, after an hour, it's a 10.
Therapist:	What do you think would be a reasonable level of pain at which to stop lifting weights?
Jim:	I can tolerate up to an 8.
Therapist:	I'm sure you can tolerate a lot of pain! But, being mindful of your doctor's recommendation to not exercise and your own desire to heal the injury, what level of pain would you want to stop at this week?

Mindful Acceptance of Thoughts, Emotions, and Physical Sensations   123

Jim:	For this week, I'd be willing to stop at a 5. I can stop working out at about twenty minutes a day. That would be a lot less than I have been doing.
Therapist:	Okay, that sounds like a plan. What you may notice is that, when you stop at a 5, your anxiety may increase because you're breaking a rule. Are you willing to use some mindfulness tools with your emotions this week?
Jim:	Yes, I can do this. But I think I might start to overexercise again once my knee starts to feel better.
Therapist:	That may happen. It sounds like, even now, your mind is giving you ideas about how to escape that anxiety and change the rules to keep you "safe." You can watch as your mind does this. It can be pretty tricky sometimes. And you can always catch it and bring yourself back to what your body needs, instead of what your mind says your body needs.

You may notice that Jim returned a few times to rules that he wanted to follow in order to reduce his anxiety level. The therapist used these opportunities as examples of how the mind works to keep Jim in the same place he's been in. In this integration of mindfulness of thought (observing thoughts that popped up in session), mindfulness of emotion (sitting with anxiety that occurs when he doesn't overexercise), and mindfulness of physical sensations (observing pain levels), the therapist guides Jim to begin the process of accepting his experience, emotionally and physically. In doing this, Jim is able to make choices about his physical activity level that are based on his body's needs, in the service of being able to return to participating in a sport he enjoys.

Mindfulness and Eating

We suggest that you discuss with your clients the various reasons for eating (such as for emotional soothing, for hunger, for escaping painful emotions, and so on) in order to assess the functions that food and eating have in their lives. As you do this, validate that most people eat for a variety of reasons, both internal and external. Your clients, for example, may eat to soothe difficult emotions or distract themselves from difficult thoughts. You may point out that if they practice mindfulness by letting go of thoughts and accepting the experience of difficult emotions, they may be better able to choose if they eat in response to hunger as opposed to thoughts and emotions.

Mindfulness can also be applied directly to eating, which has been shown to increase awareness of physiological sensations such as hunger and fullness. Fully attending to the experience of eating is something that Thich Nhat Hanh recommended when learning mindfulness. In his book *The Miracle of Mindfulness* (1976), Hanh recommends eating one meal of the day in a mindful way. Mindful eating means using all of the senses when eating: seeing your food, touching its texture, smelling it, tasting it in your mouth, and listening to the thoughts you experience as well as noticing your emotional reactions. If you are working with your clients on becoming more mindful of hunger and fullness cues, teaching mindful eating can be useful, as in the exercise below.

EXERCISE: Mindful Eating

To help prepare your clients for mindful eating on their own, we suggest that you practice this first in session with a small piece of food, such as a piece of chocolate. A suggested script for this exercise follows.

Here's a piece of candy. Just hold it in your hand for a few moments without unwrapping it. I'd like you to notice any thoughts that you have about the candy you are holding. Are you having thoughts or feelings about eating it? Maybe you're having some judgments about it, such as "Candy is a bad food," "Candy has too many calories," or "I shouldn't eat candy." If so, I'd like you to notice those as thoughts and allow them to come and go. This may happen throughout the exercise. I encourage you to simply notice any thoughts that occur and allow them to come and go; just notice them as thoughts, not as fact.

Now go ahead and feel the candy in your hand. Notice the shape of it and the texture of the wrapper. When you've thoroughly felt the candy in the wrapper, go ahead and unwrap it and hold it in your hand. Notice how different it feels without the wrapper. Is it sticky? Soft? Notice any judgments that you have about this experience.

Now go ahead and smell the candy. Notice what it smells like. Is it a familiar smell? Notice what happens when you smell the candy. Is your mouth watering? Can you almost taste it while smelling it?

Whenever you're ready, go ahead and put the candy in your mouth, but don't chew it just yet. For now, just hold it in your mouth and feel the texture of it. Can you taste it at first, or does it take a while? What does it feel like to hold it in your mouth? What is the texture like? Again, notice what thoughts or judgments you have during this experience and let them come and go.

As you hold the candy in your mouth, notice any physical reactions you may be having. Do you have an urge to chew and swallow the candy? If so, notice this as an urge, and let it come and go without giving in to it. Don't chew the candy just yet. Are you noticing that you are hungry now? Allow the candy to dissolve in your mouth and notice how the shape may change in your mouth.

When you're ready, go ahead and chew the remaining candy in your mouth. When you're chewing, notice how chewing feels. Notice how the candy feels against your teeth, and how your teeth feel against each other. Are you having thoughts about this experience? Try to notice those thoughts as separate from your experience of chewing the candy. When you've thoroughly chewed the candy, go ahead and swallow it. Feel the remaining candy slide down your throat. Notice how long you can feel it go down your throat. How long can you still taste it? Can you taste it in the back of your throat? Notice everything you can about this experience.

Now that you've chewed and swallowed the candy, notice any thoughts you're having about this experience and any judgments that may be occurring. Notice also any physical reactions you're having, the remaining flavor in your mouth, and the way your throat feels. Try to notice these physical reactions as separate from your thoughts and judgments about the experience.

When you discuss this exercise with your clients, include thoughts, emotions, and physical sensations about the experience of eating the candy or other food. This is a useful exercise for integrating mindfulness of thought, emotion, and physical sensations. You may suggest that your clients choose a meal where they have time to practice mindful eating with either the entire meal or a portion of it. See if they notice a change in the taste or quality of the food, or the amount of the food they desire to eat. Focus on the fact that those changes are experientially based, instead of based on external factors like judgments about how much they "should" eat, the time of day, what type of food the meal contains, or how many calories are in it. Daily practice of mindful eating along with mindful attention to hunger and fullness may facilitate acceptance of eating based on physical needs rather than emotional cues.

Conclusion

We have offered several exercises in this chapter aimed at mindfulness practice with regard to breathing, thoughts, emotions, physical sensations, and eating. Mindfulness is a practice, which is the way toward acceptance. It is the opposite of avoidance or unawareness. Teaching mindfulness, practicing mindfulness, and gaining a stance of acceptance toward one's experience are lifelong processes. There is no end point of "success" for these practices. Buddhist monks spend a lifetime practicing mindfulness, with no endpoint of perfection. We use the tool of mindfulness in acceptance and commitment therapy to facilitate the active process of acceptance. By experiencing versus avoiding, clients actively accept the sum total of their human experience in that moment.

In helping clients with body image dissatisfaction, the goal of mindfulness is to elicit an increased awareness of all experiences (internal and external) instead of attempting to push away certain thoughts and feelings while maintaining a narrow focus on the body. In addition to broadening what is noticed, mindfulness facilitates noticing while letting go of judgments. Noticing the body, its shape and size, will always be part of clients' experience. If done mindfully, detachment from judgments and defusion from thoughts about the body will be facilitated. Defusion from thoughts allows for behaviors to be experientially based instead of based on thoughts as being "truth." Clients may then begin to engage in behaviors they have previously avoided. For example, being mindful of the thought "I'm too ugly to go to the party" and noticing (versus reacting to) the associated anxiety that occurs in social situations will allow clients to be at the party while noticing the thoughts and anxiety. In turn, clients may become more aware of their actual experience at the party (such as the new people they may meet or how people are actually reacting to them), and how this may differ from what their mind was telling them about what the party would be like ("Everyone will avoid me and I will be laughed at"). These types of behavioral changes facilitate corrective experiences for situations that clients previously avoided.

Willingness, as discussed in previous chapters, is necessary to practice mindfulness. Given that levels of willingness vary, so will the degree to which one is mindful, and therefore the degree of acceptance one experiences. Remind your clients that acceptance is a path, not a destination, and discuss this important distinction with them. One of our mentors described the process of acceptance in this helpful way: "Gaining acceptance of a feeling or an event in life is sometimes as slow-moving as the width of a sheet of paper—barely noticeable with the turn of just one page. But, over time, diligently moving on a path of acceptance is like putting together several of those very thin sheets of paper; soon, and sometimes suddenly, you will notice a change."

In the following chapter, we will discuss the application of values clarification. Having learned some mindfulness skills for noticing and experiencing emotions, your clients are ready to embark on broadening their behaviors in life to create a more meaningful and vital existence. Because time and energy may have previously been focused on body image issues and avoiding certain life situations, your clients may not be clear about what is meaningful to them in life. Or they may be quite clear about what is meaningful to them, but they have previously avoided pursuing it. The next step in therapy is to clarify values in different domains or "directions" of life and to identify associated specific goals that align with those values. In doing so, your clients will create their own meaningful life path that is based on values instead of on avoidance.

CHAPTER 8

Clarifying Values and Defining Goals

I've learned that making a "living" is not the same thing as making a "life."

—Maya Angelou

Living a Vital Life

Why choose to move toward, rather than away from, emotional pain? To this point in the book, we have outlined a treatment that suggests that individuals experience difficult and painful emotions while letting go of often comfortable and soothing means of avoiding emotional pain. We have discussed the theoretical rationale of ACT: that avoidance only works temporarily, and in the long term paradoxically increases the emotion it intends to suppress. Research supports ACT's position that avoidance is not an effective long-term method of reducing emotional pain. From what you've learned about creative hopelessness, identifying control strategies, and learning mindfulness skills to promote experiential acceptance of emotion, it may seem as if we are suggesting that experiencing pain is the goal for your client. However, the scope of ACT is much broader than facilitating emotional experiencing. In ACT, emotional experiencing is done for the practical purpose of creating a meaningful life. A practical answer to the question "Why choose to move toward rather than away from emotional pain?" is "So you may live a fuller, more meaningful life that is consistent with your innermost values."

As we have demonstrated clinically and theoretically, avoidance of emotion produces behaviors that narrow one's behavioral repertoire. For example, if your clients avoid unpleasant feelings or emotions by continuing to focus their mental energy on their weight and shape or if their body image anxiety results in social avoidance, then their capability to attend to and build relationships lessens. When energy is consumed with avoidance practices, the capacity for living a valued life diminishes. We could also argue that this avoidance makes it harder to clarify the client's values.

Experiencing emotional pain is in the service of moving in a valued direction. But first your clients must clarify what the valued direction is and what the specific goals that define the particular value are. When clients give up their avoidance behaviors or control strategies, they will uncover pain. Engaging in values-based behaviors may increase that emotional pain. For example, clients may value developing close relationships. They may hold the belief that they first need to have more confidence in themselves or must change their appearance in order to develop those relationships. However, we would suggest that clients need not gain more confidence or change their appearance before beginning to socialize with others. Letting go of control strategies related to changing their appearance or gaining confidence (such as reassurance seeking) will be necessary in order to create space for building their values-based behavior of having close relationships. However, dropping defenses and being open to relationships can be painful in the early phases.

By engaging in avoidance-based behaviors, clients allow fear to be in the driver's seat of their life. Fear motivates their behavior instead of their values. By putting themselves in the driver's seat on the road toward their valued life, clients choose behaviors that open an opportunity to form a close relationship (perhaps attending a social event or calling an old friend) and that increase their exposure to the anxiety related to appearance and feared outcomes. Your job is to help them return, again and again, to being mindful of their experience in these values-based behaviors. Their experience will likely include difficult emotions and perhaps some negative experiences (such as rejection), but it also may include some pleasant experiences such as feeling more connected, or the simple joy of laughing with another person, or the feelings associated with beginning to make a friend. Clearly the process of creating a values-driven life is not quick and easy. If it had been easy, clients would have already moved in that direction. Moreover, it is not pain free. However, if your clients are willing to begin moving in a valued direction with their emotional pain in tow, experience and research show this process to be more vital than a narrowly lived, avoidance-based existence.

Values-Based Living: An Alternate Path

The first step of values clarification is to introduce values-based living to your clients as an alternate path to fear-based or avoidance-based living. At this juncture in therapy, your clients should have a clearer understanding of their path of fear-based or avoidance-based living—that is, they should be clear about what it is they fear related to body image, weight, eating, and other life issues, such as relationships and uncontrollable life events. They also should have identified what strategies they have tried, and may continue to try, in order to avoid those uncomfortable emotions. Additionally, having gone through the creative hopelessness process, they should understand the ineffectiveness of those avoidance strategies well. This, of course, does not mean that your clients are not engaging in any avoidance strategies. As we have pointed out, letting go of control strategies is a process—one that we all struggle with at times. The willingness to continue this will wax and wane. Mindfulness skills have been introduced as a means of gaining awareness of this, and as a tool for experiencing emotions should clients choose to do so. So, if your clients fall back into old control strategies, you can work with them on mindfulness skills to increase their awareness of when they are engaged in these strategies.

Introducing the Topic of Values to Clients

At this point, you might want to introduce your clients to the concept that you are considering an alternate life path with them—a path that is guided by what they find meaningful in life versus a path guided by avoiding what they find uncomfortable or fearful. Because body image, weight, or eating has been a prominent issue in their life, choosing a different path that is meaningful to them in a new way can feel overwhelming and unfamiliar. Some clients have been so consumed with a particular issue, problem, or avoidance strategy that there has not been time or energy to consider any other ways of living. Because of this, it's important to introduce the topic of values gently. Here is a suggested script for doing this:

So far we've discussed that you have a choice in how you deal with difficult situations and emotions: you can choose to approach difficult situations or emotions with active acceptance instead of using control strategies to avoid those emotions. These situations may involve food or body image and are likely uncomfortable for you, or they may involve other areas of life that we've been discussing that you would prefer to avoid. [You may use a specific example of your client's struggle here.] *You might want to think of this as a new path, as if you are literally choosing to walk down a new course full of all the emotions and experiences you have versus walking the old well-worn path in order to avoid that new pathway stretching out before you. So why would we ask you to walk down this new path where you'll need to observe thoughts and approach situations that you'd prefer to avoid? Why would we suggest that you "drop the rope" in your tug-of-war with the monster of unpleasant emotions? Because when you numb your thoughts or avoid situations, it limits your quality of life. This has been evident for you in a number of ways that you've shared with me.* [You may ask clients to name a few unpleasant emotions or situations that they've been avoiding.] *When you choose to approach situations you'd normally avoid, it opens up your opportunities in life. These opportunities are yours to define and explore.*

One way to think about this process is to imagine that you are in a car, driving down the road of life. You can choose to have fear in the driver's seat as you decide which turns to take. Imagine that, in this scenario, difficult emotions or challenging situations are barriers in the road (like rocks or bumps), and your fear leads you to do everything you can to drive around those barriers. Your fear and your desire to avoid difficult emotions may be so strong that you might make a sharp turn to avoid a rock in the middle of the road only to drive straight into a brick wall!

Or you can choose this other path, where you are the driver with your values as your compass—a sort of highly specialized GPS system that can provide direction on which turns to make on the road of life. The barriers or difficult situations and emotions will still be there. There will still be bumps and rocks in the road (the sadness, the pain, the disappointment), but with values providing direction, your decisions to make a turn in the road will be based on goals that are consistent with your values, as opposed to being made because of fear and avoidance. For example, you might drive right over the rock labeled "fear of rejection" if your goal is to build a relationship and to live the value of being close with human beings. You'll still feel the rock under your tires. The bumps, sometimes big, may feel jolting and painful and scary, but you'll still be headed in the direction of your values. This may seem a bit confusing right now, particularly the idea of clarifying your values and goals, but we'll explore this together. Discovering what you value in life and working toward living those values is what we'll work on over the next couple of sessions.

We suggest that you start with a worksheet to help your clients begin to explore their values. To complete the worksheet below, you will ask your clients to write for at least five minutes about what they imagine their life might be like if they had no concerns about body image, eating, or weight. You are asking your clients to suspend reality for several minutes and to imagine they really could remove their body image dissatisfaction. What would life be like? What might they do that they don't engage in now? How might they feel differently? What might their relationships be like? You can either have clients complete this worksheet as homework and bring it to session, or you can actually have them do it in session. Have clients keep their homework in a special folder so they can go back and remind themselves of their values and goals.

LIFE WITHOUT BODY IMAGE CONCERNS WORKSHEET

Have you ever wondered what life would be like if you didn't have any concerns about your weight, your eating, or your body? Use the space below to describe how your life would be different if your time were not consumed by the endless battle to achieve your ideal. If you didn't have to diet or worry about your body or weight, what would your life be like? What kinds of things would you do differently? If society didn't care what your body looked like, what would your relationships be like? For five to twenty minutes, write about the life you imagine you'd be living if you let go of your body image, eating, and weight concerns.

_____

_____

_____

_____

_____

_____

_____

_____

_____

_____

_____

_____

_____

_____

After clients complete this worksheet, ask them to read what they wrote and discuss their experience of writing and sharing the writing with you. What was different about their life, as they imagined it? Were there any new aspects of life that they have not explored because their body image dissatisfaction and associated control strategies have prevented them from doing so? From this worksheet, your clients and you may gain an initial glimpse of some valued areas of life that they have not been attending to.

If your clients have difficulty imagining what life might be like without body image or eating concerns, suggest that they consider the struggle they have been discussing with you in prior sessions. It may be that preoccupation with weight and body image was serving to avoid a struggle related to a different area of life, perhaps an uncontrollable event or relationship. In this case, ask them to imagine what life would be like if that issue disappeared from their life. Ask them to consider what life would be like if the struggle they have been attempting to avoid were actually gone.

In doing this worksheet, you ask your clients to imagine the seemingly impossible in order to bring to mind the desires, wishes, and dreams that they may believe are not viable, but which actually may be goals on the horizon that they can move toward. Point out to your clients specific components of their writing that seem to reflect their values. Asking them Socratic questions that suggest the values revealed in their writing will lead into the exercise below, which further clarifies personal values. Questions that bring out underlying assumptions and clarify the meaning of a value help clients to come to their own understanding of their life direction. For example, you can ask clients what it might mean for them to move in the direction of having closer personal relationships—what concrete steps could they take toward that value?

Defining Values and Goals

You will need to discuss the definition of values to clarify how ACT uses the term and how that differs from the cultural concept of morals. It isn't uncommon for people to associate values with morals or "shoulds." While it may be true that individual values align with cultural or societal moral principles or practices (for example, being kind to family and friends or volunteering to help people in need), our use of the term "values" is not attached to a judgment of what is moral versus immoral. Dahl and colleagues (2009) describe values as "chosen concepts linked with patterns of actions that provide a sense of meaning" (p. 9). A key element in this is that values are based on the client's sense of what is truly important, not ideas that have been prescribed by others. Simply put, an individual's values clarification in ACT is the process of discovering what is meaningful and what makes life vital for that person.

EXERCISE: Nine Valued Directions

Adapted from Pearson (in Follette & Pistorello, 2007)

It may be helpful to your clients to consider their values within various life domains. Heffner & Eifert (2004) provide nine valued domains as examples. Your client may also generate their own valued domains.

- Career

- Citizenship

- Education

- Family

- Friends

- Health

- Leisure

- Romantic Relationships

- Spirituality

You can facilitate values clarification by providing a list of the nine valued directions and asking clients to rank each direction in order of where they are currently putting their energy and time, with 1 being the most time and energy and 9 being the least (for example, Friends–3; Family–2; Career–9, and so on).

RANKING YOUR VALUED DIRECTIONS WORKSHEET

Instructions: Rate how much time and energy you put into each area or direction of your life now (1 = the most time and energy; 9 = the least time and energy).

Valued Direction	Ranking
Career	
Citizenship	
Education	
Family	
Friends	
Health	
Leisure	
Romantic Relationships	
Spirituality	

Next, rate where your time and energy would be spent in a perfect or ideal life (1 = the most time and energy; 9 = the least time and energy).

Valued Direction	Ranking
Career	
Citizenship	
Education	
Family	
Friends	
Health	
Leisure	
Romantic Relationships	
Spirituality	

Once your clients have ranked the valued directions, notice any discrepancies in numerical ranking between life now and the ideal life. This may provide a starting point for noticing what is important to clients and further specifying what directions in life they are not fulfilling. Additionally, the worksheet provides an opportunity to discuss how and why these directions are meaningful to them. You can explain that most people have some discrepancy between what is meaningful in life and how they actually live their lives. However, when there is a lot of discrepancy, people may begin to feel unhappy, unfulfilled, or restricted in their lives. The areas of discrepancy also give clues as to what directions in life clients may be avoiding. Watch for possible avoidance behaviors that suggest the client is not behaving in a way that is consistent with that value.

Goals and Values

The next step is to define attainable goals that align with each of the client's valued directions. Before moving to this step, however, clarifying the difference between goals and values is important. As we have suggested with the nine examples of valued directions, values are areas of life that are intrinsically meaningful. Goals are specific behaviors, which are associated with larger values, that may be achieved or completed. Moving in valued directions has been conceptualized as similar to following a compass to move in a direction that is consistent with the client's own "true north"—that is, toward a vital life. Goals are discrete steps that can be attained (Dahl et al., 2009). For example, if you value being a person who continues to learn new things, you can study forever and never run out of new things to learn. There will always be a next step. The Goals and Values Worksheet (below) may help illustrate the difference for your clients.

GOALS AND VALUES WORKSHEET

Instructions: Please identify three personal goals and consider what value each goal represents. Here's an example:

Goals You've Set

I want to have children someday.

I want to get an A on my next test.

I want to be accepted into medical school.

Why Are You Doing This? (Value)

To nurture children and watch them grow

Succeeding when challenged

Having a prestigious, challenging career

Goals You've Set

1. _____

2. _____

3. _____

4. _____

5. _____

Why Are You Doing This? (Value)

1. _____

2. _____

3. _____

4. _____

5. _____

Helping Your Client Develop Specific and Attainable Goals

Once your clients have an idea of the difference between goals and values, return to their completed Ranking Your Valued Directions Worksheet (above). Using the worksheet as a guide, review each direction clients have ranked and reinforce both willingness to examine difficult issues, and directions where they already have made some progress.

First, examine any direction that which is well matched on both rankings. For example, your client may have ranked career as a 4 for both now and in her ideal life. Ask her what she does in that direction of life—what types of behaviors or activities—that creates such a close match. It is in these directions that your client may be experiencing satisfaction or lower levels of avoidance or distress. She may value being a productive employee and report that she works with her supervisor to identify new sales strategies for her company, collaborates with team members to develop marketing plans, and regularly assesses the sales associated with each new program. Of course, it is fairly likely that her company will reward her hard work. However, what is more important is that she knows she works hard to help her company and there is some intrinsic value for her that goes beyond praise or pay incentives. Use these closely matched directions as examples for developing goals in other valued directions that have a discrepancy in the two rankings.

At this point, you work with your clients to develop specific and attainable goals in the valued directions that continue show a large discrepancy between the initial ranking and the second ranking. For example, if your client initially ranks friends as an 8 (very little energy or time is being placed here now), but ranks this value as a 2 on her scale of how she'd ideally like this to be, this lets you know that she has a barrier to living this direction fully (if at all). She highly values friends, but in actuality she isn't putting or can't put her energy into that direction. Try to have her identify any emotion connected to the issues associated with friends. Ask her to imagine each step involved in pursuing a friendship. At each step, ask what types of feelings, bodily sensations, or thoughts come up as you talk about this. For example, Cindy reported that even thinking about asking a coworker to lunch led to a tight feeling in her stomach and a vague sense of anxiety. She remembers being teased in school because she was shy and wore glasses. Even though Cindy is lonely, she feels safer avoiding the pain of rejection.

Second, specifically explore any avoidance behaviors that may contribute to this discrepancy (for example, "No one will want to be seen with me because of my physical appearance," "I feel anxious in social situations," or "I've never had many friends"). You may notice discrepancies related to your client's struggle that she has discussed with you in earlier sessions. Help her to see this as evidence of how avoidance has impacted her ability to live a valued life.

Third, decide on attainable goals for that area that will begin to align your client's behavior with her values. Remind your client that while she is working toward a point on the horizon, all journeys begin with small steps. Using the prior example of friends as a valued direction, specific goals might be joining a club or organization, going out for coffee with a friend or coworker, attending a social event, calling an old friend to see how he is doing, or joining a social networking site. These behaviors will likely bring up uncomfortable emotions and will be difficult. This is a good time to point out that by engaging in those behaviors, your client chooses to be in the driver's seat, with values as her compass. By doing this, she "drops the rope" of avoidance in the service of the particular value that is meaningful to her.

Achieving the "Impossible"

When a discrepancy in a valued direction exists that is not directly linked to avoidance behaviors, the discrepancy may indicate that it is not currently possible for your client to attain this goal. For example, a client coping with a chronic illness and changes in his physical capabilities who ranks health as his most valued direction may have an apparent discrepancy that does not seem to be immediately changeable. This is a good opportunity to explore his specific goals related to valuing physical health. He may be defining health-related goals as he did prior to his diagnosis and illness, which may be unrealistic under current circumstances. Acceptance would be an effective tool to use in this situation. Acceptance of a specific disease process can actually open the door for new goals that are consistent with his present health circumstances. This would be the first step in moving in this valued direction. The second step would include readjustment of personal health goals that match his current health circumstances. In this way, there is no need to readjust the value as being less personally important; rather, the client can create attainable goals that align with the valued direction. Data suggests that this is actually a very practical approach. For example, in a study of patients with type 2 diabetes, researchers found that acceptance led to better compliance with diabetes self-management and that positive changes in blood glucose were mediated by acceptance related specifically to having diabetes (Gregg, Callaghan, Hayes, & Glenn-Lawson, 2007). The following case example illustrates this dynamic.

■ Case Example: Jeremy

Jeremy is a forty-year-old African American male who was referred to you by his neurologist for symptoms of depression. He was diagnosed five years ago with multiple sclerosis and reports symptoms of depression. He relates the depression to changes in his body and physical functioning that have impacted his self-image and social life. Prior to his diagnosis, Jeremy had a long history (since high school) of being active in sports, including swimming, running, and baseball, and he had been an active member of several community groups and sports teams. Most of his friendships, both new and long-term, were developed through athletic activities. He reports also that his long-term romantic relationship is with a woman he met on a cycling team. Their earlier relationship was spent doing athletic activities together and coaching high school athletics together.

Since his diagnosis, Jeremy has developed a constellation of symptoms that have not allowed him to participate in the majority of athletic endeavors he enjoys. The damage incurred by the disease has left him with weakness in his left leg and arm, transient numbness, fatigue, and other symptoms that prevent his participation in sports. Over the past five years, the steroids used to treat exacerbations of the disease have resulted in a thirty-pound weight gain. Given the progressive and incurable nature of multiple sclerosis, he lives with the knowledge that the disease may get worse.

He presents in your office reporting that he is uncomfortable with his body and depressed about the prospect of never participating in the athletic activities that have been a pivotal part of his life. Furthermore, he is consumed with body dissatisfaction and preoccupation with changes in his muscle tone, weight, and appearance. This has resulted in anxiety and accompanying sexual dysfunction in the relationship with his girlfriend. Their relationship is barely surviving, and Jeremy reports that he feels quite alone without the social circle of athletic enthusiasts he developed over a lifetime.

A review of creative hopelessness and control as the problem reveals that Jeremy has already tried every avenue of continued participation in sports to "overcome" the disease and not "lose himself." He simply cannot physically participate anymore. He also admits that, when he was unable to participate in his usual activities, he started overeating to alleviate the emotional pain, fear, and loneliness. Also, he began to avoid intimate contact with his girlfriend when he gained weight because of fears of rejection and his own self-judgment that arises when he sees his body. Additionally, he avoids looking in mirror and shopping for clothes (because he wears larger sizes now). In order not to experience sadness, he also avoids driving past any of the sports venues where he used to attend games and trails where he used to run or cycle.

Jeremy has begun working toward letting go of the struggle of pushing away sadness by targeting the avoidance behaviors. Looking in mirrors, buying new clothing, driving past places that evoke sadness, beginning to reconnect with his girlfriend, and not overeating are all behaviors he is working on in order to experience his emotions instead of avoiding them. You have introduced mindfulness as a tool to experience his feelings related to the diagnosis and the changes he notices in his body. One day during this process, he states, "Why am I doing this? My life is pretty much screwed up anyway. I'm never going to have what I enjoy again. It seems really pointless to feel all this painful stuff when I'm never going to get what I want. This is an incurable disease. I'm only going to get worse, or at best keep the current limitations I have. What's the point?"

Using the Ranking Your Valued Directions Worksheet, you can introduce values clarification to Jeremy at this time in order to illustrate the point behind experiencing versus avoiding his emotional pain. An examination of Jeremy's rankings will help to identify specific steps to take.

Remember, for the first ranking 1 = the most time and energy and 9 = the least time and energy. Likewise, for the second ranking of the ideal in values, 1 = the most time and energy and 9 = the least time and energy.

Here's how Jeremy ranked his valued directions:

Valued Direction	Ranking 1: How I Am Living My Life	Ranking 2: My Ideal
Career	3	9
Citizenship	7	4
Education	8	8
Family	5	5
Friends	6	3

Health	1	1
Leisure	9	2
Romantic Relationships	5	7
Spirituality	4	6

Jeremy's ranking of valued directions illustrates what you might expect: there are major discrepancies in the directions of leisure, career, citizenship, and friends. Notice that he has ranked health as 1, which upon discussion reveals that he feels that direction of his life is currently in poor shape, and that he spends a great deal of time in that direction. He regularly attends doctor's appointments, has begun a new medication regime, and is doing his best at maintaining compliance with medications and a recommendation for weight loss. In his ideal ranking, he gives health a 1, indicating it is where he would like to put most of his energy and time. We provided this example to show that at times a lack of discrepancy between rankings—current and ideal—does not necessarily indicate that things are going well in that direction of life. Jeremy, for example, reports that his value for good health and his lack of it are at the root of his unhappiness. So in this case, a good match does not equal peace of mind. It does, however, indicate that he is practicing valued living in taking care of his health. If he neglected his health by being noncompliant with medications, abusing substances, or engaging in other poor health practices, his health might be in even worse shape. So at times, rankings may indicate that, while a client like Jeremy puts a lot of time and energy into a particular direction, it doesn't ensure that he will experience this direction of life in the way he would hope—that is, moving in a valued direction does not guarantee an outcome. However, what is important is that he is living the life he values.

For Jeremy, his health status has changed and may always be unpredictable. That means his health is a valued direction of life in which he may want to work on practicing acceptance and mindfulness. This may include experiencing feelings of grief and loss at the change in what "good health" means for him now.

The leisure direction offers opportunities for a change in goals. Jeremy currently ranks leisure as 9, and he admits to spending no time on leisure activities. This is a drastic change from the majority of his life, where free time was filled with leisure activities, all of which were athletic. Notably, he ranks this direction as a 2 in his ideal life. Athletics, while something that he loves and has lost, is only one activity that may be defined as leisure. The goal in your work on values clarification with Jeremy would be to process the grief related to losing athletic capability and to point out that athletics served to meet a larger value of leisure activities, and that Jeremy's task is to identify other goals that align with this valued direction. This may be quite challenging, given that Jeremy's only leisure activity has been athletics. He admits to you that he wouldn't know what to do with free time if he wasn't engaged in some type of athletic endeavor. He admits also that he does value leisure; his life motto used to be "Having fun is the most important aspect to life." Further discussion reveals that Jeremy was taught to appreciate sports by his father, whom he admired. As a child and adolescent, whenever he had free time, he spent it with his father or his friends doing some type of sport. Athletics always equaled fun, physical well-being, and quality time with friends and family. Now Jeremy's work will be to find other outlets for fun, physical well-being, and time with friends and family that take into consideration his current physical condition. Jeremy will need to shift the goals inherent in his valued direction, and he will need to grieve the loss of his old ways of living this value.

Valued life directions do not function separately as categories, but are sometimes quite interrelated. Defining and pursuing goals in one direction often causes a shift that allows another direction to become more fully lived. For Jeremy, finding other activities to live the valued direction of leisure more fully will likely also address finding new social outlets. This will begin to address the discrepancy apparent in the friends direction. Since Jeremy's friendships were based entirely on his athletic leisure activities, this area of life was subsequently negatively impacted by his illness.

Values clarification, along with other components of ACT, is most effective when it is experiential. Exercises related to values clarification, such as ranking valued directions, may feel more salient to the client when paired with an experiential exercise. In the next section, we provide a couple of experiential exercises that we recommend using with your client to facilitate values clarification.

Values Clarification: Experiential Exercises

In the routine of daily living, we often lose connection with what matters most. Getting in touch with the impermanence of life is one means of reestablishing what really matters. We have probably all heard stories of how near-death experiences or diagnoses of serious illnesses have caused people to reassess their lives and live them in more meaningful ways. Steven Hayes, one of the developers of ACT, suggests asking your clients to imagine that they have only six months to live as an experiential exercise to bring them into contact what would matter if time were limited. Try the following exercise to help your clients get in touch with the things that matter to them.

EXERCISE: Living with Intention

Adapted from Follette & Pistorello (2006)

First, ask clients if they are willing to temporarily suspend reality. If they are, ask them to close their eyes and guide them in this brief imagery:

I'd like you to close your eyes and imagine that you walk into your doctor's office. The doctor tells you that you have one year to live, but that you will be physically capable of living this last year in any way you wish. Given this limited period of time, what would you want to do? How might you live your life differently? How would your relationships change? Spend a few moments really bringing that situation into your mind. [Allow a few moments for the client to generate the image.]

As an alternative to doing this exercise in session, have clients complete the following worksheet at home and discuss it in session.

A YEAR TO LIVE: WHAT WOULD YOU DO? WORKSHEET

Consider that you have been told you have one year to live. Because this is only an exercise, pretend that you have enough physical energy to do whatever it is that you'd like to do (that is, you don't actually have an illness that prevents you from living the way you'd like to). Assuming this, consider what your personal value statement is within each domain. For example, for the domain "Family," an individual may make the value statement "I value staying closely connected with my family." Next, specify goals you would like to set in various valued domains of life. What would you like to make sure to do that would align with your values statement?

Instructions: In the values statement column, write a sentence or two that states your personal value for that particular domain in life. In the goal column, list one or two specific goals for each valued direction that you'd want to make sure to accomplish in that year.

Valued Direction	Values Statement	Goal
Career		
Citizenship		
Education		
Family		
Friends		
Health		
Leisure		
Romantic Relationships		
Spirituality		

Following completion of this worksheet, review it with your clients. Ask them to describe the goals they listed. Next, ask if they consider those goals possible now.

Our experience is that this exercise may evoke significant emotion for several reasons:

- Clients don't believe that the goals they listed are possible.

- They become aware that they are not living a values-driven life, and they believe it would require something devastating, like a terminal illness, to drive them to do so.

- Clients become aware of valued directions in life that they feel have been neglected or opportunities, relationships, or other significant things that they have lost that they feel are irreplaceable.

Situations like these (or other reasons that the exercise is painful) are wonderful opportunities to describe how pain and vitality often merge. Where there is meaning or there are values, there is often emotional pain. The merging of pain and vitality comes either from the emotional or practical difficulty that exists in living a meaningful life or in the realization that one is not living a meaningful life. Consider a funeral itself: It is often a celebration of a person's life with all the positive memories of what the person brought to others and the wonderful things she contributed. And it is in the remembering of these wonderful aspects that there is loss, with the realization that the person will never be present again. Pain is vital. It lets us know, as humans, that we are alive. It provides signals of where to turn our attention, yet it also often is a signal of when to turn away or move away from a certain experience, person, place, or thing. If life is guided by fear of emotional pain, we may miss the signals of what is important and meaningful in life. Pain, arguably as much as pleasure, guides us toward an understanding of what is valued. Therefore your clients may become clear about what is meaningful through connecting with painful losses. These painful losses may paradoxically represent valued aspects of life.

In addition, explore with your clients the belief that any of their goals are in some way unattainable or beliefs that they shouldn't focus on certain goals. Clients may believe that they wouldn't focus on meaningful goals and values unless they had only a limited period of time to live. This exercise should elucidate the fact that none of us knows exactly how long we do have to live. Therefore, given an ambiguous time limit on life, why wouldn't we begin living in a valued, meaningful way right now?

After doing this exercise (either in session or on the homework sheet), clients often discuss things they thought of during the exercise that they believe to be impossible, but which are actually quite possible. For example, clients might talk about wanting to be very healthy, but because of chronic illness or other issues, this may seem out of reach. This could lead you to discuss different ways of thinking about health, including looking at good health as a point on the horizon that one always moves toward but never fully attains. You can ask clients if they have ever heard about people who accomplished physical goals that everyone said were impossible. You could have your clients consider remarkable examples such as individuals who had lost their legs and yet completed long races, or cancer survivors who returned to competitive bicycle racing. While your clients may discount these examples as unrealistic for them, you can counter with the idea that the world is full of people doing impossible things—and it is not primarily ability that differentiates these individuals. Rather, it is the willingness to take courageous steps toward goals in valued life directions. Discuss this with your clients. Why do they believe that those goals would be unattainable? Does they need a life sentence in order to start living?

Conclusion

As with other components of ACT, such as identifying and letting go of control strategies, practicing mindfulness, and gaining acceptance, values clarification is a process, not an event. Your clients may first become clear about certain aspects of their lives that they value that are directly related to areas of struggle that you have discussed. The overall goal of values clarification is to provide a broader context for living, instead of a narrow one defined by avoidance. Given that our focus in this book is to target a reduction of body image dissatisfaction and preoccupation with image, values clarification may initially focus on the areas of life most directly impacted by this. However, just as there always may be avoidance behaviors to target, there is always room for being more congruent in living a life that is more consistent with intrinsic values. As can happen on any long journey, a number of life problems can take us off course. Checking the compass of our values can help to redirect our actions. In our next chapter, we discuss the importance of identifying barriers to valued living—those things that may take us off course. We will also review termination of treatment within an ACT model.

CHAPTER 9

Barriers to Values and Commitment to Valued Living

I am not a tentative person. Whatever I do, I give up my whole self to it.

—Edna St. Vincent Millay

Focus on Committed Action

A central focus in ACT is that treatment emphasizes moving beyond thinking about problems to developing a plan for committed action that will take clients to more vital and fulfilling lives. ACT is fundamentally a behavioral treatment, and therefore the focus on effective living is central to the process of change. As noted earlier, ACT assumes that clients are not broken, and that once clients make a decision to really let go of avoidance and control, they will be able to identify their own goals with some support from you. At this point, you can play an essential role in helping clients to move past the barriers to change that are inevitable in doing this type of work.

Barriers for the Clinician

We begin this chapter by inviting you to look at your own barriers to valued living. We have found that if therapists have not worked through their own difficulties in this area, it is easy to get caught up in the client's expressions regarding the impossibility of change. Examining your barriers is a powerful antidote to that problem. Working from this perspective provides you with the necessary tools for helping your clients to identify their own barriers to change, which we cover in the next section. We then provide specific strategies for working with these barriers, along with advice for dealing with typical sticking points.

As you work with your clients on values clarification and accordant behavior change, we suggest asking yourself this question about your own life: What barriers prevent you from living a valued life? Consider your own values and associated life goals. Is there an area of life you have not fully pursued, or perhaps an area of life that has been filled with disappointments? What factors have prevented you from pursuing certain goals in that valued area of life? What was your reaction to disappointments: to become stuck in avoiding the associated pain or to move forward with that pain?

If you haven't done so yet while reading this book, we suggest you also consider what your relationship is with your body image, weight, and eating habits. Are you dissatisfied or preoccupied with this aspect of yourself? What barriers have stood in the way of letting go of old ideas or behaviors related to body image, eating, and weight? Is weight, body image, or food a barrier to valued living in other areas of your life?

We ask these questions because as human beings none of us is exempt from pain and avoidance of it. In that way, we as clinicians also are vulnerable to the same traps of avoidance that we see in our clients. Therefore, another useful question might be this: What barriers (personal or professional) may prevent you from conducting valued clinical work? The definition of "valued clinical work" is individual and varies depending on the therapist, the client, and the client's identified struggles and goals. Identification and awareness of your values and goals with a specific client, as well as your personal values and goals, may enable you to work more effectively at an experiential level. Part of understanding personal barriers to effective psychotherapy also includes an awareness of your reactions to (that is, thoughts and feelings) about clients. *Countertransference* is the term, familiar to most clinicians, referring to therapist feelings evoked by client experiences that relate to the clinician's personal history. Most psychotherapies encourage, at varying degrees, awareness of personal historical issues that may evoke countertransference when working with clients. The type of feelings or reactions that are evoked with each client are context dependent, in that they will vary by individual therapist, client, and circumstance.

We ask you to be willing to identify barriers to working with your clients. Using mindfulness, notice any judgments you may have about your clients' identified values; identify your personal feelings about your clients; notice if you have beliefs about the potential of clients in treatment or following treatment. Hold these thoughts lightly. Notice also if you have feelings or reactions to clients based on your personal history with their struggle or a similar one. Ultimately, we encourage you as a clinician to apply willingness to your own life in the same way you ask your clients to be willing. The authenticity inherent in that process will be evident to your clients and, we believe, will produce more vital therapeutic work.

As a clinician, you will have thoughts and feelings about your clients—if you didn't, we'd be a little worried! The valence you assign to those thoughts (that is, positive versus negative) can certainly shift how you approach therapy with your clients and how you relate to them. We're asking you, as the clinician, to practice defusion from your thoughts and mindfulness of your feelings so that you make decisions based on your values as a clinician instead of based on personal judgment. This is similar to some other theoretical orientations that encourage awareness of issues of countertransference. In ACT, we ask you to use tools of mindfulness and acceptance in order to suspend your personal judgment (that is, your thoughts) and to become more aware of your feelings. Those experiences won't vanish. The thoughts may continually pop up, and the feelings may remain present; they provide useful information at times, both about you and about your clients. However, with increased awareness you will come to see that your thoughts and feelings do not represent fact; instead they represent your experience, which removes the potential barrier to your ability to be there for your clients.

As a clinician, you are theoretically susceptible to any of the same barriers to living a valued life as your clients. In addition, you are also vulnerable to the trap inherent in being the "knowing one." Since you are the one providing help—and those who need help seek you out—you can come to expect that you must know the way or the answer in your own life; that, by default, you move forward in the direction of your values. This belief, if tightly held, can lead you to get stuck in your own life. It can also hinder your ability to help your clients move forward. Therefore, while working with your clients to identify barriers to their values, we ask that you be willing to look at your own barriers in your clinical work and in your life.

Identifying Barriers with Your Clients

Nearly any experience, thought, feeling, person, place, or thing can function as a barrier to living a valued life. You have asked your clients to let go of familiar coping strategies, to experience difficult emotions, and to identify and move toward what they want in life while experiencing difficult emotions such as fear. At this juncture, your clients may perceive a number of potential barriers in order to avoid this difficult process. Likewise, you may see barriers to client values and become discouraged with your clients; you may, at times, also judge your own ability to help them, viewing your own competence or experience (or lack thereof) as a barrier. Therefore, identifying client and therapist barriers to values-consistent behavior.

Barriers can be broken into categories for easier identification. Below we discuss the four types of barriers that can affect you and your clients in therapy: societal, thoughts and feelings, behavioral, and unclear values. Recognizing these barriers can help you and your clients move forward with the therapeutic process.

Societal Barriers

It's an inescapable fact that Western society is image driven and promotes thinness as the epitome of beauty. Your client will be bombarded daily by this message through media, personal interactions, and perhaps familial influences. Popular culture and gender norms are not likely to align with a value of letting go of body image preoccupation. Nor are they likely to align with a value of experiencing negative emotion and letting go of avoidance strategies. (Consider, for example, the popularity of any new strategy for instant happiness.) As a human being, if you (as therapist) have lived in Western society for very long, you also have experienced and internalized the same image-driven messages. To a certain degree, you may hold societal beliefs about body image and the definition of beauty. Noticing these thoughts will be important in order to not align with client preoccupation with image.

For example, let's say your client is considerably obese and continues a weight-loss program based on a belief that she will be noticed more by men if she loses weight. Her identified value is to build close relationships, as she has been quite socially isolated. It may be true, based on our societal norm for beauty, that others may praise her or provide positive attention if she loses weight. There are unending examples in magazines, television, movies, and probably individuals she knows (and those you may know) who lost weight and began dating or socializing more. You may even feel pulled to provide positive feedback on her appearance if you notice weight loss; you may also notice feelings of agreement that she would be more attractive if she were not obese; you may also hope that if she loses weight she would gain the confidence needed to pursue social relationships.

In this scenario, your client still focuses on changing her exterior or appearance in order to build close relationships. She may argue that at least she isn't avoiding social situations anymore prior to losing weight. While social interaction prior to weight loss is a step in her valued direction, her barrier continues to be attachment to the societal norm of beauty and the belief that achieving this moves her in a valued direction. As long as she continues to believe that physical attractiveness will in itself build close relationships, body image preoccupation will continue to be a barrier to truly living her value.

Validating the reality that she may receive positive attention for weight loss is beneficial. Avoiding, ignoring, or attempting to change societal norms and reactions is not the most effective place to put energy in the service of helping an individual client. In order to address the barrier of attachment to societal norms as a means of building relationships, mindfulness and acceptance are useful tools. Noticing and experiencing positive reinforcement for changes in body image while also noticing and experiencing potential negative reactions to one's current body image is a useful approach. In order to demonstrate the social influence of the reactions of others, have your clients do the following exercise using guided imagery.

EXERCISE: Body in Relationship

Use this exercise to validate your clients' experience and also begin the process of questioning attachment to the expectations of others. Here is our suggested script. You may alter it as needed for individual clients.

To begin, get comfortable in your chair, close your eyes, and follow my voice as I describe various people in your life. Imagine yourself in a quiet, safe place, maybe sitting on a bench in a park. Imagine what you're wearing and how you're sitting. Just notice the experience of sitting on this park bench on a pleasant day. Notice your breathing and become very much in touch with feeling comfortable and relaxed. Now imagine someone you know approaching you. Pick someone you feel very comfortable with, someone who is very accepting of you—possibly a close friend or family member. Imagine that person walking up to you and having a brief conversation together. Notice how you feel. Do you feel comfortable or uncomfortable? How do your feelings about your body change while you are talking to this person? Do you become more aware of your body, change your position, pull at your clothes, or begin to think about your appearance with judgment? Now that person walks on. Once again you are feeling comfortable and relaxed. [Go through this experience with a series of people who are important to your client, including people who might turn up in life, such as a potential date. Use your knowledge of your client's history to select four or five people.]

Now bring yourself back to your place on the park bench. Be aware that you're feeling relaxed and comfortable, just noticing your breath and the pleasant sights around you. Now open your eyes and come back into the room.

Spend time processing your client's reactions to this exercise and discuss the specific thoughts and feelings that arose while imagining the various social interactions. Assign homework for the client to notice the thoughts, feelings, and bodily reactions that occur in real life during social interactions throughout the upcoming week.

Thoughts and Feelings as Barriers

We have emphasized the fact that efforts to push away or avoid uncomfortable thoughts and feelings eventually produce ineffective control strategies. Ultimately these efforts are also ineffective and end up increasing the frequency and distress of these experiences. Thus, experiencing all of the thoughts and feelings that are present in the moment has been encouraged in this treatment. Now we ask clients to choose values-based behaviors while experiencing some extremely uncomfortable emotions. It isn't uncommon for clients to have the belief that they cannot possibly continue to function and live life while experiencing these negative emotions or thoughts; it is not unlike the sense of dread clients report during a panic attack. Your client may have even given up the specific control strategy (for example, asking for reassurance about her body) that was getting in the way of pursuing some value (such as close social relationships), yet she may be unwilling at first to actually pursue those relationships while feeling quite anxious, doubtful, or sad, or while having the thought "I can't do this."

It is very important to notice this barrier and point it out to your client when it occurs. You may, for example, say something like this:

Ah, so you're having the thought that you can't possibly do [specify some behavior] *because you're anxious. Would you be willing to have the anxiety you're experiencing and do this* [behavior] *anyway?*

Your client's first answer might be no or maybe. This is where the rubber meets the road. Living a values-based life is not easy work. It doesn't always feel good. The point is that, as humans, we do lots of different things when we're feeling negative emotions or experiencing negative thoughts. The things we choose to do may be fear based, or they may be values based. Point out to your client that you are asking her to shift what it is she chooses to do when she has a negative thought or emotion. Instead of allowing that emotion or thought to guide her behavior, you are suggesting that she try allowing her values to guide her behavior. Here's one way of how you might say this:

Okay, so you have identified the value of being a caring person who helps others. You want to volunteer at the hospital, but when you think of that, your stomach goes into a knot and you feel anxious and ashamed. You think people will look at you and judge your appearance. You can almost hear their thoughts as they wonder why you don't control your eating and lose weight. Your fear and anxiety keep you at home and away from living the life you value. Can you just imagine having all these thoughts and feelings—and actually calling the hospital to find out about doing volunteer work? Notice that even as you imagine this, anxiety may arise, yet you can continue moving forward while experience that anxiety. You can move in your valued direction even if it is difficult and uncomfortable at first.

Behavioral Barriers

Behavioral barriers could be anything that your clients do that gets in the way of meeting a goal that aligns with their values. These behaviors might relate to a control strategy that you and a client have previously identified, or they could be something new that was never disclosed or discussed. Consider the following case example.

■ Case Example: Candace

You have been treating Candace, a nineteen-year-old college freshman, for six months. Using ACT, you have been treating her for symptoms of body dysmorphic disorder; specifically, she believes that her face is disproportional and uneven. She has engaged in several control strategies in response to this perception, including social isolation, long periods of time visually measuring the symmetry of her face in the mirror, excessive time applying makeup, and consultation with a variety of cosmetic surgeons (none of whom are willing to operate on her perceived flaws). Throughout the past three months, you have been using ACT as an intervention to target these control strategies and broaden Candace's life through values clarification. She has been interacting socially on weekends more often, states that she has begun dating someone new, and reports that she has reduced the amount of time she spends on self-evaluation. However, she continues to report intense anxiety during daytime activities such as going to class, going to the gym, and coming to see you. In session, her eye contact remains poor, and she doesn't exhibit any increased comfort during interactions with you.

In further assessment of her time spent at home and when going out in the evening, you discover that Candace has increased her alcohol use. She was honest with you from the beginning of therapy that she was using alcohol socially and that she sometimes became intoxicated. However, over the three months you've been treating her, she reports that she has begun drinking daily. She states that she drinks at least two to three glasses of wine each evening and finds that this alleviates the need to focus on her appearance in the mirror. She also has been using alcohol when socializing in order to feel less anxious.

This is a place where your own self-evaluations may become an issue. Having worked closely with Candace, you notice that you react with feelings of disappointment in your own clinical skills. You have some judgmental thoughts about not having asked more specifically about alcohol use. Suddenly you feel the progress that your client has made is destroyed. You think, "It wasn't real progress. Candace used alcohol use to make those changes easier." And then you think, "Her changes don't really count because she's been numbing out with alcohol the entire time."

Take a breath and know that, if you had thoughts like this, you may have feelings associated with your values connected to these thoughts. First, most clinicians want their clients to improve. (You probably would not be reading this book if you didn't have a value related to this!) When a client does not improve or you feel you missed something about your client, you are disappointed. Perhaps the client has not moved in a direction that you hoped she would. In this case, your client is most likely still experiencing a great deal of fear and pain—and she has kept a secret from you. Notice this thought without judgment, but just an issue to be addressed. She may have kept the secret for several reasons. In this case, part of Candace's reason for keeping the secret is that she wanted to please you and follow through with her stated goals. Your clients may want to please you as much as you want to see them improve. These are perfectly acceptable feelings and desires; they are only barriers if they aren't ever discussed.

You have this discussion with Candace following her disclosure.

Therapist: First of all, I want to thank you for being honest with me.

Candace: Well, you asked what was making the socialization easier while daytime activities were still so tough. And I just couldn't lie to you anymore. I've feel like I've been cheating.

Therapist: How does drinking feel like cheating?

Candace: I guess because it takes away all my feelings. My anxiety and shame about my appearance just go away, and then I can do what I've been wanting to. However, I don't feel anything really—I'm just numb. And I know that much of this therapy has focused on how important it is to have whatever feelings are happening. So, in that way, it feels like cheating.

Therapist: I can appreciate that you want to do this work "right." However, this is your life. Drinking is not necessarily bad, but it seems like there may be some concerns you are experiencing with daily drinking. Is it getting in the way of anything?

Candace: Well, at first drinking didn't seem like it got in the way of anything. I met someone and started dating. I had more relaxing afternoons without all that time fixating on my appearance. But then I'd wake up in the morning and face terrible anxiety during the day. Nothing was getting better during the day—not school, not coming to see you, not being in public at the grocery store or the library. Unless I had at least some alcohol, I felt pretty much the same as I did before this treatment. Oh, that feels really bad to say.

Therapist: What feels bad about that?

Candace: Well, I just said I didn't think this treatment was working. I feel bad about that.

Therapist: Well, has that been your experience? That this treatment isn't working in the ways you'd hoped it would?

Candace: Yes. But at the same time, I want it to work. I want to be able to do all the things I'm doing while I'm drinking, but I want to do them sober. I want to enjoy them. So I want all the things we talked about in values clarification. And I also agree with all the control strategies that we talked about and how those don't work. So I think this treatment could work, but why hasn't it?

Therapist: I can't tell you for sure. But let's go back first to what effect the drinking has. You said it numbed your emotions, right?

Candace: Yes.

Therapist: Do you see any similarities with the effect of the alcohol and the effect of what you used to do to control anxiety?

Client: You mean staying in my house all the time?

Therapist: Yes. Staying in your house and asking people you did interact with for reassurance about how you look.

Candace: Well, yes, they all reduce my anxiety. But at least with drinking, I wasn't alone. I got to do all the activities we talked about. Well, except for the daytime activities.

Therapist: Sure. I can see how you felt like it would work. Ultimately, though, it is doing the very same thing: taking you away from experiencing the emotions and thoughts that are ultimately there anyway. When you can't use the alcohol (for example, during the day), the same beliefs and feelings are present.

Candace: Well, I actually did think about drinking one morning. But I didn't because I knew that would be a real problem. And that's when I decided to tell you. I could tell it just wasn't working the way I wanted it to.

Therapist:	How is that?
Candace:	I want to be able to socialize and have a full life all the time, not just when I can drink or do something to decrease my anxiety.
Therapist:	It is pretty limiting, isn't it, to feel controlled by an emotion?
Candace:	It's horrible!
Therapist:	So, guess what? The drinking is a barrier to what you really want. And these barriers will show up. The important thing is that you noticed it and you talked about it. It doesn't mean to me that you can't have what you want.

In this scenario, the you identified that Candace had a behavioral barrier of drinking alcohol to decrease anxiety. You also clarified that she wants to change this behavior because it doesn't align with her value of wanting to participate in all areas of her life (not just because Candace felt like she was cheating in therapy). With all clients, barriers will be present. It is important to normalize this and predict that clients might have thoughts about having failed or disappointed themselves or you. Once again, these are just thoughts, which provide another opportunity to practice defusion (distancing from the thoughts) with your clients. Bringing clients back to their experience of their own lives and the control strategies they've been using is always the most effective way to guide them in a decision of whether they want to change from an unworkable control strategy to a more effective acceptance strategy.

Unclear Values as a Barrier

Is it really your value, or is it someone else's value? This barrier may occur for both you and your clients. As a therapist, you will want certain things for your clients. You may see goals that you'd like to see them achieve. These may be very well-reasoned, delightful goals. However, if they are not the client's personal goals or values, the work is not authentically the client's. ACT is a less therapist-directed therapy than many psychotherapeutic approaches; it is absolutely a collaborative effort between you and your clients. In helping your clients clarify their values and goals, it is most effective to give ultimate deference to your clients. If you see that a goal is perhaps "lofty" or in your opinion unachievable in some way, notice that as a thought you have. It may be that you are right. That doesn't matter as much as clients finding out for themselves, through experience, if the goal is indeed well matched to their values, and if it is achievable, reasonable, and so on. Your work as therapist is to be aware of your own personal values, those that you would want for your clients, and to mindfully reorient to the goals and values your clients have specified.

A related issue is helping clients to disentangle their goals and values from those that may be significantly influenced by their cultural context. That is the water in which we all swim. It may be that your clients have described values and accordant goals that they believe would be right or healthy, or those that they have been told are good in some way.

Values are inherently influenced by the context in which one has lived, and is presently living. Taking into account contextual variables such as culture and family, consider if the values specified by your clients are based on their life experience or are based on thoughts about what they should value. For example, the client's mother may have told her for years that she would be much happier if she were more like her cousin, who is blonde, petite, and dresses in all the latest fashions. It might be difficult for your client to let go of a message that was repeated so often over the years. And we are not trying to make her mother a bad person here. The message could have been sent with love as the mother struggled with her own painful feelings when she saw her daughter struggle. At the same time, it is important for the client to find her own values and goals, If she cannot find her own truth, it will likely be quite difficult for her to move forward, because her values are not based on her own experience but rather on rules she learned as a child. The difference between these is seen in this example: "I value eating healthy because my doctor told me to eat healthy foods and I know I should" (verbally based or rule based) versus "I value eating healthy because, even though unhealthy foods taste good, I feel better physically when I make healthy food choices."

Sometimes there is also a rule or law that aligns with the stated value. For example, a client with diabetes might state, "I value being healthy, and my doctor told me that eating some of my favorite foods is very dangerous in managing my insulin." A client with anger management problems might state, "I value not harming other people when I become angry, and physically harming people is against the law." When your clients repeatedly struggle to follow through with goals that align with a stated value, examine if that value is truly theirs. It may be authentically a client's value, but he may not yet be connected to how it aligns with his experience in life. Alternately, the stated value may be entirely based on verbal rules (that is, what he has been told is right) or social control. In that case, the client is basically controlled by *pliance*, or rule following. If this is the case, you may need to do more work on values clarification and help your client to contact the cost of "living by the rules." You may, for example, have your client describe what his life would be like if you had shown up when he was a little boy and could help him plan any life he could imagine. From there, you would begin to deconstruct the "magic life" into components that could be labeled values and goals. Your client may have never been reinforced for noticing and labeling his own values. Dreaming of a valued life may be very frightening, as the client may immediately come in contact with the pain of his current situation. As you gently help your client to identify what his heartfelt values are, your own reinforcement of those wants can serve as an initial foundation for working with the client on developing his sense of self. In this case, it may be helpful to do experiential exercises. The exercises throughout this book are examples of experiential exercises that examine both your clients' fear and the feeling of what it would be like to really speak the truth of valued life directions. For example, the Body in Relationship script can allow clients to imaginarily experience their reaction to social interactions and how those reactions impact their movement toward valued directions.

Discussing Barriers to Values with Your Clients

Begin with a discussion of the four categories of barriers—societal, thoughts and feelings, behavioral, and unclear values. Find out which barriers your clients identify with. Also ask yourself which ones you identify with as a therapist and in your personal life. If a barrier seems to interfere with your work with a client, bring this up in session.

For example, your client may have not openly expressed concerns about you as the therapist that are interfering with the client's participation in the therapy you provide. In that case, you may have to suggest this as one issue. For example, you may brainstorm a list of barriers with the client, with each of you throwing out ideas. You could be the one to suggest things such as "This therapist seems too young" or "This therapy is just really confusing and maybe I should try something else I read about." Your nondefensive stance can open the door for client concerns and validate client willingness to discuss uncomfortable issues. Awareness of these will inevitably help you both to move the therapeutic work, and thereby your client's life, in a valued direction. At this point in ACT, any barrier that may stand in the way of your client letting go of old behaviors and moving in a valued direction is worth discussion.

The next step is specifically identifying your clients' barriers to their identified values. The following client worksheet is designed to help clients clarify barriers. Have your clients take time in session to complete this worksheet, identifying what specifically they value in each domain, and then identifying two or three barriers that get in the way of living that value. Your clients may refer back to the exercises completed while working on values clarification (see chapter 8).

WHAT BARRIERS DO YOU FACE?
BARRIERS TO VALUES WORKSHEET

Think about each of your values and consider what stands in the way of pursing these values. For each valued domain, make a values statement for that domain, and then list the barriers that prevent you from moving in that values direction. We've included an example for the first valued domain—career. You may use the same values statement form the Year To Live: What Would You Do exercise in chapter 8 or you may choose to create another one.

Career

Values Statement: *To work in a field in which I can help other people*

Barriers:

1. *Most helping professions require a college degree, and I don't have one.*

2. *My current job as a highway toll worker does not really involve helping people, but I am scared to quit because it is secure and I don't want to lose that security.*

3. *A job search is too stressful, and I don't think I could handle the stress of looking for a job in the helping professions.*

Career

Values statement: _____

_____

Barriers: _____

_____

_____

_____

_____

_____

Citizenship

Values statement: _____

_____

Barriers: _____

_____

_____

_____

_____

_____

_____

Education

Values statement: _____

_____

Barriers: _____

_____

_____

_____

_____

_____

_____

Family

Values statement: _____

_____

Barriers: _____

_____

_____

_____

_____

_____

_____

Friends

Values statement: _____

_____

Barriers: _____

_____

_____

_____

_____

_____

_____

Health

Values statement: _____

_____

Barriers: _____

_____

_____

_____

_____

_____

_____

Leisure

Values statement: _____

_____

Barriers: _____

_____

_____

_____

_____

_____

_____

Romantic Relationships

Values statement: _____

_____

Barriers: _____

_____

_____

_____

_____

_____

Spirituality

Values statement: _____

_____

Barriers: _____

_____

_____

_____

_____

_____

After your clients complete this worksheet, spend some time discussing each section. For each barrier, assess when and how this barrier may arise. You may find it useful to identify which category the barrier falls into (societal rules, avoidant thoughts or feelings, behavior, unclear value). Clients may feel overwhelmed by looking at each category of values and the potential barriers that exist in living life in a valued way. Remind them that they have their entire life to move in the direction of the values they have identified. Living a valued life is a process, not a goal, just as being mindful and emotional experiencing are life processes. ACT provides your clients with a new way of approaching life. Each day presents a new opportunity to live in a way that is consistent with the values they have identified and the goals they have specified. The worksheet is not a week plan or a month plan, but a life plan, which may be revised at any time.

Now, in the final section of this chapter, we will examine specific ways for you to work with clients to overcome barriers. Part of this work is helping clients to notice that barriers are unavoidable and that what is important is developing a strategy to surmount difficulties that they may encounter.

Commitment to Valued Living

Throughout each component of the ACT work, your clients will move through varying levels of willingness to change by letting go of old behaviors and adopting new ones. This aligns in some ways with a theory that may be familiar: Prochaska and DiClemente's (1992) theory on the stages of change. In this theory, individuals move between stages of readiness for behavior change—from denial (precontemplation) to action, and back to precontemplation again, for example. In this same way, your clients may at times seem very aware of their thoughts and feelings and feel very clear about their values; at other times they may feel confused, discouraged, and fused with their thoughts and feelings, believing them to be their truth. As the therapist, it is your job to bring your clients again and again gently back to that place of awareness. Also, as the therapist, it is your job to encourage willingness through reminding your clients of their past behaviors that were not workable or effective, and of the future goals and values that they have identified.

We have found that making a verbal commitment to moving in a valued direction is often quite helpful for clients as they're choosing to move toward emotional experiencing versus avoidance, awareness versus denial, mindfulness versus mindlessness, and values-based behavior versus fear-based behavior or exclusively rule-based behavior. Your clients will struggle with each of these processes. Therefore, it is very important to create a practice, in sessions, of committing and recommitting to this path. To begin the process of commitment, we suggest an exercise in which your clients verbalize their specified values, the potential barriers to those values, and their commitment to experiencing difficult feelings as they pursue their values-based goals.

They can verbalize these to you by reviewing the work they completed during the values clarification part of treatment and the Barriers to Values Worksheet (above). Or they may want to make a statement at the end of each session about how they want to walk the world in the next week: What do they want to do that is meaningful? What behavior that is taking them away from a values-based, vital life do they plan to stop doing? What interactions with other people do they plan to have, and how do they hope those interactions will be? We have provided some examples of statements by clients that elucidate commitment to moving in a valued direction:

■ "This week I want to notice what I appreciate about my children when I'm talking with them, instead of constantly criticizing them. This will be hard to stop doing, because I fear that if I don't say all the negative things I notice, they will end up suffering or making a mistake because I didn't say something. But I know my criticizing is hurtful and pushing us apart. So I'm committing to noticing the aspects of my kids that I enjoy and love."

■ "This week, instead of avoiding it, I'm committing to looking at myself in the mirror each morning and practicing mindfulness of the negative thoughts I have. Even though it's painful and anxiety provoking to look at my body, avoiding it only makes me feel worse—it's like I don't deserve to be seen. So I'm going to let myself have some anxiety while looking in the mirror and work on detaching from the thoughts so they eventually will not define me."

■ "This week I'm going to commit to eating three meals each day, instead of skipping lunch. I hate feeling my stomach with food in it during the day because it feels physically uncomfortable and anxiety provoking. I always fear I'm gaining weight unless I'm hungry. But I know that's been ineffective because I always end up overeating at night anyway. So even though it will be uncomfortable, I really value treating my body well and want to begin the process of doing this by eating lunch."

These examples, written with specific behavioral goals in mind, are based on values. You may have your clients write down these types of commitment statements for each valued direction, or you can keep it more focused on what is relevant for them in a specific session.

Committing to living a valued life, even with barriers that may arise, is an active process. Commitment is the process of taking action. In session, we recommend that you ask your clients to write down their commitments and potential barriers, then verbally make a statement to you in session or to a loved one at home about following through with this. We recommend that you use the Commitment to Valued Living Worksheet (below) for this.

COMMITMENT TO VALUED LIVING WORKSHEET

I am making a commitment today to take action on the following goals:

_____

_____

_____

_____

These goals represent the values I have in life, which include:

_____

_____

_____

_____

As I pursue these values, there will be some barriers that will be present. These may include:

_____

_____

_____

_____

It is my intention to move toward my values, instead of away from them, by following though with the goals I've mentioned, even with the barriers that come up. I've made some plans about how to address those barriers when they do arise. Some ways I plan to cope with the barriers to living the life I want are:

_____

_____

_____

_____

Using these tools, the barriers I face will no longer actually prevent me from living my most vital, valued life. I am sharing this with you today because you matter to me, my values matter to me, and it's important that I stick to this commitment of living in this new way, even when it becomes difficult.

Conclusion

The process of identifying clients' most cherished or wished for values is at the heart of ACT. This treatment is not about simply accepting things as they are; rather, it is focused on moving clients into committed action that can lead to a vital life that will be rich in choices, experiences, and emotions. There is nothing easy about this path—it involves living out in the open and experiencing life as it happens—and there will be obstacles and barriers along the way. Remind your clients that this is all a part of the journey and that we all have to get up and dust ourselves off at times, adjusting our stance to find our own "true north"—the direction we wish to move in our lives. And the journey continues.

CHAPTER 10

Adapting ACT to Group Therapy

When spider webs unite, they can tie up a lion.

—Ethiopian proverb

Benefits of Group Therapy

In previous chapters, we described acceptance and commitment therapy techniques to support individuals who experience body image dissatisfaction. In this chapter, we'll describe how this approach can be implemented in a group therapy setting.

Group therapy can be an adjunct to individual therapy or the sole modality of treatment. Group participants tend to pay less per session than they would pay for an individual therapy session, making group therapy a cost-effective treatment option. Groups also offer therapeutic benefits, as participants learn from and support each other. For people who have been socially isolated, groups provide exposure to social interaction.

Groups also provide social contingencies that encourage motivation for and participation in treatment.

ACT group therapy protocols have been developed for a variety of psychological problems that are characterized by maladaptive avoidance behavior. The group therapy protocols that have been used in research studies can be accessed at www.contextual psychology.org/treatment_protocols. Each protocol describes how to implement structured, time-limited group therapy for problems such as self-harm (Gratz & Gunderson, 2006), polysubstance abuse (Hayes, Wilson, et al., 2004), chronic pain (McCracken, Vowles, & Eccleston, 2005), and depression (Zettle & Raines, 1989). Published research supports the efficacy of ACT group therapy in outcome studies, including randomized clinical trials, correlational studies, case studies, and component analysis studies. A list of the research support can be found at www.contextualpsychology.org/Research_Summaries.

Practical Suggestions for Implementing Group Therapy

Before you implement group therapy, brainstorm and plan the details for how your group will be conducted. The following sections list several questions you should consider as you develop an ACT body image group.

Open vs. Closed Groups

The first question to ask yourself is whether you will conduct an open or closed group. Most of the published ACT research has been conducted on closed therapy groups, in which group members enroll at the same time and new participants are not included after the initial session. In this case, you orient all members to the group at the same time, typically in the first session.

However, in settings that have rolling admissions, open therapy groups are more practical. Open groups allow new members to join an existing group at any time. If an open group is implemented, it would be beneficial for new participants to meet individually with you prior to their first ACT group session. You can provide an overview of the ACT approach, answer questions, and give examples of activities that have been recently completed during the group sessions. This orientation is helpful to integrate new members without needing to take time to reexplain and repeat the ACT philosophy each time a new member joins. In addition, Yellowlees (1988) recommends that new participants of open therapy groups enroll in pairs to avoid being singled out as the new person.

Group Size and Makeup

A group size of five to eight members tends to be ideal. Typically participants are more likely to share—and benefit—from smaller groups. Before enrolling participants, decide whether the group will be homogenous (similar characteristics among members) or heterogeneous (diverse characteristics among members). Consider the questions below to determine if the group should be limited by gender, age, severity of body image concern, or population:

- **Gender:** Is the group intended for females or males only, or will the group be mixed?

- **Age:** Is the group for adults only, adolescents only, or is there no age restriction?

- **Severity of body image concern:** This can range from normative discontent to an eating disorder diagnosis. Will all levels of severity be eligible, or will the group be restricted to one part of the severity continuum?

- **Population:** Is the group intended for specific populations, such as gastric bypass patients, high school females, athletes, women who have given birth within the last year, homosexual men, or any other target populations?

You need to weigh pros and cons of homogenous versus heterogeneous members when developing a group. For example, homogeneity can be helpful to focus sessions on specific topics most relevant to the participants, but it can also limit the diversity of perspectives and experiences among group members. Ask yourself what your goals are and what objectives you would like the group to achieve.

Format of Sessions and Topics

After the group membership has been determined, the next step is to develop a structured format. The chapters in this book can provide a framework for determining the number of sessions and the topics to be addressed in each session. For example, a twelve-week closed therapy group may be structured to include an initial session for introductions and orientation to ACT, followed by two sessions of each component (creative hopelessness, control as the problem, mindfulness and acceptance, values clarification, and barriers to valued living), then end with a final wrap-up or graduation session. Another option is to develop a group based on a specific component of ACT, such as a six-week group that focuses on mindfulness and acceptance of the thoughts, feelings, and bodily sensations associated with body image dissatisfaction (see chapter 7 for topics to include in a mindfulness-specific group).

ACT Group Techniques

Throughout this book, we have described techniques that can be administered in individual therapy sessions. Most of these techniques also can be included or adapted for group therapy. In addition, you can create your own ACT-consistent group activities. The sections below offer examples of some group-based exercises that can be included in an ACT body image group.

Thoughts Are Inevitable, Behavior Is Optional

The purpose of the following exercises is to indicate that some thoughts occur automatically. Although we cannot prevent some thoughts from occurring, we can control how much we buy into them—and we can choose to take effective action even when they occur.

EXERCISE: Thoughts Are Inevitable, Behavior Is Optional

This exercise is made up of three subexercises. These three subexercises can be used together in one group therapy session.

Mary Had a Little…

Invite group members to participate in an activity to identify how the mind works. Ask group members to fill in the blanks of the following phrases:

"Mary had a little _____."

"The United States of _____."

"A penny saved is a penny _____."

After filling in the blanks, the group discusses how some thoughts automatically occur. You might say something like this:

Somehow, through life experience, we learned that Mary had a little lamb and our minds automatically generate the thought "lamb" when prompted with "Mary had a little _____." As a result of life experiences, your mind has been "programmed" to generate certain thoughts, including the negative thoughts about yourself or your bodies.

Then the group may discuss some personal examples of body image situations that prompt negative thoughts, such as what thoughts automatically pop up when they are in the grocery store, at the gym, or shopping for new clothes.

Explain that ACT does not aim to eliminate negative, automatic thoughts, and then have the group participate in the following exercise to understand why ACT does not incorporate thought-changing techniques.

Remember the Numbers, Forget the Numbers

Tell the group that they must remember three very important numbers and that you will refer to these numbers throughout the group. Then say, "The numbers are 1, 2, and 3." Next, you ask, "What are the numbers?" Inevitably the group will respond to your question with "1, 2, and 3," and you then offer a million dollars to the person who can forget those numbers.

Even with a million dollars on the line in this exercise, the numbers will not go away. Likewise, automatic thoughts are not easy to eliminate. Instead of changing thoughts, ACT treatment focuses on helping clients to choose values-based behaviors when the thoughts emerge. Clients learn that they cannot control whether automatic thoughts occur, but they can control how they behave when the thoughts do occur. The group then participates in an activity to practice choosing values-driven behaviors.

The Sealed Envelope

(Materials needed: slips of paper and envelopes)

Before the group therapy session, take slips of paper and write on each slip a situation that might trigger an automatic thought, such as "Putting on a pair of jeans that fit too tightly," "Being invited by a friend to go to the gym," "Feeling full after a meal," or "Being offered a high-calorie food at a party." Place one slip of paper in each envelope, being certain that you have an envelope for each group member.

During the session, give each group member a sealed envelope. Tell the group not to open the envelopes until you instruct them to do so. Ask the group to mindfully observe and discuss any automatic thoughts and feelings that emerge from the uncertainty associated with receiving the envelope. One by one, participants are invited to open their envelopes and read aloud the situation. The group then discusses automatic thoughts that are likely to emerge in that situation and the behavioral options, including values-based options, that can be chosen.

Eye Contact for Acceptance and Willingness

The Thoughts Are Inevitable, Behavior Is Optional exercises help clients cope with general situations that trigger uncomfortable thoughts and feelings. If you are interested in focusing on social situations specifically, the following Eye Contact exercise provides an experiential opportunity for your group to practice acceptance and willingness in a social situation.

EXERCISE: Eye Contact

(Materials needed: a piece of paper and a pen or pencil for each participant)

This exercise is especially helpful for clients with body image problems who struggle to build intimate interpersonal relationships because they feel insecure or fearful of how others will judge them based on their body. The exercise requires willingness to experience discomfort in the service of building intimacy with another human being. When participants look at each other, they may have thoughts that the other is judging them or they may worry about how they look. They may notice anxiety, often expressed by nervous giggles. The goal of the exercise is to notice the discomfort that arises when one is totally present and vulnerable with another human being.

Give the participants a blank sheet of paper and pen or pencil. Ask them to draw their own eyes—nothing else—only the eyes. Participants are then assigned a partner. If possible, partners should not be close friends, and it may be useful to select partners at random by drawing names from a hat. After partners are selected, explain that, in a moment, each pair will face each other and maintain eye contact. This is not a stare-down and partners should not say, do, or communicate anything other than looking into each other's eyes. The purpose of this activity is to notice how they experience being totally present with another human being. Group members should remain committed to looking into the eyes of their partner, even if they experience thoughts to stop, feelings of boredom, fear of being judged, concerns about how they look, or whatever else arises. The pairs then look silently into each other's eyes for at least five minutes.

After the activity, the group can discuss the thoughts and feelings they experienced during the eye contact. Typically clients report that they wondered what the other person was thinking about them. In this case, you might ask if they've had real-life interpersonal experiences that elicited similar thoughts and feelings of judgment. If so, how did they respond to these thoughts and feelings in real life? Did they respond differently to the thoughts and feelings today, and what was the result of making a choice to be willing to experience discomfort in the service of connecting with another human being?

The group can also discuss their core values in relationships and how moving toward those values may require willingness to be vulnerable with others. (The term *core values* refers to the values that are discussed in the previous chapters on clarifying values and commitment to values.) Following the discussion on intimacy, participants take the drawings they created of their own eyes and write a message to their partner concerning their personal reaction to the partner's willingness to be present with them. The drawing of the eyes with the personal message is then given to the partner.

Two participants in an ACT training once practiced this technique with each other and embraced when the exercised ended. They had not met before the workshop, but the experience of sitting eye to eye allowed each to feel deeply connected to the other.

Urge Surfing

Marlatt and Gordon (1985) developed "urge surfing" as part of relapse prevention for substance abuse, and this technique is applicable to ACT. Clients with eating related problems may experience urges to binge, purge, restrict, and so on. Urge surfing involves acceptance that urges will occur. Although treatment will not eliminate urges, clients can learn to respond more effectively when urges do occur. In ACT, you may say, "In what valued direction are your feet currently taking you?" which means "Will satisfying the urge bring you closer to or further away from your core values?"

Through urge surfing, clients can learn to experience urges without giving in to them. Instead of trying to distract themselves or fight an urge, clients learn to "surf" the urge as if riding a wave in the ocean. You may draw an inverted-U to represent the wave pattern of an urge as it gradually rises, reaches peak intensity, then gradually dissipates. Explain that clients often do not experience the dissipation of an urge because they satisfy the urge before it crests. In this case, if clients give in as the urge rises, they may only experience urges as getting stronger and stronger without ever experiencing the reality that urges do pass. The purpose of urge surfing is not to make the craving go away, but to be willing to experience the urge as it runs its natural course. Some urge surfing techniques include writing in a journal to describe the thoughts and feelings and bodily sensations associated with the urge. Or clients can make urge surfboards, as we describe in the exercise below.

EXERCISE: Making Urge Surfboards

(Materials needed: pieces of paper cut in the shape of surfboards; colored pens, pencils, or other art materials with which to decorate the surfboards; laminating paper)

Give each group member a piece of paper cut in the shape of a surfboard. Ask participants to draw, write, and decorate their surfboards with urge-surfing information, such as "This urge will build, then pass," "Ride the urge wave," or "If you ride it out, the wave will carry you safely to the shore." Participants can also pass their surfboards around so that group members can write words of encouragement to each other. At the end of group, members can share these creative representations with each other. If available, laminating paper can be used to preserve the surfboards so clients can use them as bookmarks, or carry them in a purse or wallet to refer to when urges occur.

The Big Orange Splot

The Big Orange Splot (Pinkwater, 1977) is a children's book that teaches the value of acceptance. Body image clients can relate to the message in this story, which teaches how acceptance of physical imperfection can lead one in a valued direction.

EXERCISE: Splots to Dreams

(Materials needed: sheets of paper; pencils or pens; crayons or colored markers; other art materials for decorating; one large orange felt-tip marker; *The Big Orange Splot,* by D. M. Pinkwater)

At the start of group, give participants a sheet of paper and ask them to trace one of their hands on the paper. As each participant finishes, take an orange marker and scribble a big splot on each drawing. Ask participants to mindfully observe and express their thoughts and feelings about having their pictures spoiled.

Then read *The Big Orange Splot* (Pinkwater, 1977) to the group. This children's book is about a neighborhood in which all of the houses look exactly alike until a bird drops a can of orange paint onto the home of Mr. Plumbean. Instead of cleaning up the big orange splot from his roof, Mr. Plumbean repaints his home with a jungle theme that incorporates the orange splot. At first the neighbors are appalled, but after talking to Mr. Plumbean, all his neighbors transform their own homes to represent their dreams: a castle, a ship, a hot-air balloon, and so on.

Have the participants discuss the story. Here are some possible discussion topics:

- How can being different inspire oneself and others?

- How does creating a valued life involve facing opposition and complaints from others?

- How is the body the home of our core values?

- How can group members accept and incorporate, rather than change, the "splots" or imperfections of their bodies?

After the discussion, bring out crayons, markers, and other art materials. Invite participants to incorporate the big orange splot on their hand drawings into a creative representation of their core values and dreams. When finished, have participants share their work with the group.

The Dash

One ACT exercise involves writing your own epitaph (Hayes et al., 1999). A variation of this exercise for group therapy is based on "The Dash," a poem by Linda Ellis. A copy of the poem, set to moving music and images, can be found at www.lindaellisonline.com. The poem describes how each epitaph is marked by a date of birth and a date of death, but the most important part is the dash in between, representing the time alive on earth.

EXERCISE: The Dash Between the Years

(Materials needed: a ball of yarn and the poem "The Dash" by Linda Ellis)

If possible, in advance of the session ask participants to prepare a values statement (as described in chapter 8 of this book) that reflects what they would like their life to stand for. If you choose to do this, you can use the values statements during the course of the session. Participants may read the values statements aloud during the group, or they may choose parts to discuss in the group.

When clients arrive to group, if you have access to audiovisual equipment in your therapy room, you can share the online presentation of the poem during group. As an alternative, you can prepare hard copies of the poem (after obtaining the author's permission to reproduce the poem) to hand out to each member. In this case, ask each participant to read a verse.

After the poem has been shared with the group, ask participants to sit in a circle. Give the ball of yarn to one member of the group. She ties a piece around one of her fingers, shares what she would like her dash to be like, and then throws the yarn to another participant, who repeats this process. Participants respond spontaneously what they would like their dash to be like.

In the end, a web of "dashes" of yarn is created to visually represent how each life is meaningfully connected to the others. You can then cut the strings to give each member his or her own "dash" to keep.

Participants can then discuss their reactions to listening to what their peers have shared during this exercise. Typically participants will reflect how much they value each other and how meaningful the other group members are to them.

Mindful Movement

Leisure is a valued domain. Some clients with body image concerns avoid certain activities due to body discomfort, while others may engage in compulsive exercise in an attempt to control body weight or shape. Such avoidance and excessive exercise are not done in the service of the client's core leisure values. Mindful movement is a technique to help clients participate in recreational activities that satisfy core leisure values. Mindful movement involves listening to the body in order to stop moving when the body is hurt or tired and to identify activities that elicit pleasure and honor clients' core leisure values.

Group members can make a list of movement activities that are chosen on the basis of leisure values, such as biking, flying kites, sledding, yoga, gardening, or walking a dog. Each group member can then set a goal to participate in a specific valued leisure activity for the week. Members can discuss a plan for allowing themselves to experience the activity mindfully, appreciating each moment and observing the thoughts, feelings, and bodily sensations that arise during the activity. Members can also ask questions and receive feedback from each other. For example, a participant may share that she struggles with doing movement activities in the service of leisure values because her primary movement activity, jumping rope at the gym, is in the service of losing weight. A peer may encourage her to notice the difference between how she has been jumping rope versus how children jump rope (playing and enjoying the moment). The client can then set a goal to jump rope in the mindful way children do and also to be aware of any thoughts, feelings, or emotions that arise during the activity.

Handling Barriers to Treatment

This section will present a case example of a situation that may arise in an ACT body image group and how you can effectively handle barriers to treatment like this. The case demonstrates two issues that group therapists need to be prepared to handle: (1) a group member says or does something that creates discomfort among the group members, and (2) a group member offers ACT-inconsistent advice to another member.

■ Case Example: Genie

Genie is a socially isolated, twenty-six-year-old woman with a ten-year history of body image dissatisfaction. She was seeing an individual therapist who recommended a body image group. During her first group session, Genie reaches into her purse and pulls out a graphic drawing she has created of her body. She begins to cry and screams, "I hate myself." The other members freeze up in silence. Genie's behavior clearly disturbs them.

As the ACT group therapist, how would you handle this situation? Think for a moment before reading further.

The discomfort in the room is quite obvious, which presents a great opportunity to model ACT in action. That means not avoiding the discomfort by changing the subject or trying to talk Genie and other members into feeling better. An ACT therapist would never say, "Don't worry, Genie. Things will get better. Why don't you tell us what you like about your body instead?"

Instead it is important for you and other group members to accept, without judgment, Genie's discomfort as well as your own. Statements such as "Your anger [tears, or whatever] are welcome here" are particularly helpful. Another option would be for you to model mindfulness and say, "I am feeling _____ right now. I just want you to know that I am being mindful of how I feel in this moment." With your facilitation, the other group members should be encouraged to model responding in a similar ACT-consistent manner. Other members may add statements like "That drawing is hard for me to look at because it makes me realize how much pain you are in." Group members may also share examples of empathy and acceptance, such as "There were times when I felt horrible about my body too, but I learned that I can't let that image define who I am or what I do in my life."

What if another group member suggests that Genie shred the drawing and put it in the trash? Again, think for a moment before reading further.

ACT-inconsistent advice provides a great opportunity to review the ACT approach with the group. Although shredding the drawing would be an option, it is not ACT consistent. The group may discuss how destroying the drawing does not eliminate the underlying body dissatisfaction that Genie has, and there is no way to throw away the body image thoughts and feelings that occur inside her skin. Instead you could suggest that Genie keep her drawing and carry it with her as a metaphor for going through her daily life and moving toward valued directions even if she feels disgusted about her body. You can also encourage the other group members to draw or write their body image thoughts during the session to carry throughout the week. By involving the entire group in the activity, the session does not focus solely on Genie's body image dissatisfaction per se; it allows all members to practice mindfulness of their own body image dissatisfaction, willingness to have it, and commitment to live a valued life even if it is present.

Conclusion

Group therapy is a cost-effective and therapeutic treatment option. ACT group therapy protocols have been developed and are empirically supported for a variety of experiential avoidance disorders. You can refer to the previous chapters in this book to develop topics and structure for an ACT body image group for homogenous or heterogeneous populations. This chapter provided examples of additional techniques that are suitable for a group format and discussed the importance of maintaining an ACT perspective in a therapy group.

AFTERWORD

Endings and New Beginnings

There will come a time when you believe everything is finished.
That will be the beginning.

—Louis L'Amour

There is no definitive endpoint of ACT work because it is a lifelong process. It is a way of living that broadens behavior choices and produces vitality, and it can wax and wane in terms of willingness to experience discomfort in the service of living a valued life. As a practitioner, you may have used this book for a circumscribed or brief treatment in a medical setting; you may have used this in your private practice as an adjunct to other therapeutic work or as a stand-alone treatment; or if you work in a college counseling center, you may have implemented this in group or individual format. Termination or the ending of treatment will differ by setting.

If clients will not be returning to see you for treatment, we suggest you provide them with an ACT self-help book such as *ACT for Anorexia* (Heffner & Eifert, 2004), which targets similar body image and disordered eating patterns with exercises and worksheets that your clients can implement independently. Another ACT self-help book, *Get Out of Your Mind and Into Your Life* (Hayes & Smith, 2005), is not directed toward any specific clinical problem or population and is widely applicable to clients for independent use.

If your work with a client will be ongoing, we suggest that you continue to integrate components of ACT into therapy. If you work primarily from a different theoretical orientation (for example, psychodynamic, cognitive behavioral, humanistic-existential) and have used this book to supplement to your work in addressing body image dissatisfaction with your clients, we hope that you have found this treatment to be consistent with your work. Body image dissatisfaction doesn't exist as a problem in a box, separated from other aspects of life. The interconnected nature of body image issues touches all areas of your clients' lives. Therefore, we encourage you to continue integrating mindfulness, acceptance, and other components of ACT into your work.

If you are an ACT therapist and have used this book to guide you in working with body image dissatisfaction, we hope we've provided you with some content-specific guidance on applying the components of ACT. Body image dissatisfaction is just one problem associated with eating disorders, but it also occurs in high rates across age cohorts of women and men without clinically diagnosed eating disorders. We anticipate, and hope, that this book will be helpful to practitioners with clients of diverse ages and with diverse presenting problems.

Ending therapy as a practitioner of ACT, or as a behavior therapist in general, includes assessment of the extent to which changes made in therapy are generalized outside of therapy, assessment of existing areas of life that are ineffective or problematic for the client, and attention to the therapeutic relationship as the client experienced it. Of course, the ending of therapy doesn't always occur when the client is "ready"; many factors may influence when and why the client chooses to end treatment. Wherever you are at the end of therapy is acceptable. You may have thoughts, judgments, wishes, and hopes about what could have, should have, or might have happened. In the end, what did occur between you and your client is what matters. The therapeutic relationship is as important as the behavior changes that occur (or don't occur) outside of session. To experience acceptance from another human being is part of the experience of being a client working with an ACT therapist. Your commitment to introducing an experience of acceptance to your clients may be the most enduring aspect of ACT for them. That experience of acceptance during their work with you may both enable and sustain them as they seek to accept, commit, and take action in living a life that is an expression of their deepest values. In a very real way, the end of therapy with you may be a new life beginning for your client.

References

Allison, D. B., Mentore, J. L., Heo, M., Chandler, L. P., Cappelleri, J. C., Infante, M. C., et al. (1999). Antipsychotic-induced weight gain: A comprehensive research synthesis. *American Journal of Psychiatry, 156,* 1686–1696.

Allison, K. C., & Park, C. L. (2004). A prospective study of disordered eating among sorority and nonsorority women. *International Journal of Eating Disorders, 35,* 354–358.

American Psychiatric Association. (2000). *Diagnostic and statistical manual of mental disorders* (4th ed., text revision). Washington, DC: Author.

Arnow, B., Kenardy, J., & Agras, W. S. (1992). Binge eating among the obese: A descriptive study. *Journal of Behavioral Medicine, 15,* 155–170.

Bach, P. A., & Moran, D. J. (2008). *ACT in practice: Case conceptualization in acceptance and commitment therapy.* Oakland, CA: New Harbinger Publications.

Barak, Y., Lampl, Y., Sarova-Oinchas, I., & Achiron, A. (1999). Self and body esteem perception in multiple sclerosis. *Behavioral Neurology, 11,* 159–161.

Barlow, D. H. (2002). *Anxiety and its disorders: The nature and treatment of anxiety and panic* (2nd ed.). New York: Guilford Press.

Beck, R. W., Cleary, P. A., Trobe, J. D., Kaufman, D. I., Kupersmith, M. J., Paty, D., et al. (1993). The effect of corticosteroids for acute optic neuritis on the subsequent development of multiple sclerosis. *New England Journal of Medicine, 329,* 1764–1769.

Bennett, K., & Stevens, R. (1996). Weight anxiety in older women. *European Eating Disorders Review, 4,* 32–39.

Beren, S., Hayden, H., Wilfley, D., & Grilo, C. (1996). The influence of sexual orientation on body dissatisfaction in adult men and women. *International Journal of Eating Disorders, 20*, 135–141.

Billingham, R. E., & Patterson, J. E. (1998). Body dissatisfaction and sexual victimization among college women. *Psychological Reports, 82*, 907–911.

Bishop, S. R., Lau, M., Shapiro, S., Carlson, L., Anderson, N., Carmody, J., et al. (2004). Mindfulness: A proposed operational definition. *Clinical Psychology: Science and Practice, 11*, 230–241.

Bond, F. W., & Bunce, D. (2003). The role of acceptance and job control in mental health, job satisfaction, and work performance. *Journal of Applied Psychology, 88*, 1057–1067.

Bond, F. W., Hayes, S. C., Baer, R. A., Carpenter, K. M., Orcutt, H. K., Waltz, T., et al. (2009). Preliminary psychometric properties of the Acceptance and Action Questionnaire–II: A revised measure of psychological flexibility and acceptance. Manuscript submitted for publication.

Bowen, S., Witkiewitz, K., Dillworth, T. M., Chawla, N., Simpson, T. L., Ostafin, B. D., et al. (2006). Mindfulness meditation and substance use in an incarcerated population. *Psychology of Addictive Behaviors, 20*, 343–347.

Briere, J., & Scott, C. (2007). Assessment of trauma symptoms in eating disordered populations. *Eating Disorders, 15,* 347–358.

Bryant-Waugh, R. J., Cooper, P. J., Taylor, C. L., & Lask, B. D. (1996). The use of the Eating Disorder Examination with children: A pilot study. *International Journal of Eating Disorders, 19*, 391–397.

Burlingame, G. M., Fuhriman, A., Paul, S., & Ogles, B. M. (1989). Implementing a time-limited therapy program: Differential effects of training and experience. *Psychotherapy: Theory, Research, Practice, Training, 26*, 303–313.

Burns, D. D., & Nolen-Hoeksema, S. (1992). Therapeutic empathy and recovery from depression in cognitive-behavioral therapy: A structural equation model. *Journal of Consulting and Clinical Psychology, 60*, 441–449.

Carroll, P., Tiggemann, M., & Wade, T. (1999). The role of body dissatisfaction and bingeing in the self-esteem of women with type II diabetes. *Journal of Behavioral Medicine, 22*, 59–74.

Cash, T. F. (1994). The Situational Inventory of Body-Image Dysphoria: Contextual assessment of a negative body image. *Behavior Therapist, 17*, 133–134.

Cash, T. F. (2002). The Situational Inventory of Body-Image Dysphoria: Psychometric evidence and development of a short form. *International Journal of Eating Disorders, 32*, 362–366.

Cash, T. F., & Fleming, E. C. (2002). The impact of body-image experiences: Development of the Body Image Quality of Life Inventory. *International Journal of Eating Disorders, 31*, 455–460.

Chambless, D. L., & Ollendick, T. H. (2001). Empirically supported psychological interventions: Controversies and evidence. *Annual Review of Psychology, 52*, 685–716.

Clark, A., Skouteris, H., Wertheim, E. H., Milgrom, J., & Paxton, S. J. (2009). The relationship between depression and body dissatisfaction across pregnancy and the postpartum: A prospective study. *Journal of Health Psychology, 14*, 27–35.

Clemency, C. E. (2009, May). Behavioral foundations for disordered eating among performers. Paper presented at the annual meeting of the Association of Behavior Analysis, Phoenix, AZ.

Cockell, S. J., Geller, J., & Linden, W. (2002). The development of a decisional balance scale for anorexia nervosa. *European Eating Disorders Review, 10*, 359–375.

Connor-Greene, P. A., Striegel-Moore, R. H., & Cronan, S. (1994). Perceived social climate and weight preoccupation in college women. *Eating Disorders: The Journal of Treatment and Prevention, 2*, 126–134.

Craighead, L. W. (2008). *The appetite awareness workbook: How to listen to your body and overcome bingeing, overeating, and obsession with food.* Oakland, CA: New Harbinger Publications.

Dahl, J. C., Plumb, J. C., Stewart, I., & Lundgren, T. (2009). *The art and science of valuing in psychotherapy: Helping clients discover, explore, and commit to valued action using acceptance and commitment therapy.* Oakland, CA: New Harbinger Publications.

Dahl, J., Wilson, K. G., Luciano, C., & Hayes, S. C. (2005). *Acceptance and commitment therapy for chronic pain.* Reno, NV: Context Press.

Denmark-Wahnefried, W., Rimer, B. K., & Winer, E. P. (1997). Weight gain in women with breast cancer. *Journal of the American Dietetic Association, 97*, 519–525.

Dicker, S. L., & Craighead, L. W. (2004). Appetite-focused cognitive-behavioral therapy in the treatment of binge eating with purging. *Cognitive and Behavioral Practice, 11*, 213–221.

Didie, E. R., Tortolani, C., Walters, M., Menard, W., Fay, C., & Phillips, K. A. (2006). Social functioning in body dysmorphic disorder: Assessment considerations. *Psychiatry Quarterly, 77*, 223–229.

Elmore, D., & de Castro, J. M. (1990). Meal patterns of normal, untreated bulimia nervosa and recovered bulimic women. *Physiology and Behavior, 49*, 99–105.

Erkolahti, R. K., Ilonen, T., and Saarijarvi, S. (2003). Self-image of adolescents with diabetes mellitus type I and rheumatoid arthritis. *Nordic Journal of Psychiatry, 57*, 309–312.

Fairburn, C. G., & Cooper, Z. (1993). The Eating Disorder Examination (12th ed.). In C. G. Fairburn & G. T. Wilson (Eds.), *Binge eating: Nature, assessment, and treatment* (pp. 317–360). New York: Guilford Press.

Fairburn, C. G., Marcus, M. D., & Wilson, G. T. (1993). Cognitive-behavioral therapy for binge eating and bulimia nervosa: A comprehensive treatment manual. In C. G. Fairburn & G. T. Wilson (Eds.), *Binge eating: Nature, assessment, and treatment* (pp. 361–404). New York: Guilford Press.

Filiault, S. M. (2007). Measuring up in the bedroom: Muscle, thinness, and men's sex lives. *International Journal of Men's Health, 6,* 127–142.

Fletcher, L., & Hayes, S. C. (2005). Acceptance and commitment therapy, relational frame theory, and a functional analytic conceptualization of mindfulness. *Journal of Rational-Emotive and Cognitive Behavior Therapy, 23,* 315–336.

Follette, V., & Pistorello, J. (2007). *Finding life beyond trauma: Using acceptance and commitment therapy to heal from post-traumatic stress and trauma-related problems.* Oakland, CA: New Harbinger.

Follette, V. M., Pistorello, J., & Pearson, A. (2007) Creating a Valued life. In V. M. Follette & J. Pistorello, *Finding life beyond trauma: Using acceptance and commitment therapy to heal from post-traumatic stress and trauma-related problems* (pp. 165–190). Oakland, CA: New Harbinger Publications.

Forman, E., Hoffman, K., McGrath, K., Herbert, J., Brandsma, L., & Lowe, M. (2007). A comparison of acceptance- and control-based strategies for coping with food cravings: An analog study. *Behaviour Research and Therapy, 45,* 2372–2386.

Frohman, E. M. (2007). Corticosteroids for multiple sclerosis: Application for treating exacerbations. *Neurotherapeutics, 4,* 618–626.

Ganem, P. A., & Morera, O. (2009). Does body dissatisfaction predict mental health outcomes in a sample of predominately Hispanic college students? *Personality and Individual Differences, 46,* 557–561.

Garner, D. M. (2004). Eating Disorders Inventory 3: Professional manual. Lutz, FL: Psychological Assessment Resources.

Garner, D. M., Olmsted, M. P., Bohr, Y., & Garfinkel, P. E. (1982). The Eating Attitudes Test: Psychometric features and clinical correlates. *Psychological Medicine, 12,* 871–878.

Goldfarb, L. A., Dykens, E. M., & Gerrard, M. (1985). The Goldfarb Fear of Fat Scale. *Journal of Personality Assessment, 49,* 329–332.

Goretti, B., Portaccio, E., Zipoli, V., Hakiki, B., Siracusa, G., Sorbi, S., et al. (2009). Coping strategies, psychological variables, and their relationship with quality of life in multiple sclerosis. *Neurological Science, 30,* 15–20.

Gratz, K. L., & Gunderson, J. G. (2006). Preliminary data on an acceptance-based emotion regulation group intervention for deliberate self-harm among women with borderline personality disorder. *Behavior Therapy, 37*, 25–35.

Gregg, J., Callaghan, G., Hayes, S., & Glenn-Lawson, J. (2007). Improving diabetes self-management through acceptance, mindfulness, and values: A randomized controlled trial. *Journal of Consulting and Clinical Psychology, 75*, 336–343.

Grossbard, J. R., Lee, C. M., Neighbors, C., & Larimer, M. E. (2009). Body image concerns and contingent self-esteem in male and female college students. *Sex Roles, 60*, 198–207.

Halligan, F. R., & Reznioff, M. (1985). Personality factors and change with multiple sclerosis. *Journal of Consulting and Clinical Psychology, 53*, 547–548.

Hanh, T. N. (1976). *The miracle of mindfulness: A manual on meditation.* Boston, MA: Beacon Press.

Hanson, J. (2005). Should your lips be zipped? How therapist self-disclosure and nondisclosure affects clients. *Counseling and Psychotherapy Research, 5*, 96–104.

Hardy, R., & Kuh, D. (2002). Change in psychological and vasomotor symptom reported during menopause. *Social Science and Medicine, 55*, 1975–1988.

Harris, S. M. (1995). Body image attitudes and the social development of college women. *Journal of Psychology, 129*, 315–329.

Hayes, S. C., Barnes-Holmes, D., & Roche, B. (Eds.). (2001). *Relational frame theory: A post-Skinnerian account of human language and cognition.* New York: Plenum Press.

Hayes, S. C., & Pankey, J. (2002). Experiential avoidance, cognitive fusion, and an ACT approach to anorexia nervosa. *Cognitive and Behavioral Practice, 9*, 243–247.

Hayes, S. C., & Smith, S. (2005). *Get out of your mind and into your life.* Oakland, CA: New Harbinger Publications.

Hayes, S. C., & Strosahl, K. D. (Eds.). (2004). *A practical guide to acceptance and commitment therapy.* New York: Springer.

Hayes, S. C., Strosahl, K. D., Bunting, K., Twohig, M., & Wilson, K. G. (2004). What is acceptance and commitment therapy? In S. C. Hayes and K. D. Strosahl (Eds.), *A practical guide to acceptance and commitment therapy* (pp. 3–29). New York: Springer.

Hayes, S. C., Strosahl, K. D., & Wilson, K. G. (1999). *Acceptance and commitment therapy: An experiential approach to behavior change.* New York: Guilford Press.

Hayes, S. C., Strosahl, K. D., Wilson, K. G., Bissett, R. T., Pistorello, J., Toarmino, D., et al. (2004). Measuring experiential avoidance: A preliminary test of a working model. *Psychological Record, 54*, 553–578.

Hayes, S. C., Wilson, K. G., Gifford, E. V., Bissett, R., Piasecki, M., Batten, S. V., et al. (2004). A randomized controlled trial of twelve-step facilitation and acceptance and commitment therapy with polysubstance abusing methadone maintained opiate addicts. *Behavior Therapy, 35*, 667–688.

Hayes, S. C., Wilson, K. G., Gifford, E. V., Follette, V. M., & Strosahl, K. D. (1996). Experiential avoidance and behavioral disorders: A functional dimensional approach to diagnosis and treatment. *Journal of Consulting and Clinical Psychology, 64*, 1152–1168.

Heatherton, T. F., & Baumeister, R. F. (1991). Binge eating as escape from self-awareness. *Psychological Bulletin, 110*, 86–108.

Heffner, M. H., & Eifert, G. H. (2004). *The anorexia workbook: How to accept yourself, heal your suffering, and reclaim your life.* Oakland, CA: New Harbinger Publications.

Heffner, M., Sperry, J., Eifert, G. H., & Detweiler, M. (2002). Acceptance and commitment therapy in the treatment of an adolescent female with anorexia nervosa: A case example. *Cognitive and Behavioral Practice, 9*, 232–236.

Helms, R. L., O'Hea, E. L., & Corso, M. (2008). Body image issues in women with breast cancer. *Psychology, Health, and Medicine, 13*, 313–325.

Hesse-Biber, S. (1992). Report on a panel longitudinal study of college women's eating patterns and eating disorders. *Health Care for Women International, 13*, 375–391.

Holm-Denoma, J. M., Scaringi, V., Gordon, K. H., Van Orden, K. A., & Joiner, T. E. (2009). Eating disorder symptoms among undergraduate varsity athletes, club athletes, independent exercisers, and nonexercisers. *International Journal of Eating Disorders, 42*, 47–53.

Hurston, Z. N. (1991). *Their eyes were watching God.* Urbana: University of Illinois Press.

Keel, P. K., Dorer, D. J., Franko, D. L., Jackson, S. C., & Herzog, D. B. (2005). Postremission predictors of relapse in women with eating disorders. *American Journal of Psychiatry, 162*, 2263–2268.

Kimmel, S. B., & Mahalik, J. R. (2005). Body image concerns of gay men: The roles of minority stress and conformity to masculine norms. *Journal of Consulting and Clinical Psychology, 73*, 1185–1190.

Lakkis, J., Ricciardelli, L. A., & Williams, R. J. (1999). Role of sexual and gender-related traits in disordered eating. *Sex Roles, 41*, 1–16.

Langer-Gould, A., Moses, H. H., & Murray, J. (2004). Strategies for managing the side effects of treatments for multiple sclerosis. *Neurology, 63*, S35–S41.

Lerner, R. M., Skinner, E. A., & Sorell, G. T. (1980). Methodological implications of contextual/dialectic theories of development. *Human Development, 23*, 855–856.

Levitt, J. L. (2007). Treating eating disorder patients who have had traumatic experiences: A self-regulatory approach. *Eating Disorders, 15*, 359–372.

Lewis, D. M., & Cachelin, F. M. (2001). Body image, body dissatisfaction, and eating attitudes in midlife and elderly women. *Eating Disorders, 9*, 29–39.

Lillis, J., & Hayes, S. C. (2008). Measuring avoidance and inflexibility in weight related problems. *International Journal of Behavior Consulting and Therapy, 4*, 30–40.

Lillis, J., Hayes, S. C., Bunting, K., & Masuda, A. (2009). Teaching acceptance and mindfulness to improve the lives of the obese: A preliminary test of a theoretical model. *Annals of Behavioral Medicine, 37*, 58–69.

Linehan, M. M. (1993). *Cognitive-behavioral treatment of borderline personality disorder.* New York: Guilford Press.

List, M. A., D'Antonio, L. L., Cella, D. F., Siston, A., Mumby, P., Haraf, D., et al. (1996). The Performance Status Scale for head and neck cancer patients and the Functional Assessment of Cancer Therapy Head and Neck Scale: A study of utility and validity. *Cancer, 77*, 2294–2301.

Liu, H. S. (2007). Changes of satisfaction with appearance and working status for head and neck tumor patients. *Journal of Clinical Nursing, 17*, 1930–1938.

Lockhart, J. S. (2000). Nurses' perceptions of head and neck oncology patients after surgery: Severity of facial disfigurement and patient gender. *Plastic Surgery Nursing, 20*, 68–80.

Luoma, J. B., Hayes, S. C., & Walser, R. D. (2007). *Learning ACT: An acceptance and commitment therapy skills-training manual for therapists.* Oakland, CA: New Harbinger Publications.

Mannucci, E., Ricca, V., Barciulli, E., Di Bernardo, M., Travaglini, R., Cabras, P. L., et al. (1999). Quality of life and overweight: The Obesity Related Well-Being (ORWELL 97) questionnaire. *Addictive Behaviors, 24*, 345–357.

Marlatt, G. A., & Gordon, J. R. (Eds.). (1985). *Relapse prevention: Maintenance strategies in the treatment of addictive behaviors.* New York: Guilford Press.

Masand, P. (2000). Weight gain associated with psychotropic drugs. *Expert Opinion on Pharmacotherapy, 1*, 377–389.

McCracken, L. M., Vowles, K. E., & Eccleston, C. (2005). Acceptance-based treatment for persons with complex, long-standing chronic pain: A preliminary analysis of treatment outcome in comparison to a waiting phase. *Behaviour Research and Therapy, 43*, 1335–1346.

McFarland, M. B., & Kaminski, P. L. (2009). Men, muscles, and mood: The relationship between self-concept, dysphoria, and body image disturbances. *Eating Behaviors, 10*, 68–70.

McKinley, N. M. (2006). The developmental and cultural contexts of objectified body consciousness: A longitudinal analysis of two cohorts of women. *Developmental Psychology, 42*, 679–687.

McLaren, L., Beck, C. A., Patten, S. B., Fick, G. H., & Adair, C. E. (2008). The relationship between body mass index and mental health: A population-based study of the effects of the definition of mental health. *Journal of Social Psychiatry and Psychiatric Epidemiology, 43*, 63–71.

McLaren, L., Hardy, R., & Kuh, D. (2003). Women's body satisfaction at midlife and lifetime body size: A prospective study. *Health Psychology, 22*, 370–377.

McLaren, L., & Kuh, D. (2004). Body dissatisfaction in midlife women. *Journal of Women and Aging, 16*, 35–54.

Mintz, L. B., & Betz, N. E. (1988). Prevalence and correlates of eating disordered behaviors among undergraduate women. *Journal of Counseling Psychology, 35*, 463–471.

Mizes, S. J., Christiano, B. A., Madison, J., Post, G., Seime, R., & Varnado, P. (2000). Development of the Mizes Anorectic Cognitions Questionnaire–Revised: Psychometric properties and factor structure in a large sample of eating disorder patients. *International Journal of Eating Disorders, 28*, 415–421.

Mizes, S. J., & Klegses, R. C. (1989). Validity, reliability, and factor structure of the Anorectic Cognitions Questionnaire. *Addictive Behaviors, 14*, 589–594.

Mussell, M. P., Binford, R. B., & Fulkerson, J. A. (2000). Eating disorders: Summary of risk factors, prevention programming, and prevention research. *Counseling Psychologist, 28*, 764–796.

Myers, T. D., Smith, J. R., Wertheim, M. S., Egan, R. A., Shults, W. T., & Rosenbaum, J. T. (2004). Use of corticosteroid sparing systemic immunosuppression for treatment of corticosteroid dependent optic neuritis not associated with demyelinating disease. *British Journal of Ophthalmology, 88*, 673–680.

Niemeier, H. M. (2004). Clinical implications of disordered eating attitudes and behaviors in college women. *Dissertation Abstracts International: Section B—The Physical Sciences and Engineering, 65*, 1035.

Niemeier, H. M., Craighead, L. W., Pung, M. A., & Elder, K. A. (2002, November). Reliability, validity, and sensitivity to change of the Preoccupation with Eating, Weight, and Shape Scale. Paper presented at conference of the Association for Behavior Therapy, Reno, NV.

Orsillo, S., & Roemer, L. (2005). *Acceptance and mindfulness-based approaches to anxiety: Conceptualization and treatment.* New York: Springer Science and Business Media.

Pearson, A. (2009). Acceptance and commitment therapy as a workshop intervention for body image dissatisfaction and disordered eating attitudes. Unpublished doctoral dissertation, University of Nevada, Reno.

Pinkwater, D. M. (1977). *The big orange splot.* New York: Scholastic.

Plankey, M., Bacchetti, P., Jin, C., Grimes, B., Hyman, C., Cohen, M., et al. (2009). Self-perception of body fat changes and HAART adherence in the women's interagency HIV study. *AIDS Behavior, 13*, 53–59.

Pope, H., Phillips, K., & Olivardia, R. (2000). *The Adonis complex.* New York: Free Press.

Prochaska, J. O., & DiClemente, C. C. (1992). *Stages of change in the modification of problem behaviors.* Newbury Park, CA: Sage.

Protinsky, H., & Marek, L. I. (1997). Insights into the treatment of eating disorders: A qualitative approach. *Family Therapy, 24*, 63–69.

Quintard, B., & Lakdja, F. (2008). Assessing the effect of beauty treatments on psychological distress, body image, and coping: A longitudinal study of patients undergoing surgical procedures for breast cancer. *Psycho-Oncology, 17*, 1032–1038.

Rasmussen-Hall, M. L. (2007). Distress intolerance, experiential avoidance, and alexithymia: Assessing aspects of emotion dysregulation in undergraduate women with and without histories of deliberate self-harm and binge/purge behavior. Doctoral dissertation, University of Nevada, Reno. *Dissertation Abstracts International: Section B—The Physical Sciences & Engineering, 67*(9-B), 5420.

Raudenbush, B., & Zellner, D. A. (1997). Nobody's satisfied: Effects of abnormal eating behaviors and actual perceived weight status on body image satisfaction in males and females. *Journal of Social and Clinical Psychology, 16*, 95–110.

Reboussin, B. A., Rejeski, W. J., Martin, K. A., Callahan, K., Dunn, A. L., King, A. C., et al. (2000). Correlates of satisfaction with body function and body appearance in middle and older aged adults: The Activity Counseling Trial (ACT). *Psychology and Health, 15*, 239–254.

Reed, D. L., Thompson, J. K., Brannick, M. T., & Sacco, W. P. (1991). Development and validation of the Physical Appearance State and Trait Anxiety Scale (PASTAS). *Journal of Anxiety Disorders, 5*, 323–332.

Rosen, J. C., Srebnik, D., Saltzberg, E., & Wendt, S. (1991). Development of a body image avoidance questionnaire. *Psychological Assessment, 3*, 32–37.

Ruggiero, L., Williamson, D., Davis, C. J., Schlundt, D. G., & Carey, M. P. (1988). Forbidden Food Survey: Measure of bulimic's anticipated emotional reactions to specific foods. *Addictive Behaviors, 13*, 267–274.

Schmidt, U., & Treasure, J. (2006). Anorexia nervosa: Valued and visible. A cognitive-interpersonal maintenance model and its implications for research and practice. *British Journal of Clinical Psychology, 45*, 343–366.

Schwitzer, A. M., Rodriguez, L. E., Thomas, C., & Salimi, L. (2001). The eating disorders NOS diagnosis profile among college women. *Journal of College Health, 49*, 157–166.

Seddon, K., & Waller, G. (2000). Emotional processing and bulimic psychopathology: Age as a factor among nonclinical women. *International Journal of Eating Disorders, 28*, 364–369.

Segal, Z. V., Williams, J. M. G., & Teasdale, J. D. (2001). *Mindfulness-based cognitive behavioral therapy for depression: A new approach to preventing relapse.* New York: Guilford Press.

Sheehan, J., Sherman, K. A., Lam, T., & Boyages, J. (2008). Regret associated with the decision for breast reconstruction: The association of negative body image, distress, and surgery characteristics with decision regret. *Psychology and Health, 23*, 207–219.

Siegert, R. J., & Abernethy, D. A. (2005). Depression in multiple sclerosis: A review. *Journal of Neurology, Neurosurgery, and Psychiatry, 76*, 469–475.

Siever, M. D. (1994). Sexual orientation and gender as factors in socioculturally acquired vulnerability to body dissatisfaction and eating disorders. *Journal of Consulting and Clinical Psychology, 62*, 252–260.

Smith, M. L., & Glass, G. V. (1977). Meta-analysis of psychotherapy outcome studies. *American Psychologist, 32*, 752–760.

Stanbury, R., & Graham, E. (1998). Systemic corticosteroid therapy: Side effects and their management. *British Journal of Ophthalmology, 82*, 704–708.

Teasdale, J. D., Moore, R. G., Hayhurst, H., Pope, M., Williams, S., & Segal, Z. V. (2002). Metacognitive awareness and prevention of relapse in depression: Empirical evidence. *Journal of Consulting and Clinical Psychology, 70*, 275–287.

Terrell, J. E., Manavati, K., Esclamado, R. M., Bradford, C. R., & Wolf, G. T. (1999). Health impact of head and neck cancer. *Otolaryngology-Head and Neck Surgery, 120*, 852–859.

Thompson, K. J., Heiburg, L. J., Altabe, M., & Tantleff-Duff, S. T. (2002). *Exacting beauty: Theory, assessment, and treatment of body image disturbance.* Washington DC: American Psychological Association.

Tiggemann, M., & Lynch, J. E. (2001). Body image across the life span in adult women: The role of self-objectification. *Developmental Psychology, 37*, 243–253.

Tylka, T. L. (2004). The relation between body dissatisfaction and eating disorder symptomatology: An analysis of moderating variables. *Journal of Counseling Psychology, 51*, 178–191.

Tylka, T. L., & Subich, L. M. (2002). Women's perceptions of the effectiveness and safety of maladaptive weight control techniques. *Journal of Counseling and Development, 80*, 101–110.

Vanina, Y., Podolskaya, M. D., Sedky, K., Shahab, H., Siddiqui, A., Firoz, M., et al. (2002). Body weight changes associated with psychopharmacology. *Psychiatric Services, 3*, 842–847.

Webber, E. (1994). Psychological characteristics of binging and nonbinging obese women. *Journal of Psychology: Interdisciplinary and Applied, 128*(3), 339–351.

Wegner, D., & Zanakos, S. (1994). Chronic thought suppression. *Journal of Personality, 62*, 615–640.

Weiderman, M. W., Sansone, R. A., & Sansone, L. A. (1999). Obesity among sexually abused women: An adaptive function for some? *Women and Health, 29*, 90–100.

Wells, A., & Davies, M. I. (1994). The Thought Control Questionnaire: A measure of individual differences in the control of unwanted thoughts. *Behaviour Research and Therapy, 32*, 871–878.

Williamson, D. A., Davis, C. J., Bennett, S. M., Goreczny, A. J., & Gleaves, D. H. (1989). Development of a simple procedure for assessing body image disturbances. *Journal of Behavioral Assessment, 11*, 433–446.

Williamson, D. A., Womble, L. G., Zucker, N. L., Reas, D. L., White, M. A., Blouin, D. C., et al. (2000). Body Image Assessment for Obesity (BIA-O): Development of a new procedure. *International Journal of Obesity, 24*, 1326–1332.

Yellowlees, P. (1988). Group psychotherapy in anorexia nervosa. *International Journal of Eating Disorders, 7*, 649–655.

Zettle, R. D., & Raines, J. C. (1989). Group cognitive and contextual therapies in treatment of depression. *Journal of Clinical Psychology, 45*, 438–445.

Adria N. Pearson, Ph.D., received her doctorate in clinical psychology from the University of Nevada, Reno, and completed her internship at the VA Long Beach Healthcare System. Pearson has presented at national conferences on the topic of body image and eating disorders and has written articles in peer-reviewed journals on mindfulness, acceptance, and trauma. She is currently a post-doctoral fellow at the VA Long Beach Healthcare System and lives in the greater Los Angeles area.

Michelle Heffner, Ph.D., is a licensed psychologist in Nevada and coauthor of *The Anorexia Workbook*. She has written and developed professional book chapters, online continuing education courses, and peer-reviewed journal articles.

Victoria M. Follette, Ph.D., is Foundation Professor of Psychology at the University of Nevada, Reno, and a clinical scientist specializing in interpersonal violence and body image problems.

Foreword writer **Steven C. Hayes, Ph.D.**, is University of Nevada Foundation Professor of Psychology at the University of Nevada, Reno. An author of thirty books and nearly 400 scientific articles, he has focused his career on understanding language and cognition functionally and applying this perspective to prevention and intervention, primarily acceptance and commitment therapy.

Index

A

ABCs of Behavior worksheet, 93-95
abstinence violation model, 77
acceptance, 33-34; defusion and, 33;
    description of, 71; disordered eating
    and, 90; eye contact for, 171-172;
    importance of experiencing, 180;
    mindfulness and, 106-107, 126;
    process of, 126-127; self-as-context
    and, 32-33; therapeutic stance and,
    68-69. *See also* willingness
Acceptance and Action Questionnaire
    (AAQ/AAQ-2), 31-32
Acceptance and Action Questionnaire for
    Weight-Related Difficulties (AAQ-W),
    32
acceptance and commitment therapy
    (ACT): assessment measures used in,
    28-32; barriers to treatment in, 44-46;
    basic tenets of, 69-70, 71; body image
    dissatisfaction and, 12, 19, 25-35; case
    examples of using, 46-50; clinical
    training in, 42-44; cognitive fusion
    and, 22-23; core processes of, 26-27;
    developing competency in, 41-42;
    emotional pain and, 18; experiential
    avoidance and, 24-25; group therapy
with, 167-177; historical context of,
    19-20; integrating assessment data
    with, 32-35; introducing to clients,
    55-72; learning to use, 37-42; length
    and frequency of, 39-40; lifelong
    process of, 179; one-day workshop
    on, 90; overarching themes of, 26-28;
    recommended resources on, 18-19;
    relational frame theory and, 21-22;
    sequence of, 40; tailoring to client
    needs, 39-41; termination of, 40-41,
    179-180; theoretical bases of, 20-25;
    therapeutic relationship in, 41, 67-69,
    180; treatment components in, 26
*Acceptance and Commitment Therapy for
    Chronic Pain* (Dahl, Wilson, Luciano,
    and Hayes), 50
ACT for Anorexia (Heffner and Eifert),
    47, 179
*ACT in Practice: Case Conceptualization
    in Acceptance and Commitment Therapy*
    (Bach and Moran), 19
action: behavior change as, 69-70, 71. *See
    also* committed action
Adonis complex, 6
alcohol abuse, 24
alexithymia, 90
alliance building, 67-68

Angelou, Maya, 129
anorexia, 13, 14, 24. *See also* eating
  disorders
Anorexia Workbook, The (Heffner and
  Eifert), 19
appetite awareness training, 120
Approaching Difficult Situations exercise,
  116-118
assessment: integrating ACT with, 32-35;
  measures used for, 28-32; progress
  indicated through, 40-41
assessment measures: of body image
  dissatisfaction and disordered eating
  pathology, 30-31; of experiential
  avoidance and psychological flexibility,
  31-32; of thought suppression, 78;
  of weight dissatisfaction and desired
  weight, 29-30
athletes, 8-9
avoidance. *See* experiential avoidance
avoidance-driven behavior, 96-97

B

barriers to treatment, 44-46; eliminating
  resistance as, 45-46; handling in group
  therapy, 175-176; workability and, 46
barriers to valued living, 35, 147-165;
  behavioral barriers, 152-156; clinician
  barriers, 148-149; discussing with
  clients, 157-162; societal barriers, 149-
  151; thoughts and feelings, 151-152;
  unclear values, 155-156
Barriers to Values worksheet, 158-161
behavior: ABCs of Behavior worksheet,
  93-95; avoidance-driven vs. values-
  driven, 96-97; barriers to values based
  on, 152-155; reinforcing consequences
  of, 96
behavior change: action as basis of, 69-70,
  71; contact with the present moment
  and, 34; theory on the stages of, 162
behavior therapy, 19-20
behavioral barriers, 152-156
beliefs about thoughts, 113
Big Orange Splot, The (Pinkwater), 173-
  174

binge eating, 79, 90. *See also* eating
  disorders
body dysmorphic disorder (BDD), 13
body image, 6
Body Image Assessment (BIA), 29
Body Image Assessment for Obesity
  (BIA-O), 29-30
Body Image Avoidance Questionnaire
  (BIAQ), 30
body image dissatisfaction: ACT and, 12,
  19, 25-35; assessment measures for,
  30-31; avoidance strategies and, 79-80;
  body mass index and, 6, 15; case
  examples of, 46-50; client storytelling
  about, 57-63; complexity of, 3-12;
  cultural differences and, 13-14;
  definition of, 3; eating disorders and,
  12-13, 25; experiential factors in, 8-9;
  exploring with clients, 56-57; gender
  differences and, 6-7, 13-14; historical
  context of, 4-5; medical conditions
  and, 9-11; medication compliance and,
  11-12, 15; necessity of interventions
  for, 14-15; therapeutic issues with,
  12-15; women and, 5-6; worksheet on
  living without, 133
Body Image Quality of Life Inventory
  (BIQLI), 30
Body in Relationship exercise, 150-151
body mass index (BMI), 6, 15, 29
body silhouette preferences, 29-30
body-to-mind letters, 61
breast cancer, 10-11
breathing, mindful, 108-111; exercise on,
  108-109; instructions on practicing,
  111
bulimia, 13,n 14, 24. *See also* eating
  disorders

C

cachexia, 10
cancer, 10-11
career values, 158
change-based approach, 45
chemotherapy, 11
childhood sexual abuse, 8

choice, 69, 71

chronic health conditions. *See* medical conditions

citizenship values, 158-159

client-centered therapy, 46

clients: barriers to valued living, 149-162; introducing ACT to, 55-72; new control strategies of, 89-91; storytelling about body dissatisfaction, 57-63; tailoring treatment to needs of, 39-41; therapeutic relationship with, 41, 67-69, 180; workability discussed with, 63-64

clinical training, 42-44

clinicians: barriers to valued living, 148-149; therapeutic relationship and, 41, 67-69, 180

closed therapy groups, 168

cognitive behavioral therapy (CBT): eating disorders and, 14; historical success of, 19-20; mindfulness-based, 105

cognitive defusion, 33, 106, 113-114, 126

cognitive fusion, 22-23, 120

commitment: alliance building and, 67-68; to valued living, 162-164

Commitment to Valued Living worksheet, 164

committed action, 35, 147; contact with the present moment and, 34; values clarification and, 34-35

consultation groups, 43

contact with the present moment, 34

contextualpsychology.org website, 41, 42, 43, 168

control, exercise on exploring, 67

control strategies, 56-57; creative hopelessness and, 73-76; examples of common, 59-60; experiential avoidance and, 76-80; new vs. old, 90-92

core processes of ACT, 26-27

core values, 172

countertransference, 148

creative hopelessness, 73-87; achieving, 86; control strategies and, 73-76; experiential avoidance and, 76-80;

facilitating with clients, 80-86; metaphors for experiencing, 82-86

cultural considerations: barriers to values and, 155-156; body image dissatisfaction and, 13-14

D

"Dash, The" (Ellis), 174

Dash Between the Years exercise, 174-175

defusion, 33, 106, 113-114, 126

diabetes, 9-10

Diagnostic and Statistical Manual of Mental Disorders, 20

dialectical behavior therapy (DBT), 105

dieting, excessive, 79

difficult situations: exercise on approaching, 116-118; worksheet on identifying, 117

digging, use of term, 86

disease processes: acceptance of, 140; body image dissatisfaction and, 9-11

disordered eating. *See* eating disorders

E

eating, mindful, 120, 124-126

Eating Attitudes Test (EAT-26), 30

Eating Disorder Examination (EDE), 28, 30

Eating Disorder Examination for Children (ChEDE), 28

Eating Disorder Inventory-III (EDI-III), 30

eating disorders: acceptance as solution to, 90; body image dissatisfaction and, 12-13, 25; case examples of, 47, 48, 49; experiential avoidance and, 24-25, 78-79; measures for assessing, 30-31; mindful eating and, 120; prevention programs for, 14; research on ACT and, 19

education values, 159

Einstein, Albert, 73

Ellis, Linda, 174

emotions: active experiencing of, 112; allowing in clients, 86; as barriers, 151-152; importance of processing,

119; in-session experience of, 101-102, 119; mindfulness of, 115-120; painful, 17-18, 129-130; standing with, 118; suppression of thoughts and, 77; willingness to experience, 101-102

empirically supported treatment, 14

ending ACT treatment, 40-41, 179-180

excessive dieting, 79

exercises: Approaching Difficult Situations, 116-118; Body in Relationship, 150-151; The Dash Between the Years, 174-175; Eye Contact, 171-172; How Long Have You Been Struggling?, 62-63; Living with Intention, 143-145; Making Urge Surfboards, 173; Man in the Hole Metaphor, 83; Milk, Milk, Milk, 114; Mindful Eating, 125-126; Mindful Mirror, 118-119; Mindfulness of Breath, 108-109; Mind-to-Body and Body-to-Mind Letters, 61; Polygraph Metaphor, 84-85; Splots to Dreams, 173-174; Things You'd Like to Control and Cannot Control, 67; Thoughts Are Inevitable, Behavior Is Optional, 170-171; Tug-of-War Metaphor, 99-101. *See also* worksheets

experiential avoidance, 24-25; behavior driven by, 96-97; body image dissatisfaction and, 79-80; control strategies and, 76-80; definition of, 24; disordered eating as, 24-25, 78-79; values-based living and, 130-131

eye contact, 101, 119, 171-172

Eye Contact exercise, 171-172

F

facial disfigurement, 11

family values, 159

feelings. *See* emotions

Forbidden Food Survey (FFS), 30

frequency of treatment, 40

friends, values about, 159

fusion, 22-23, 120

G

gay men, 6-7

gender considerations: body image dissatisfaction and, 6-7, 13-14; therapy groups and, 169

Get Out of Your Mind and Into Your Life (Hayes and Smith), 47, 179

goals, 137-143; committed action based on, 35; dealing with discrepancies in, 140-143; developing specific and attainable, 139-143. *See also* values

Goals and Values worksheet, 138

Goldfarb Fear of Fat Scale (GFFS), 31

Greek myths, 4

group therapy, 167-177; ACT techniques used in, 169-175; benefits of, 167-168; handling barriers to treatment in, 175-176; open vs. closed groups in, 168; protocols for ACT in, 168; session formats and topics in, 169; size and makeup of groups in, 168-169

H

HAART regimen, 11-12

Hanh, Thich Nhat, 105, 106, 124

Hayes, Steven, 44, 101, 143

head and neck cancer, 11

health: values related to, 140-142, 160. *See also* medical conditions

hunger, mindfulness of, 120

Hurston, Zora Neal, 55

I

Identifying Difficult Situations worksheet, 117

informed consent, 56

in-session willingness, 101-102

L

L'Amour, Louis, 179

Learning ACT: An Acceptance and Commitment Therapy Skills-Training Manual for Therapists (Luoma, Hayes, and Walser), 19

leisure, values about, 160, 175
length of treatment, 39
lesbians, 7
Life Beyond Trauma (Follette and
    Pistorello), 47
Life Without Body Image Concerns
    worksheet, 133
Living with Intention exercise, 143-145
Longfellow, Henry Wadsworth, 89
long-term consequences of behavior, 96

M

Making Urge Surfboards exercise, 173
Man in the Hole Metaphor, 83
Mary Had a Little... exercise, 170
measures. *See* assessment measures
medical conditions: acceptance of, 140;
    body image dissatisfaction and, 9-11
medication compliance, 11-12, 15
men: body image dissatisfaction in, 6-7.
    See also gender considerations
metaphors: Man in the Hole, 83;
    Polygraph, 84-85; Tug-of-War, 99-101.
    See also exercises
Milk, Milk, Milk exercise, 114
Millay, Edna St. Vincent, 147
Mindful Eating exercise, 125-126
Mindful Mirror exercise, 118-119
mindful movement, 175
mindfulness, 105-127; acceptance and,
    106-107, 126; of breath, 108-111;
    conceptualizations of, 106; defusion
    and, 33; eating with, 120, 124-126;
    of emotions, 115-120; experience and,
    112; introducing to clients, 107-108;
    operational definition of, 106; origins
    of, 105; of physical sensations, 120-
    124; reasons for learning, 107-108;
    self-as-context and, 33; third-wave
    therapies and, 20; of thoughts, 113-
    115, 119-120; willingness and, 126
mind-to-body letters, 61
minority stress, 7
Miracle of Mindfulness, The (Hanh), 124
mirror exercise, 118-119

Mizes Anorectic Cognitions (MAC)
    questionnaire, 31
morals vs. values, 134
movement, mindful, 175
multiple sclerosis (MS), 10

N

negative reinforcement, 96
new control strategies, 90-92
nonjudgment, 68-69
normative discontent, 14

O

Obesity-Related Well-Being (ORWELL
    97) questionnaire, 31
objective binge eating, 79
one-day ACT workshops, 90
open therapy groups, 168

P

pain: emotional, 17-18, 129-130; suffering
    vs., 64-66; values clarified by, 145
Physical Appearance State and Trait
    Anxiety Scale–State Version
    (PASTAS-S), 31
physiological mindfulness, 120-124
Pinkwater, D. M., 173
pliance, 156
Polygraph Metaphor, 84-85
positive reinforcement, 96
*Practical Guide to Acceptance and
    Commitment Therapy, A* (Hayes and
    Strosahl), 19
Preoccupation with Eating, Weight, and
    Shape (PEWS) scale, 31
present moment awareness, 34
psychological flexibility, 27
psychological inflexibility, 23
psychotropic medications, 12
purging, 79

Q

questions, Socratic, 134

R

reinforcement, 96
rejection, fear of, 57
relational frame theory (RFT), 21-22
Remember the Numbers, Forget the Numbers exercise, 170-171
resistance: eliminating as a barrier, 45-46; exercise on struggling with, 84-85
romantic relationships, 161
rule following, 156

S

Saint-Exupéry, Antoine de, 17
Sappho, 3
Sealed Envelope exercise, 171
self-as-context, 32-33
self-concept, 32
self-disclosure, 41
self-esteem, 7
self-objectification, 9
sequence of treatment, 40
sexual abuse, 8
short-term consequences of behavior, 96
silence: emotional experiencing and, 101, 118, 119; in-session periods of, 101
Situational Inventory of Body-Image Dysphoria (SIBID), 31
societal barriers, 149-151
Socratic questions, 134
spirituality, values about, 161
Splots to Dreams exercise, 173-174
storytelling about body dissatisfaction, 57-63
subjective binge eating, 79
substance abuse, 24
suffering vs. pain, 64-66
suppression, thought, 77-78

T

tapes-in-the-mind metaphor, 113-114, 119-120
termination of treatment, 40-41, 179-180
therapeutic relationship, 41, 67-69, 180
third-wave therapies, 20

Thought Control Questionnaire (TCQ), 31
thoughts: as barriers, 151-152; beliefs about, 113; exercises on defusing, 114, 170-171; mindfulness of, 113-115, 119-120; suppression of, 77-78
Thoughts Are Inevitable, Behavior Is Optional exercises, 170-171
training in ACT, 42-44
trauma, 8
treatment: barriers to, 44-46, 175-176; components of, 26; frequency of, 40; length of, 39; resistance to, 45-46; scope of, 41-42; sequence of, 40; tailoring to client needs, 39-41; termination of, 40-41, 179-180
Tug-of-War Metaphor, 99-101

U

urge surfing, 172-173

V

valued directions: commitment to moving in, 162-164; discrepancies identifying, 140-143; exercise on considering, 135; worksheet for ranking, 136
valued living: barriers to, 35, 147-165; commitment to, 162-164
values: barriers to, 35, 147-165; behavior driven by, 96-97; clarification of, 34-35, 135-137, 143-145; commitment to living based on, 162-164; definitions of, 34, 134; domains of, 135, 158-161; emotional pain and, 129-130, 145; exercise on contacting, 143-145; goals and, 137-143; introducing the topic of, 131-134; morals vs., 134; unclear, 155-156
values clarification, 34-35; barriers related to, 155-156; discrepancies revealed through, 140-143; experiential exercise on, 143-145; life directions and, 135-137
Van Gogh, Vincent, 37
verbal referents, 21

Vipassana meditation, 105
vital living, 129-130

W

weight: assessment of desired, 29-30;
    dissatisfaction assessment, 29
White Bear Suppression Inventory, 78
willingness, 33, 97-102; definition
    of, 97; exercise on experiencing,
    99-101; eye contact for, 171-172;
    in-session encouragement of, 101-
    102; mindfulness and, 126. *See also*
    acceptance
women: body image dissatisfaction in,
    5-6. *See also* gender considerations
workability, 46, 63-64
worksheets: ABCs of Behavior,
    93-95; Barriers to Values, 158-161;
    Commitment to Valued Living, 164;
    Goals and Values, 138; Identifying
    Difficult Situations, 117; Life Without
    Body Image Concerns, 133; A Year to
    Live, 144. *See also* exercises
workshops on ACT, 43

Y

A Year to Live worksheet, 144

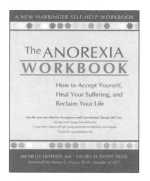

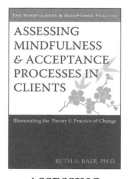